A Voyage Around
the Second Letter of Peter

A Voyage Around
the Second Letter of Peter

Collected Essays

Terrance Callan

⌖PICKWICK *Publications* · Eugene, Oregon

A VOYAGE AROUND THE SECOND LETTER OF PETER
Collected Essays

Copyright © 2020 Terrance Callan. All rights reserved. Except for brief quotations in critical publications or reviews, no part of this book may be reproduced in any manner without prior written permission from the publisher. Write: Permissions, Wipf and Stock Publishers, 199 W. 8th Ave., Suite 3, Eugene, OR 97401.

Pickwick Publications
An Imprint of Wipf and Stock Publishers
199 W. 8th Ave., Suite 3
Eugene, OR 97401

www.wipfandstock.com

PAPERBACK ISBN: 978-1-5326-9410-3
HARDCOVER ISBN: 978-1-5326-9411-0
EBOOK ISBN: 978-1-5326-9412-7

Cataloguing-in-Publication data:

Names: Callan, Terrance.

Title: A voyage around the second letter of peter : collected essays. / Terrance Callan.

Description: Eugene, OR: Pickwick Publications, 2020. | Includes bibliographical references.

Identifiers: ISBN 978-1-5326-9410-3 (paperback) | ISBN 978-1-5326-9411-0 (hardcover) | ISBN 978-1-5326-9412-7 (ebook)

Subjects: LCSH: Bible. Peter, 2nd—Criticism, interpretation, etc.

Classification: BS2795.2 C35 2020 (print) | BS2795.2 (ebook)

Manufactured in the U.S.A.   MARCH 8, 2020

For Jane, Terry, and Annie

Contents

Abbreviations | ix
Introduction | xv

1   Use of the Letter of Jude by the Second Letter of Peter | 1
2   The Christology of the Second Letter of Peter | 24
3   The Soteriology of the Second Letter of Peter | 38
4   The Style of the Second Letter of Peter | 51
5   The Syntax of 2 Peter 1:1–7 | 73
6   A Note on 2 Peter 1:19–20 | 83
7   Rhetography and Rhetology of Apocalyptic Discourse in 2 Peter | 92
8   Comparison of Humans to Animals in 2 Peter 2:10b–22 | 118
9   The Gospels of Matthew and John in the Second Letter of Peter | 134
10 Faith and Faithfulness in 2 Peter | 148
11 Reading the Earliest Copies of 2 Peter | 163
12 The Second Letter of Peter, Josephus, and Gnosticism | 185

Appendix A | 203
Appendix B | 212
Appendix C | 213
Bibliography | 215

Abbreviations

General

CE	Common Era
c.	approximately
cf.	compare
col., cols.	column, columns
ed., eds.	editor, editors
e.g.	for example
etc.	and so forth
i.e.	that is
n.	note
NT	New Testament
St.	Saint
v., vv.	verse, verses
vol.	volume

Bible Texts and Versions

33	Minuscule 33
A	Codex Alexandrinus
LXX	Septuagint
P72	Papyrus 72

Ancient Authors and Writings

1 Clem.	1 Clement
2 Clem.	2 Clement
1 En.	1 Enoch (Ethiopic Apocalypse)
2 Bar.	2 Baruch (Syriac Apocalypse)

Aristotle

Eth. Nic.	Nichomachean Ethics

Babylonian Talmud

b. B. Metz.	Bava Metzi'a
b. Bek.	Bekorot
b. Shabb.	Shabbat
b. Tem.	Temurah

Clement of Alexandria

Strom.	*Stromata*

Dead Sea Scrolls

1QH	Thanksgiving Hymns

Diodorus Siculus

Hist.	*Bibliotheca historica*

Epiphanius

Pan.	*Refutation of All Heresies*

Eusebius of Caesarea

Praep. ev.   *Praeparatio evangelica*

Hippolytus

Haer.   *Refutation of All Heresies*

Ignatius of Antioch

Eph.   *To the Ephesians*
Magn.   *To the Magnesians*
Smyrn.   *To the Smyrnaeans*

Irenaeus

Haer.   *Against Heresies*

Josephus

Ant.   *Jewish Antiquities*
Ag. Ap.   *Against Apion*
J.W.   *Jewish War*

Justin Martyr

1 Apol.   *First Apology*
Dial.   *Dialogue with Trypho*

Philo

Abr.   *De Abrahamo*
Aet.   *De aeternitate mundi*

Agr.	*De agricultura*
Cher.	*De cherubim*
Conf.	*De confusione linguarum*
Congr.	*De congressu eruditionis gratia*
Contempl.	*De vita contemplativa*
Decal.	*De decalogo*
Det.	*Quod deterius potiori insidari soleat*
Deus	*Quod Deus sit immutabilis*
Ebr.	*De ebrietate*
Fug.	*De fuga et inventione*
Gig.	*De gigantibus*
Her.	*Quis rerum divinarum heres sit*
Jos.	*De Iosepho*
Leg. 1, 2, 3	*Legum allegoriae I, II, III*
Migr.	*De migratione Abrahami*
Mos. 1, 2	*De vita Mosis I, II*
Mut.	*De mutatione nominum*
Opif.	*De opificio mundi*
Plant.	*De plantatione*
Post.	*De posteritate Caini*
Praem.	*De praemiis et poenis*
Prob.	*Quod omnis probus liber sit*
Prov. 1, 2	*De providentia I, II*
QE 1, 2	*Quaestiones et solutiones in Exodum I, II*
QG 1, 2, 3, 4	*Quaestiones et solutions in Genesin I, II, III, IV*
Sacr.	*De sacrificiis Abelis et Caini*
Somn. 1, 2	*De somniis I, II*
Spec. 1, 2, 3, 4	*De specialibus legibus I, II, III, IV*
Virt.	*De virtutibus*

Plato

Resp.	*Republic*
Tim.	*Timaeus*

Pliny the Elder

Nat.	*Naturalis historia*

Pliny the Younger

Ep.	*Epistulae*

Pss. Sol.	Psalms of Solomon

Shepherd of Hermas

Vis.	Vision

Suetonius

Domit.	*Life of Domitian*

Targums

Frg. Tg.	Fragmentary Targum
Tg. Neof.	Targum Neofiti
Tg. Ps.-J.	Targum Pseudo-Jonathan

Testaments of the Twelve Patriarchs

T. Levi	Testament of Levi

Modern Works

ANF	*Ante-Nicene Fathers: The Writings of the Fathers Down to AD 325*. Edited and translated by Alexander Roberts, James Donaldson, and A. Cleveland Coxe. 10 vols. New York: Christian Literature Publishing, 1885.
NHC	Nag Hammadi Codices
NovTSup	Supplements to Novum Testamentum
PG	Patrologia graeca [*Patrologiae cursus completus*: Series graeca]. Edited by J.-P. Migne. 162 vols. Paris, 1857–1886.
PL	Patrologia latina [*Patrologiae cursus completus*: Series latina]. Edited by J.-P. Migne. 217 vols. Paris, 1844–1864.
P. Oxy.	*The Oxyrhynchus Papyri*. Edited and translated by Bernard P. Grenfell and Arthur S. Hunt. 15 vols. London: Egypt Exploration Society, 1898–1922.
TDNT	*Theological Dictionary of the New Testament*. Edited by Gerhard Kittel and Gerhard Friedrich. Translated by Geoffrey W. Bromiley. 10 vols. Grand Rapids: Eerdmans, 1964–76.
WUNT	Wissenschaftliche Untersuchungen zum Neuen Testament
ZNW	*Zeitschrift für die neutestamentliche Wissenschaft und die Kunde der älteren Kirche*

Introduction

My concentrated exploration of the Second Letter of Peter began a little over twenty years ago. I was teaching "Introduction to the New Testament" in spring of 1997 and as part of that discussed the literary relationship between 2 Peter and Jude. My students asked questions that made me realize my understanding of the relationship was rather superficial. Soon, I embarked on a detailed investigation of the relationship, the results of which are presented in the first essay of this collection, "Use of the Letter of Jude by the Second Letter of Peter." This essay takes as its starting point the widely accepted view that 2 Peter used Jude and describes exactly what 2 Peter did with Jude in making use of it.

I showed this essay to Duane F. Watson, another student of 2 Peter. He suggested that I look at 2 Peter through the lens developed by Vernon Robbins in two books, *The Tapestry of Early Christian Discourse: Rhetoric, Society and Ideology* and *Exploring the Texture of Texts: A Guide to Socio-Rhetorical Interpretation*. When I did so, what seemed most interesting about 2 Peter was its theological content, what Robbins called its "sacred texture." The most important aspects of 2 Peter's sacred texture are presented in the essays on "The Christology of the Second Letter of Peter" and "The Soteriology of the Second Letter of Peter." The first of these argues that 2 Peter has a notably high Christology; the second argues that 2 Peter's soteriology is the basis for its ethics and eschatology.

Most interpreters of 2 Peter have commented on its style, usually in negative terms. I set out to investigate the style of 2 Peter thoroughly, and the results are presented in "The Style of the Second Letter of Peter."[1] This essay argues that 2 Peter is stylistically ambitious and written in the grand Asian style. Few other examples of writing in this style have survived, and most find it inferior to the Attic style of most surviving contemporary Greek

---

1. I later investigated the style of Galatians in a similar way; see Callan, "Style of Galatians."

literature. This essay was written at about the same time as Thomas J. Kraus, *Sprache, Stil und historischer Ort des zweiten Petrusbriefes* and consequently did not take it into account. I have never returned to the topic of 2 Peter's style in a way that would allow for interaction with Kraus's treatment. Kraus, however, has critiqued my essay in his article "'Anders und doch Teil des Ganzen!?' oder Über Asianismus, das 'Verwunderliche' an 2 Petr und 'Verwunderliches' über ihn."

Interpreters of 2 Peter disagree about whether 2 Peter 1:3–4 continues 1:1–2, is an independent sentence, or begins a sentence that continues in vv. 5–7. "The Syntax of 2 Peter 1:1–7" argues for the last of these views.

"A Note on 2 Peter 1:19–20" argues that the phrase "in your hearts" in 2 Peter 1:19, which is almost always seen as modifying the verb "rises" earlier in the verse, should instead be seen as modifying the participle "knowing" that follows it in verse 20. Stanley E. Porter and Andrew W. Pitts responded to this argument in their essay, "τοῦτο πρῶτον γινώσκοντες ὅτι in 2 Peter 1:20 and Hellenistic Epistolary Convention."

I was invited to contribute a paper on 2 Peter to a section titled "Methodological Reassessments of the Letters of James, Peter, and Jude" at the 2007 annual meeting of the Society of Biblical Literature. I decided to discuss 2 Peter using further development of Vernon Robbins's socio-rhetorical interpretation. The result was the essay "Rhetography and Rhetology of Apocalyptic Discourse in Second Peter." Subsequent to his identification of the textures of texts in the books mentioned earlier, Robbins identified various kinds of discourse found in early Christian texts, including apocalyptic discourse. He also distinguished between the rhetography of a text, i.e., the way it evokes mental images, and the rhetology of a text, i.e., its argumentation. My essay analyzes these two aspects of those portions of 2 Peter that constitute apocalyptic discourse. I later developed a complete interpretation of 2 Peter along the same lines in *Acknowledging the Divine Benefactor: The Second Letter of Peter*.

Another paper presented at the "Methodological Reassessments of the Letters of James, Peter, and Jude" section in 2007 was Robert Paul Seesengood's "'Irrational Animals, Creatures of Instinct, Bred to Be Caught and Killed': Hybridity, Alterity, and Name-Calling in 2 Peter 2." This paper moved me to investigate 2 Peter's references to animals. Three times in a relatively short section of 2 Peter, the author compares those he opposes to animals. "Comparison of Humans to Animals in 2 Peter 2:10b–22" analyses these references. In 2 Peter's context, comparison of humans to animals is common; it can be neutral, positive, or negative. Second Peter's comparisons are negative.

INTRODUCTION   xvii

I was invited to contribute a paper on 2 Peter to the "Letters of James, Peter, and Jude" section on the theme Letters of Peter and Q/Early Jesus Tradition at the 2011 annual meeting of the Society of Biblical Literature. My contribution was "The Gospels of Matthew and John in the Second Letter of Peter." This essay argues that 2 Peter refers to the Gospel of Matthew in two places and the Gospel of John in another, and that 2 Peter echoes the Gospel of John in yet another passage.

At about the same time I was invited to contribute an essay on 2 Peter to a planned volume on the theme of faith and faithfulness in Hebrews and the Catholic Epistles. My contribution was "Faith and Faithfulness in 2 Peter." This essay argues that faith, mentioned only twice, and faithfulness, not mentioned at all in 2 Peter, are reconfigured into knowledge and virtue in 2 Peter, both of which 2 Peter discusses rather extensively.

It is well known that all the manuscripts of the New Testament differ from one another in greater and lesser degrees. These differences have been studied intensively in the effort to establish the most likely original text. They have also been studied to some extent to determine the character of the scribes who wrote them. Little attention has been paid to the meaning of the manuscripts themselves. Since those who first used these manuscripts probably knew the New Testament only from the single manuscript they possessed, I thought it would be interesting to consider the meaning of 2 Peter as it is found in the earliest manuscripts we possess. The result is "Reading the Earliest Copies of 2 Peter."[2] This essay finds that the copy of 2 Peter in Codex Vaticanus is very similar to the critical text of today. The copy of 2 Peter in Papyrus 72 puts more emphasis on the divinity of Jesus; the copy of 2 Peter in Codex Sinaiticus puts more emphasis on the distinction between Jesus and God. Appended to this essay collection is a previously unpublished description of the meaning of the copies of 2 Peter found in Codices Alexandrinus and Ephraemi Syri Rescriptus.

Finally, I was invited to contribute a paper to a volume titled *2 Peter and the Apocalypse of Peter: Towards a New Perspective*, responding to Jörg Frey's 2016 Radboud Prestige Lectures in New Testament. My contribution was "The Second Letter of Peter, Josephus, and Gnosticism." This essay revives two old scholarly hypotheses, arguing that 2 Peter used the writings of Josephus, and that 2 Peter argued against Gnostics.

These essays can be grouped in two broad categories. Some of them focus on the understanding of 2 Peter in itself; others focus on its relationship to its cultural environment. The essays in the first group are those on

---

2. I later examined the earliest copy of Galatians in a similar way; see Callan, "Reading the Earliest Copy of Galatians."

the Christology and soteriology of 2 Peter, its style, the interpretation of 2 Peter 1:1–7 and 1:19–20, the rhetography and rhetoric of 2 Peter, and the theme of faith and faithfulness in 2 Peter. Of course, these essays use the cultural context of 2 Peter as a means to its interpretation, but they focus on the interpretation of 2 Peter. The remaining essays focus on the cultural environment, namely the essays on 2 Peter's use of Jude, its comparison of humans to animals, its use of Matthew and John, the meaning of various manuscripts of 2 Peter, and its relationship to Josephus and Gnosticism. These essays also use its cultural context to interpret 2 Peter but focus on the cultural context.

The essays in the first group can be further divided into two subgroups. Most of the essays focus on the message of the text—how to construe 2 Peter 1:1–7 and 1:19–20, 2 Peter's Christology and soteriology, and the theme of faith and faithfulness in 2 Peter. The other two focus on the expression of its message—its style and its rhetography and rhetoric.

The essays in the second group discuss 2 Peter's use of literary sources available to it—Jude, Matthew, John, and Josephus—and its use of a topic common in its cultural environment—comparison of humans to animals. One of them also argues that 2 Peter opposed Gnostic Christians. And another explores different ways 2 Peter would have been understood by those who read it in the earliest manuscripts we have.

All of this hardly constitutes a complete interpretation of 2 Peter. Rather, these essays illuminate various aspects of 2 Peter but leave other aspects still in the dark. I hope both light and darkness will assist others in further exploration of 2 Peter.

Original Publications

"The Christology of the Second Letter of Peter." *Biblica* 82 (2001) 253–63.
"The Soteriology of the Second Letter of Peter." *Biblica* 82 (2001) 549–59.
"The Style of the Second Letter of Peter." *Biblica* 84 (2003) 202–24.
"Use of the Letter of Jude by the Second Letter of Peter." *Biblica* 85 (2004) 42–64.
"The Syntax of 2 Peter 1:1–7." *Catholic Biblical Quarterly* 67 (2005) 632–40.
"A Note on 2 Peter 1:19–20." *Journal of Biblical Literature* 125 (2006) 143–50.
"Comparison of Humans to Animals in 2 Peter 2:10b–22." *Biblica* 90 (2009) 101–113.
"Rhetography and Rhetoric of Apocalyptic Discourse in Second Peter." In *Reading Second Peter with New Eyes*, edited by Robert L. Webb and Duane F. Watson, 59–90. Library of New Testament Studies 382. London: T & T Clark, 2010.
"Reading the Earliest Copies of 2 Peter." *Biblica* 93 (2012) 427–50.
"The Gospels of Matthew and John in the Second Letter of Peter." In *James, 1 and 2 Peter, and Early Jesus Traditions*, edited by Alicia J. Batten and John S. Kloppenborg, 166–80. Library of New Testament Studies 478. London: Bloomsbury, 2014.

"Faith and Faithfulness in 2 Peter." *Biblical Research* 61 (2016) 62–76.

"The Second Letter of Peter, Josephus and Gnosticism." In *2 Peter and the Apocalypse of Peter: Towards a New Perspective*, edited by Jörg Frey, Matthijs den Dulk, and Jan G. van der Watt, 128–46. Biblical Interpretation Series 174. Leiden: Brill, 2019.

All are reprinted here with permission of the original publisher. "Rhetography and Rhetology of Apocalyptic Discourse in Second Peter" and "The Gospels of Matthew and John in the Second Letter of Peter" are used by permission of Bloomsbury Publishing Plc.

1

Use of the Letter of Jude by the Second Letter of Peter

It seems obvious to all readers that there is some kind of close relationship between Jude and 2 Peter. For good reasons, it is now widely accepted that 2 Peter is dependent on Jude.[1] This is so much the case that authors at times overstate this dependence, saying that 2 Peter has simply incorporated Jude.[2] A closer examination shows that the relationship is not this simple. The author of 2 Peter adapted Jude 4–18 in 2 Pet 2:1–3:3. The purpose of this paper is to offer a detailed description and explanation of this adaptation. I will describe at the level of vocabulary and syntax the way 2 Peter has modified Jude and attempt to understand the significance of these modifications.

For the most part, 2 Peter has not adapted Jude by quoting it directly. While 2 Peter contains many of the words and some phrases found in Jude, no sentence of Jude is quoted in 2 Peter. Twice, however, clauses of Jude are used in 2 Peter with little change. These passages are

Jude 13b/2 Peter 2:17b

---

1. For this view, see Sidebottom, *James, Jude, and 2 Peter*, 68–69; Kelly, *Peter and Jude*, 226–27; Senior, *1 and 2 Peter*, 102; Bauckham, *Jude, 2 Peter*, 142–43; Neyrey, *2 Peter, Jude*, 122; Perkins, *First and Second Peter*, 178; and most recently Gilmour, *Significance of Parallels*, 90–91, 120. Watson has argued for the priority of Jude on rhetorical grounds (*Invention, Arrangement, and Style*, 160–87).

2. See, for example, Marxsen, *Introduction*, 241; Koester, *History and Literature*, 56; Ehrman, *New Testament*, 394.

| οἷς ὁ ζόφος τοῦ σκότους εἰς αἰῶνα τετήρηται | οἷς ὁ ζόφος τοῦ σκότους τετήρηται |

and Jude 17–18/2 Peter 3:2–3

17 Ὑμεῖς δέ, ἀγαπητοί,	
μνήσθητε τῶν ῥημάτων τῶν προειρημένων ὑπὸ τῶν ἀποστόλων τοῦ κυρίου ἡμῶν Ἰησοῦ Χριστοῦ·	3:2 μνησθῆναι τῶν προειρημένων ῥημάτων ὑπὸ τῶν ἁγίων προφητῶν καὶ τῆς τῶν ἀποστόλων ὑμῶν ἐντολῆς τοῦ κυρίου καὶ σωτῆρος,
18 ὅτι ἔλεγον ὑμῖν·[ὅτι] Ἐπ' ἐσχάτου [τοῦ] χρόνου ἔσονται ἐμπαῖκται κατὰ τὰς ἑαυτῶν ἐπιθυμίας πορευόμενοι τῶν ἀσεβειῶν.	3:3 τοῦτο πρῶτον γινώσκοντες ὅτι ἐλεύσονται ἐπ' ἐσχάτων τῶν ἡμερῶν [ἐν] ἐμπαιγμονῇ ἐμπαῖκται κατὰ τὰς ἰδίας ἐπιθυμίας αὐτῶν πορευόμενοι

It seems that 2 Peter's use of Jude can best be described as a rather free paraphrase.³ Working from the written text of Jude, the author of 2 Peter re-wrote Jude, avoiding direct quotation but using much of Jude's language. The procedure was similar to that used by the author of a paper like this one, who paraphrases the work of others in developing his/her own presentation.⁴

Jude 4–18 consists of 311 words. Second Peter 2:1–3:3 incorporated 80 of these words directly and substituted synonyms for another 7 of these words. In these ways, 2 Peter 2:1–3:3 used 28 percent of the vocabulary of Jude 4–18. 22 of the 87 words of Jude 4–18 used in 2 Peter 2:1–3:3, or 25 percent of them, are found in the two clauses that are virtual quotations from Jude, i.e., 2 Peter 2:17b and 3:2–3. Another 23 words (26 percent) are used by 2 Peter in the same syntactical structures as found in Jude: participial phrases (2 Peter 2:1, 10), clauses (2 Peter 2:11–12, 17), an adjective-noun phrase (2 Peter 2:12), and direct address (2 Peter 3:1). The remaining 42 of the words taken by 2 Peter 2:1–3:3 from Jude 4–18, or 48 percent of them, are used in syntactical structures different than those found in Jude. All of this clearly indicates the degree to which 2 Peter has reworked Jude.

Second Peter 2:1–3:3 consists of 426 words. The 87 of these words that are taken from Jude 4–18 constitute 20 percent of the total. This is another indication of how completely 2 Peter has reworked Jude.

3. Sidebottom, *James, Jude, and 2 Peter*, 95, 112.

4. Bauckham says, "This dependence is never slavish. The author takes what he wants from Jude, whether ideas or words, and uses it in a composition that is very much his own.... It is characteristic of our author's use of Jude that he gets an idea from Jude and then gives it a fresh twist or development of his own" (*Jude, 2 Peter*, 236, 260).

The principal purpose of 2 Peter is to argue against those who denied that Jesus would come again.[5] This is most explicit in 3:4–10, but the earlier part of the letter prepares for this explicit argument. As part of that preparation, in 2:1–3:3 the author of 2 Peter criticized false teachers who would arise among its addressees. This section of the letter criticized both the content of their teaching and the immoral behavior that flowed from it. Jude is mainly a critique of the immoral behavior of its opponents.[6] However, the author of 2 Peter adapted Jude to serve as an argument against both the teaching and the behavior of its opponents. In order to do so, 2 Peter made rather free use of Jude.

In adapting Jude, the author of 2 Peter also changed Jude's critique of a group presently confronting its readers into prediction of a group that will confront the readers of 2 Peter in the future. This may have been required by the fiction that the author is Peter, writing in the past. This was not difficult to do; it was mainly a matter of changing the aorist of Jude 4 into future tense in 2 Peter 2:1–3. Jude 5–7, 9 describe historical precedents for the error of Jude's present opponents, and Jude 17–18 contains a prediction of their arrival; both of these served 2 Peter's purpose without alteration of tense. And Jude's description of its opponents in present tense in vv. 8, 10–13, 16 could be used as a description of the future opponents predicted by 2 Peter, taking its meaning in 2 Peter from the tense of 2:1–3. However, the author of 2 Peter made several other changes in the tense of the verbs he took from Jude; these will be noted below.

In what follows I will consider each section of 2 Peter 2:1–3:3 in turn and discuss the way the author has used Jude in that section.

Jude 4(–5)/2 Peter 2:1–3

	2:1 Ἐγένοντο δὲ καὶ ψευδοπροφῆται ἐν τῷ λαῷ, ὡς καὶ ἐν ὑμῖν ἔσονται ψευδοδιδάσκαλοι, οἵτινες

---

5. Kelly, *Peter and Jude*, 229; Bauckham, *Jude, 2 Peter*, 154–57; Watson, *Invention, Arrangement, and Style*, 82. Neyrey describes the purpose of the letter as opposition to those "who rejected traditional theodicy" (*2 Peter, Jude*, 122).

6. For descriptions of the purpose of Jude, see Bauckham, *Jude, 2 Peter*, 11–13; Watson, *Invention, Arrangement, and Style*, 29–30; Neyrey, *2 Peter, Jude*, 31–32; Thurén, "Hey Jude!"

4 <u>παρεισέδυσαν</u> γάρ τινες ἄνθρωποι, οἱ <u>πάλαι</u> προγεγραμμένοι εἰς τοῦτο <u>τὸ κρίμα</u>, ἀσεβεῖς, τὴν τοῦ θεοῦ ἡμῶν χάριτα μετατιθέντες εἰς <u>ἀσέλγειαν</u>	<u>παρεισάξουσιν</u> αἱρέσεις <u>ἀπωλείας</u>,
καὶ τὸν μόνον <u>δεσπότην</u> καὶ κύριον ἡμῶν Ἰησοῦν Χριστὸν <u>ἀρνούμενοι</u>.	καὶ τὸν ἀγοράσαντα αὐτοὺς <u>δεσπότην</u> <u>ἀρνούμενοι</u>, ἐπάγοντες ἑαυτοῖς ταχινὴν <u>ἀπώλειαν</u>·
	2:2 καὶ πολλοὶ ἐξακολουθήσουσιν αὐτῶν ταῖς <u>ἀσελγείαις</u>, δι' οὓς ἡ ὁδὸς τῆς ἀληθείας βλασφημηθήσεται· 2:3 καὶ ἐν πλεονεξίᾳ πλαστοῖς λόγοις ὑμᾶς ἐμπορεύσονται· οἷς <u>τὸ</u> <u>κρίμα</u> <u>ἔκπαλαι</u> οὐκ ἀργεῖ, καὶ ἡ <u>ἀπώλεια</u> αὐτῶν οὐ νυστάζει.
5 Ὑπομνῆσαι δὲ ὑμᾶς βούλομαι, εἰδότας ὑμᾶς πάντα, ὅτι [ὁ] κύριος ἅπαξ <u>λαὸν</u> ἐκ γῆς Αἰγύπτου σώσας τὸ δεύτερον τοὺς μὴ πιστεύσαντας <u>ἀπώλεσεν</u>.	

In addition to changing its tense, the author of 2 Peter made other changes in Jude 4 (and 5) in adapting it in 2:1–3. The author of 2 Peter began his condemnation of future opponents by saying that false prophets arose among the people, i.e., the people of Israel. Only then did he say that false teachers will likewise appear in the future. The reference to false prophets created a chiastic relationship between 2 Peter 2:1–3 and 1:16–21. The false prophets of 2:1a are a negative counterpart of the true prophets mentioned in 1:19–21; the false teachers of 2:1b–3 are a negative counterpart of the apostolic teachers mentioned in 1:16–18.[7] In this way the author of 2 Peter connected the critique of false teachers in 2:1–3:3 with the earlier part of the letter.

Second Peter 2:1a seems to be an adaptation of Jude 5.[8] For Jude, this was the first of a series of historical precedents for condemnation of the author's opponents, namely, the Lord's salvation of the people of Israel from Egypt and later destruction of those who did not believe. Second Peter did not make use of this as a precedent. However, it may underlie the reference to the false prophets that arose among the people. Second Peter may have taken the word "people" from Jude 5. And 2 Peter may assume that it was

---

7. Bauckham, *Jude, 2 Peter*, 236; Watson, *Invention, Arrangement, and Style*, 106.

8. Watson, *Invention, Arrangement, and Style*, 173–74. Watson attributes to Fornberg the suggestion that adaptation of Jude 5 in 2 Pet 2:1 explains why Jude 5 is not included in the list of examples in 2 Pet 2:4–10a (173).

the presence of false prophets in Israel that led some not to believe and to be destroyed.

The remainder of 2 Peter 2:1–3 is more directly related to Jude 4. The latter is a very compact description of those whom Jude criticizes. They are described in a main clause and further described in three participial phrases and an adjective. Second Peter 2:1b–3 rearranged and elaborated these elements. The main clause of Jude 4 says, "Certain people have stolen in among you." Second Peter 2:1b specifies the people as false teachers. The author of 2 Peter replaced "have stolen in among you" with "will be among you." He then added a relative clause describing the false teachers as ones "who will secretly bring in destructive opinions." The verb of this clause has the same prefixes (i.e., παρεισ) as the verb in the main clause of Jude 4. Jude criticized the presence of certain people and their way of life; 2 Peter changed this into a critique of those who will be present and teach falsely in the future. This false teaching is denial of the second coming of Christ.[9] Second Peter says that their opinions are destructive, that they bring destruction on themselves (v. 1), and that their destruction is not asleep (v. 3). This emphasis on destruction may owe something to Jude's reference to God's destruction of unbelievers in v. 5. This repetition of the word "destruction" in close proximity in three different cases constitutes a figure of speech called polyptoton.

After adapting the main clause of Jude 4, 2 Peter passed over a participial phrase, an adjective, and another participial phrase, and went directly to the final participial phrase with which Jude described its opponents, i.e., they "deny our only Master and Lord, Jesus Christ." For the author of 2 Peter, this is the most important criticism of his opponents. From Jude, 2 Peter took only the words "denying the Master." But 2 Peter replaced the adjective "only" and the phrase "and our Lord Jesus Christ," with two participial phrases. The first describes the Master as the one "who bought them"; the second observes that by this denial, they bring "swift destruction on themselves." Describing Jesus as the Master "who bought them" emphasized the heinousness of denying him. Second Peter's second elaboration made the consequences of denying the Master explicit.

By moving the phrase "denying the Master" forward, the author of 2 Peter made it a description of the content of the false teaching he opposes. In Jude 4 the phrase probably spells out what Jude sees as the implications of the opponents' manner of life. For 2 Peter it summarizes the teaching of the opponents, i.e., their denial of the second coming of Jesus, as well as the behavior that follows from this teaching (cf. 2:2).[10] Also in line with 2 Peter's

---

9. Fornberg, *Early Church*, 36.
10. Watson (*Invention, Arrangement, and Style*, 174) and Neyrey (*2 Peter, Jude*,

use of the material of Jude to criticize teachers, 2 Peter 2:2 adds that many will follow them. Watson suggests that this also forms an *inclusio* with the author's denial in 1:16 that he and others followed cleverly devised myths.[11] This is another way the author of 2 Peter connected 2:1–3:3 with the earlier part of the letter.

The second participial phrase of Jude 4 says that its opponents "pervert the grace of our God into licentiousness." Of this, 2 Peter 2:2 used only the word "licentiousness" and made it plural rather than singular. The verse says that many will follow the "licentiousnesses" of the false teachers, and that on account of them, the way of truth will be maligned; the latter may be an allusion to Isa 52:5.[12] The reference to the "way of truth" anticipates use of similar language in 2 Peter 2:15 and 21. Fornberg argues that licentiousness here does not have its ordinary meaning of "sexual immorality" but instead refers to the opponents' doctrinal error.[13] To me, it seems more likely that it does have its ordinary meaning and that sexual immorality is seen as a consequence of the opponents' doctrinal error. The accusation of sexual immorality is repeated in 2:10, 13–14, 18; 3:3. Second Peter 2:3 adds that in their greed the false teachers will make a profit of the readers with false words. The accusation of greed anticipates the similar accusation in 2:14–15.[14]

The first participial phrase of Jude 4 says that its opponents "long ago were designated for this condemnation." Of this, 2 Peter 2:3 used the term "condemnation" and a slightly different form of the adverb "long ago"; here, as elsewhere, the author of 2 Peter shows a preference for unusual vocabulary. Second Peter 2:3 made "condemnation" the subject of a new clause and said of the false teachers that their "condemnation, pronounced against them long ago, is not idle, and their destruction is not asleep." Sometimes use of the present tense in this clause is seen as a failure to sustain the fiction that Peter is the author of the letter. Bauckham sees it as an intentional shift to allow direct argument with the opponents; such a shift is possible because attribution of the letter to Peter is a convention that the readers

---

188–89) think the opponents deny Jesus by denying his second coming. Bauckham argues that the opponents deny Jesus by teaching and practicing immorality (*Jude, 2 Peter*, 241). Kelly thinks their denial took both forms (*Peter and Jude*, 320).

11. Watson, *Invention, Arrangement, and Style*, 106–7.

12. Bauckham, *Jude, 2 Peter*, 242; Watson, *Invention, Arrangement, and Style*, 109.

13. Fornberg, *Early Church*, 37–38.

14. Accusations of immorality and greed were conventional in contemporary polemic and may not be reliable indications of the actual behavior of those attacked by 2 Peter. On this, see Johnson, "New Testament's Anti-Jewish Slander," esp. 432.

understand.¹⁵ Watson argues that it is a futuristic use of the present tense.¹⁶ The author of 2 Peter argues the truth of 2:3 in vv. 4–10a.

Thus 2 Peter 2:1–3 is a thorough revision of Jude 4–5. This revision served to connect the material 2 Peter adapted from Jude with the earlier part of 2 Peter, to predict the coming of false teachers, and to introduce the main things for which they would be criticized in 2 Peter 2:4–3:3. The author of 2 Peter rewrote the main clause and final participial phrase of Jude 4 in 2 Peter 2:1; he rewrote the second participial phrase from Jude 4 in 2 Peter 2:2; and he rewrote the first participial phrase from Jude 4 in 2 Peter 2:3. Second Peter's reference to the people of Israel in 2:1 and its three references to destruction of the false teachers in 2:1, 3 may have been suggested by Jude 5.

Jude 5–8a/2 Peter 2:4–10a

5 Ὑπομνῆσαι δὲ ὑμᾶς βούλομαι, εἰδότας ὑμᾶς πάντα, ὅτι [ὁ] κύριος ἅπαξ λαὸν ἐκ γῆς Αἰγύπτου σώσας τὸ δεύτερον τοὺς μὴ πιστεύσαντας ἀπώλεσεν,	
6 <u>ἀγγέλους</u> τε τοὺς μὴ τηρήσαντας τὴν ἑαυτῶν ἀρχὴν ἀλλὰ ἀπολιπόντας τὸ ἴδιον οἰκητήριον <u>εἰς</u> <u>κρίσιν</u> μεγάλης ἡμέρας <u>δεσμοῖς</u> ἀϊδίοις ὑπὸ <u>ζόφον</u> <u>τετήρηκεν,</u>	2:4 Εἰ γὰρ ὁ θεὸς <u>ἀγγέλων</u> ἁμαρτησάντων οὐκ ἐφείσατο, ἀλλὰ <u>σειραῖς</u> <u>ζόφου</u> ταρταρώσας παρέδωκεν <u>εἰς</u> <u>κρίσιν</u> <u>τηρουμένους,</u>
	2:5 καὶ ἀρχαίου κόσμου οὐκ ἐφείσατο, ἀλλὰ ὄγδοον Νῶε δικαιοσύνης κήρυκα ἐφύλαξεν κατακλυσμὸν κόσμῳ ἀσεβῶν ἐπάξας,
7 ὡς <u>Σόδομα</u> <u>καὶ</u> <u>Γόμορρα</u> καὶ αἱ περὶ αὐτὰς <u>πόλεις</u> τὸν ὅμοιον τρόπον τούτοις ἐκπορνεύσασαι καὶ <u>ἀπελθοῦσαι</u> <u>ὀπίσω</u> <u>σαρκὸς</u> ἑτέρας,	2:6 καὶ <u>πόλεις</u> <u>Σοδόμων</u> <u>καὶ</u> <u>Γομόρρας</u> τεφρώσας [καταστροφῇ] κατέκρινεν,
πρόκεινται <u>δεῖγμα</u> πυρὸς αἰωνίου δίκην ὑπέχουσαι.	<u>ὑπόδειγμα</u> μελλόντων ἀσεβέ[σ]ιν τεθεικώς,

---

15. Bauckham, *Jude, 2 Peter*, 245.
16. Watson, *Invention, Arrangement, and Style*, 110–11.

	2:7 καὶ δίκαιον Λὼτ καταπονούμενον ὑπὸ τῆς τῶν ἀθέσμων ἐν ἀσελγείᾳ ἀναστροφῆς ἐρρύσατο
	2:8 βλέμματι γὰρ καὶ ἀκοῇ ὁ δίκαιος ἐγκατοικῶν ἐν αὐτοῖς ἡμέραν ἐξ ἡμέρας ψυχὴν δικαίαν ἀνόμοις ἔργοις ἐβασάνιζεν
	2:9 οἶδεν κύριος εὐσεβεῖς ἐκ πειρασμοῦ ῥύεσθαι, ἀδίκους δὲ εἰς ἡμέραν κρίσεως κολαζομένους τηρεῖν,
8 Ὁμοίως μέντοι καὶ οὗτοι ἐνυπνιαζόμενοι <u>σάρκα</u> μὲν <u>μιαίνουσιν</u> <u>κυριότητα</u> δὲ ἀθετοῦσιν	2:10 μάλιστα δὲ τοὺς <u>ὀπίσω</u> <u>σαρκὸς</u> ἐν ἐπιθυμίᾳ <u>μιασμοῦ</u> <u>πορευομένους</u> καὶ <u>κυριότητος</u> καταφρονοῦντας.

Jude 5–7 is a single sentence reminding readers of historical precedents for God's condemnation of sinners, as a prelude to critique of its opponents in v. 8. Second Peter 2:4–10a revised this material considerably. Apart from what may be an oblique reference to it in 2 Peter 2:1, 2 Peter passed over the precedent in Jude 5. Second Peter 2:4–10a begins with the precedent in Jude 6, i.e., God's condemnation of the sinful angels. Jude 5–7 simply narrates its precedents; 2 Peter 2:4–10a incorporates them into a long and elaborate conditional sentence. After beginning "If God" in v. 4, there follow three conditional clauses in vv. 4, 5, 6–8; vv. 9–10 (which incorporate part of Jude 8) provide the conclusion, "then the Lord."[17] In this way, the author of 2 Peter transformed Jude's list of precedents for punishment of sinners and critique of its opponents into a refutation of the false teachers' denial of a final judgment. At the same time, this refutation served as a warning that the false teachers will be condemned. The author of 2 Peter began 2:4–10a with the word "for" to indicate that this section is the basis for the assertion in 2:3b that the condemnation of the false teachers is not idle or asleep.

The first two conditional clauses in vv. 4 and 5 have the same verb, "If God did not spare." In v. 4 the author speaks about God's not sparing the angels and in v. 5 about God's not sparing the ancient world at the time of the flood. The former is taken from Jude 6. The author of 2 Peter added the latter both because it serves his present purpose and it prepares for a reference to the flood in 3:5–6. The author may also have added it in view of the following reference to the destruction of Sodom and Gomorrah (2 Peter

---

17. According to Bauckham (*Jude, 2 Peter*, 246–47) and Neyrey (*2 Peter, Jude*, 196–97), the author of 2 Peter here relies not only on Jude but also on the tradition that underlies Jude. This tradition also underlies Sir 16:6–23.

2:6). The two constitute precedents for destruction of the world by water and fire (cf. 2 Peter 3:5–7).[18]

Jude 6 describes the angels in two participial phrases as ones "who did not keep their own position, but left their proper dwelling," referring to Genesis 6:1–4 as elaborated in extra-biblical writings like 1 Enoch.[19] Second Peter 2:4 replaced these phrases with a single participle describing the angels as ones who had sinned. This gives much less information about exactly what they did wrong but also makes the reason for their condemnation (i.e., their sin) clearer to someone who does not recognize the story to which reference is being made. The author of 2 Peter may have been trying to minimize reference to non-biblical literature.[20]

Jude 6 says that God "has kept [the angels] in eternal chains in deepest darkness for the judgment of the great day."[21] Second Peter 2:4 says that God "cast the angels into hell and committed them to chains of deepest darkness to be kept until the judgment." The author of 2 Peter changed the main verb of the clause from "kept" to "committed," perhaps to emphasize that God was responsible for putting the angels in chains and not merely for keeping them there. The author of 2 Peter made this still more emphatic by adding a participle to say that God cast the angels into hell.[22] Second Peter used a different word for "chains" than that used in Jude 6 and eliminated the adjective "eternal," perhaps because the idea that the chains are eternal conflicts with the idea that the angels are subject to judgment in the future. Second Peter also changed "chains in deepest darkness" into "chains of deepest darkness," suggesting that the chains were not literal chains, but that the chains consisted of darkness.[23] Second Peter changed the main verb of Jude 6, i.e., "kept," into a participle, using it to say that God was keeping the angels for judgment. The author of 2 Peter omitted the phrase "of the

---

18. Fornberg, *Early Church*, 41; Bauckham, *Jude, 2 Peter*, 252; Watson, *Invention, Arrangement, and Style*, 113.

19. For a parallel to this language, see 1 En. 12.4.

20. Kelly, *Peter and Jude*, 331.

21. This echoes 1 En. 10.4, 6, 11–14; 22.11; 91.15.

22. He also makes use of a Greek verb, ταρταροω = cast into hell, that is reminiscent of the Greek myth of the Titans who were cast into hell, though he probably derives its use from Hellenistic Jewish authors (Kelly, *Peter and Jude*, 331; Bauckham, *Jude, 2 Peter*, 249). Neyrey says this usage suggests that 2 Peter was written for a multi-cultural audience (*2 Peter, Jude*, 198, 202).

23. Bauckham, *Jude, 2 Peter*, 249. Fornberg argues that 2 Pet 2:4 says that the angels were committed to pits (σιροις) of deepest darkness, rather than chains (σειραις). He further argues that σιροις is "religious vocabulary originally derived from the Eleusinian Mysteries" (*Early Church*, 53).

great day," which modifies judgment in Jude 6. Perhaps he thought it added nothing to the meaning.

Second Peter's second conditional clause (v. 5) cites the precedent of the flood, "[If God] did not spare the ancient world." This obviously provided another precedent for God's punishment of evildoers. However, it also allowed 2 Peter to introduce a precedent for God's salvation of the righteous, i.e., the salvation of Noah and his family. This precedent is not found in Jude.

Second Peter's third conditional clause (v. 6-8) cites the precedent of Sodom and Gomorrah, "[If God] condemned them." Jude 7 says, "Sodom and Gomorrah and the surrounding cities, which, in the same manner as they [i.e., the angels], indulged in sexual immorality and pursued other flesh, serve as an example by undergoing a punishment of eternal fire." Second Peter omitted any reference to other cities and to the specific nature of their sin. The latter is mentioned in general terms in 2:7 and then taken up in 2:10, which we will discuss below. The author of 2 Peter changed the main verb of Jude 7 from "serve" to "condemned," making it clear that God was responsible for the destruction of Sodom and Gomorrah. Second Peter changed the description of the destruction from "undergoing a punishment of eternal fire" to "having turned [them] to ashes." Perhaps the author thought this was a more accurate description of the fate of the two cities. Second Peter rewrote Jude's "serve as an example" as "made them an example of what is coming to the ungodly"; this makes more explicit both that God is the one who made an example of Sodom and Gomorrah and how they function as an example. The author of 2 Peter replaced "serve" with the participle "made," and used a slightly different word for "example."

The second part of 2 Peter's third conditional clause (vv. 7-8) cites the precedent of Lot. This is another precedent for God's salvation of the righteous. God saved the righteous Lot from the destruction of Sodom and Gomorrah. The salvation of Lot is not mentioned in Jude.[24]

The main, concluding clause of this long sentence begins in 2 Peter 2:9. If the preceding clauses are true (vv. 4-8), then God obviously knows how to rescue the godly and punish the unrighteous. The conclusion has no counterpart in Jude. However, the author of 2 Peter used material from Jude 7-8 to develop the second part of this conclusion in v. 10a. Here the author describes the unrighteous in more detail and strongly implies that the false teachers are among them. To do this, the author rewrote Jude 8. Jude 8 describes its opponents as dreamers who "also defile the flesh, reject authority, and slander the glorious ones." Second Peter 2:10a omitted descriptions of

---

24. Noah and Lot are also linked in Luke 17:26-30.

the opponents as "dreamers"; it was probably not appropriate as a description of the false teachers. In 2 Peter 2:10a the author replaced the first two clauses of Jude 8 with participial phrases. The author of 2 Peter replaced the first clause of Jude 8 with a participial phrase taken from Jude 7. The latter described Sodom and Gomorrah as having gone after other flesh. In 2 Peter 2:10a the author replaced the aorist participle with the present participle of a synonymous verb, making the phrase a description of ongoing behavior. He also eliminated the adjective "other"; this was appropriate to describe the sin of Sodom and Gomorrah (and of the angels) but was apparently not suited to describe the sin of the false teachers. The author of 2 Peter added the prepositional phrase "in desire of defilement." This makes more explicit the meaning of going after flesh. It also uses a noun, "defilement," that is cognate with the verb "defile" used in Jude 8.

The second clause of Jude 8 says that the opponents "reject authority." Second Peter 2:10a replaced "reject" with "despise." Perhaps the author of 2 Peter thought that Jude's language conceded too much power to the opponents, or perhaps "despise" simply fit his situation better.

Thus 2 Peter 2:4–10a is a thorough revision of Jude 5–8a. Passing over Jude 5, 2 Peter incorporated Jude 6–8a into a long conditional sentence consisting of three conditional clauses (vv. 4–8) and a conclusion (vv. 9–10a). The historical precedents cited in Jude 6–7, 2 Peter fashioned into two of the three conditional clauses; to these the author added a third. In this way 2 Peter created a list of precedents supporting the conclusion that God both punishes the unrighteous and rescues the godly. Second Peter used the first part of Jude 8 to describe the false teachers it opposes as unrighteous.

Jude 8b–11/2 Peter 2:10b–16

8b δόξας δὲ βλασφημοῦσιν.	2:10b Τολμηταί, αὐθάδεις, δόξας οὐ τρέμουσιν, βλασφημοῦντες,
9 ὁ δὲ Μιχαὴλ ὁ ἀρχάγγελος, ὅτε τῷ διαβόλῳ διακρινόμενος διελέγετο περὶ τοῦ Μωϋσέως σώματος, οὐκ ἐτόλμησεν κρίσιν ἐπενεγκεῖν βλασφημίας, ἀλλὰ εἶπεν· Ἐπιτιμήσαι σοι κύριος.	2:11 ὅπου ἄγγελοι ἰσχύϊ καὶ δυνάμει μείζονες ὄντες οὐ φέρουσιν κατ' αὐτῶν παρὰ κυρίου βλάσφημον κρίσιν.
10 οὗτοι δὲ ὅσα μὲν οὐκ οἴδασιν βλασφημοῦσιν, ὅσα δὲ φυσικῶς ὡς τὰ ἄλογα ζῷα ἐπίστανται, ἐν τούτοις φθείρονται.	2:12 οὗτοι δέ, ὡς ἄλογα ζῷα γεγεννημένα φυσικὰ εἰς ἅλωσιν καὶ φθοράν ἐν οἷς ἀγνοοῦσιν βλασφημοῦντες, ἐν τῇ φθορᾷ αὐτῶν καὶ φθαρήσονται

	2:13 ἀδικούμενοι μισθὸν ἀδικίας, ἡδονὴν ἡγούμενοι τὴν ἐν ἡμέρᾳ τρυφήν, <u>σπίλοι</u> καὶ μῶμοι ἐντρυφῶντες <u>ἐν ταῖς</u> ἀπάταις αὐτῶν <u>συνευωχούμενοι</u> ὑμῖν, 2:14 ὀφθαλμοὺς ἔχοντες μεστοὺς μοιχαλίδος καὶ ἀκαταπαύστους ἁμαρτίας, δελεάζοντες ψυχὰς ἀστηρίκτους, καρδίαν γεγυμνασμένην πλεονεξίας ἔχοντες, κατάρας τέκνα·
11 οὐαὶ αὐτοῖς, ὅτι <u>τῇ ὁδῷ</u> τοῦ Κάϊν ἐπορεύθησαν, καὶ τῇ <u>πλάνῃ</u> τοῦ <u>Βαλαὰμ μισθοῦ</u> ἐξεχύθησαν, καὶ τῇ ἀντιλογίᾳ τοῦ Κόρε ἀπώλοντο.	2:15 καταλείποντες εὐθεῖαν <u>ὁδὸν</u> <u>ἐπλανήθησαν</u>, ἐξακολουθήσαντες <u>τῇ ὁδῷ</u> <u>τοῦ Βαλαὰμ</u> τοῦ Βοσὸρ, ὃς <u>μισθὸν</u> ἀδικίας ἠγάπησεν
	2:16 ἔλεγξιν δὲ ἔσχεν ἰδίας παρανομίας· ὑποζύγιον ἄφωνον ἐν ἀνθρώπου φωνῇ φθεγξάμενον ἐκώλυσεν τὴν τοῦ προφήτου παραφρονίαν.

The third clause of Jude 8 says that the opponents "slander the glorious ones." Jude 9 then mentions an incident when the archangel Michael refrained from a judgment of slander. In 2 Peter 2:10b–11 the author separated the final clause of Jude 8 from the previous two clauses, revised it, made it the beginning of a new sentence, and incorporated a revised version of Jude 9 into this sentence. One reason for this may have been to make explicit the implicit connection between Jude 8b and 9.

The author of 2 Peter expanded Jude 8b, emphasizing the audacity of the behavior described: "Bold and willful, they are not afraid to slander the glorious ones." The author of 2 Peter added two adjectives to describe the false teachers, i.e., bold and willful. The word "bold" is probably taken from Jude 9.[25] Second Peter replaced "slander," the main verb of Jude 8b, with "they are not afraid," implying that the false teachers should fear to behave as they do. Second Peter then converted "slander" into a participle and used it describe the behavior of the false teachers as slandering the glorious ones.

Jude 9 describes a specific incident when the archangel Michael was not bold to bring a judgment of slander against the devil. This contrasts with the behavior of Jude's opponents as described in vv. 8 and 10. The author of 2 Peter rewrote this in much more general terms and incorporated it into the sentence begun in v. 10b in order to make the contrast with the behavior described there sharper. Second Peter 2:10b says that the false teachers are not afraid to slander the glorious ones; v. 11 says that the angels do not bring

---

25. Bauckham, *Jude, 2 Peter*, 260; Neyrey, *2 Peter, Jude*, 208.

a slanderous judgment against them, i.e., either the glorious ones or the false teachers.[26]

Second Peter replaced the reference to Michael the archangel with a reference to angels in general and omitted the clause in Jude that describes the occasion when Michael did not bring a judgment of slander against the devil, i.e., when the two contended over the body of Moses. For some reason, the specific incident mentioned by Jude did not serve 2 Peter's purpose, and the author replaced it with a reference to the behavior of angels in general. Having used the adjective "bold" in 2:10b, the author of 2 Peter omitted the cognate verb "dare" from the main clause of Jude 9 and replaced it with "bring." In addition, as Fornberg observes, the author of 2 Peter changed the tense of the main verb from the aorist of Jude 9 to present tense, transforming a reference to a specific incident into a description of repeated behavior. The author of 2 Peter also changed the quotation of Michael's words into the phrase "from the Lord."[27] Bauckham adds that the author of 2 Peter replaced Jude's implication that the judgment of slander would be against the devil with the statement that it would be "against them."[28]

The author of 2 Peter may have made these changes because he was unfamiliar with the incident mentioned in Jude 9[29] or wary of referring to an incident not recorded in the Bible and found only in apocryphal writings.[30] Or perhaps an incident in which Michael refrained from bringing a judgment of slander against the devil did not form a sufficient contrast to the behavior of the false teachers described in 2 Peter 2:10b. The author adds that the angels are "greater in might and power" than either the false teachers or the glorious ones[31] in order to sharpen the contrast between the false teachers and the angels. The author of 2 Peter changed Jude's "condemnation of slander" into "slanderous judgment" in order to make the meaning of the phrase clearer.[32] All of this made the behavior of the angels a clear contrast to that of the false teachers. However, the reader remains uncertain on what basis the author describes the behavior of the angels in this way.

---

26. Bauckham (*Jude, 2 Peter*, 261) opts for the former. Perkins interprets 2 Pet 2:11 as a statement that the angels do not bring the blasphemous judgments of the opponents into the heavenly court as evidence against them (*First and Second Peter*, 184).

27. Fornberg, *Early Church*, 54.

28. Bauckham, *Jude, 2 Peter*, 261.

29. Bauckham, *Jude, 2 Peter*, 260.

30. Kelly, *Peter and Jude*, 338; Neyrey, *2 Peter, Jude*, 208.

31. Kelly (*Peter and Jude*, 338) and Fornberg (*Early Church*, 54) argue for the latter. Bauckham (*Jude, 2 Peter*, 262) regards it as "slightly more natural."

32. Bauckham, *Jude, 2 Peter*, 261.

Jude 10–11 are a further criticism of Jude's opponents. Second Peter 2:12–16 is an adaptation of this material to continue 2 Peter's description of the false teachers begun in 2 Peter 2:10. Jude 10 criticizes the opponents in two carefully constructed parallel clauses: "These slander whatever they do not understand, and they are destroyed by those things that, like irrational animals, they know by instinct." Second Peter 2:12 revised this to emphasize the comparison with irrational animals.[33] The author of 2 Peter put this comparison first. He inserted the phrase "like irrational animals," from the second clause of Jude 10, immediately after "these," giving prominence to the assertion that the false teachers are like irrational animals. The author also changed the adverb "by instinct," from the second clause of Jude 10, into an adjective, "of instinct," and used it to describe irrational animals. He then described them further as having a very limited purpose—"born to be caught and killed." The author of 2 Peter converted "slander," the main verb of Jude 10's first clause, into a participle and used it to describe the false teachers as slandering what they do not understand. Second Peter also replaced Jude 10's words for "whatever they do not understand" with synonyms.

Finally, the author says, "In their destruction they also will be destroyed." This is 2 Peter's revision of the second clause of Jude 10. Having already used "by instinct" and the comparison with irrational animals, the author of 2 Peter omitted Jude 10's statement that the opponents do know some things. The remainder of Jude 10's second clause says, "By these they are destroyed." The author of 2 Peter changed the tense of the verb from present to future and replaced "by these" with "in their destruction." The antecedent of "their" is unclear; the most likely possibilities are that it refers to the irrational animals or the ones slandered by the false teachers.[34] This seems less clear than the text of Jude that underlies it; however, Jude's statement that the opponents are destroyed by the things they know by instinct is far from transparent. Repetition of the root meaning "destruction" (φθορ-/φθαρ-) three times in 2 Peter 2:12 is paronomasia. Second Peter 2:13a further describes the future destruction of the false teachers as "suffering the penalty for doing wrong." Repetition of the root meaning "wrongdoing" (ἀδικ-) twice in this verse is another example of paronomasia.

The remainder of 2 Peter 2:13–14 is further description of the false teachers. The author of 2 Peter took the description of them as "blots" and as "feasting with" the readers from Jude 12, using a cognate of the word for

---

33. Fornberg argues that the purpose of this revision is to deny "all understanding to the adversaries" (*Early Church*, 48–49).

34. Bauckham, *Jude, 2 Peter*, 263–64.

"blots" in Jude 12.³⁵ Otherwise, this material has no counterpart in Jude. In 2 Peter 2:13 the author coupled "blots," taken from Jude, with blemishes, and so prepared for his use of the phrase "without blot or blemish" in 3:14. Bauckham thinks that the phrase "indulging in their deceits (ἀπάταις) while they feast with you" may contain a pun on Jude 12—"blots on your love feasts (ἀγάπαις), feasting with you."³⁶ Senior suggests that the author of 2 Peter changed love feasts to deceits either because love feasts were not a custom in the churches he addresses or because they had not been abused by his opponents.³⁷ Perkins suggests that 2 Peter is trying to obviate any suspicion that the feasting occurs at formal celebrations of the Christian church.³⁸

Second Peter 2:15 is an adaptation of Jude 11. Jude 11 compares the opponents to Cain, Balaam, and Korah. Second Peter omitted any reference to the first and third, though it adapted the image of the "way" from Jude's reference to Cain.³⁹ The description of the false teachers as accursed children at the end of 2 Peter 2:14 may also have been suggested by Jude's reference to Cain, the accursed child of Adam and Eve (Gen 4:11). The author may have thought it more effective to make a single comparison at greater length than three very brief comparisons. In addition, comparison with Balaam may have been particularly appropriate following an accusation that the false teachers are greedy.⁴⁰ Senior suggests that the author of 2 Peter focused on Balaam because "his credentials as prophet and wise man fit the false teachers."⁴¹

Jude 11 says of the opponents that "they went the way of Cain and abandoned themselves to Balaam's error for the sake of gain." Second Peter 2:15 says of the false teachers, "Having left the straight way, they have erred, having followed the way of Balaam, son of Bosor, who loved the gain of wrongdoing." Using the word "way" twice in different cases is polyptoton. Jude 11 says that the opponents have gone the way of Cain; 2 Peter 2:15 expressed a similar idea more generally and in negative terms, i.e., the false teachers have left the straight way. This refers back to the language of 2 Peter 2:2 and anticipates a similar statement in 2:21. Jude 11 says that

---

35. Kelly, *Peter and Jude*, 341; Fornberg, *Early Church*, 49–50; Bauckham, *Jude, 2 Peter*, 265–66; Neyrey, *2 Peter, Jude*, 209–10.

36. Bauckham, *Jude, 2 Peter*, 260, 266; so also Watson, *Invention, Arrangement, and Style*, 117.

37. Senior, *1 and 2 Peter*, 124.

38. Perkins, *First and Second Peter*, 185.

39. Bauckham, *Jude, 2 Peter*, 267; Neyrey, *2 Peter, Jude*, 210.

40. Bauckham, *Jude, 2 Peter*, 260.

41. Senior, *1 and 2 Peter*, 125; cf. Fornberg, *Early Church*, 39–40.

the opponents abandoned themselves to Balaam's error for the sake of gain. The author of 2 Peter replaced "abandoned themselves to error" with "have erred," using a verb cognate to the noun "error" found in Jude 11. The author then explained how they have gone astray with the phrase "having followed the way of Balaam." This phrase is patterned on Jude 11's statement that the opponents followed the way of Cain. The author of 2 Peter then transformed Jude 11's statement that the opponents acted for the sake of gain in following Balaam into a description of Balaam as one "who loved the gain of wrongdoing." To this, 2 Peter added 2:16, describing the rebuke of Balaam for his transgression. Jude says nothing about this.

Thus 2 Peter 2:10b–16 is a thorough revision of Jude 8b–11. In 2 Peter 2:10b–11 the author separated the final clause of Jude 8 from the preceding two clauses and joined to it a revised version of Jude 9. In 2 Peter 2:12 the author followed Jude 10 more closely, though still making substantial changes. The author of 2 Peter added 2:13–14, making some use of Jude 12. In 2 Peter 2:15 the author used one of the three elements of Jude 11. He expanded upon it and developed it further by the addition of 2 Peter 2:16. From a rhetorical point of view, one can say that here and in the following section of 2 Peter, the author reworked a portion of Jude that attempted to prove Jude's thesis, into a digression in which the author of 2 Peter denounced his opponents.[42]

Jude 12–16 / 2 Peter 2:17–22

12 οὗτοί εἰσιν οἱ ἐν ταῖς ἀγάπαις ὑμῶν σπιλάδες συνευωχούμενοι ἀφόβως ἑαυτοὺς ποιμαίνοντες,	2:17 Οὗτοί εἰσιν
νεφέλαι ἄνυδροι ὑπὸ ἀνέμων παραφερόμεναι, δένδρα φθινοπωρινὰ ἄκαρπα δὶς ἀποθανόντα ἐκριζωθέντα, 13 κύματα ἄγρια θαλάσσης ἐπαφρίζοντα τὰς ἑαυτῶν αἰσχύνας, ἀστέρες πλανῆται	πηγαὶ ἄνυδροι καὶ ὁμίχλαι ὑπὸ λαίλαπος ἐλαυνόμεναι,
οἷς ὁ ζόφος τοῦ σκότους εἰς αἰῶνα τετήρηται.	οἷς ὁ ζόφος τοῦ σκότους τετήρηται.

---

42. Watson, *Invention, Arrangement, and Style*, 48–49, 114–15.

14 Προεφήτευσεν δὲ καὶ τούτοις ἕβδομος ἀπὸ Ἀδὰμ Ἑνὼχ λέγων· Ἰδοὺ ἦλθεν κύριος ἐν ἁγίαις μυριάσιν αὐτοῦ, 15 ποιῆσαι κρίσιν κατὰ πάντων καὶ ἐλέγξαι πᾶσαν ψυχὴν περὶ πάντων τῶν ἔργων ἀσεβείας αὐτῶν ὧν ἠσέβησαν καὶ περὶ πάντων τῶν σκληρῶν ὧν ἐλάλησαν κατ' αὐτοῦ ἁμαρτωλοὶ ἀσεβεῖς.	
16 οὗτοί εἰσιν γογγυσταί, μεμψίμοιροι, κατὰ τὰς <u>ἐπιθυμίας</u> ἑαυτῶν πορευόμενοι, καὶ τὸ στόμα αὐτῶν λαλεῖ <u>ὑπέρογκα</u>, θαυμάζοντες πρόσωπα ὠφελείας χάριν.	2:18 <u>ὑπέρογκα</u> γὰρ ματαιότητος φθεγγόμενοι δελεάζουσιν ἐν <u>ἐπιθυμίαις</u> σαρκὸς ἀσελγείαις τοὺς ὀλίγως ἀποφεύγοντας τοὺς ἐν πλάνῃ ἀναστρεφομένους,
	2:19 ἐλευθερίαν αὐτοῖς ἐπαγγελλόμενοι, αὐτοὶ δοῦλοι ὑπάρχοντες τῆς φθορᾶς· ᾧ γάρ τις ἥττηται, τούτῳ δεδούλωται. 2:20 εἰ γὰρ ἀποφυγόντες τὰ μιάσματα τοῦ κόσμου ἐν ἐπιγνώσει τοῦ κυρίου [ἡμῶν] καὶ σωτῆρος Ἰησοῦ Χριστοῦ, τούτοις δὲ πάλιν ἐμπλακέντες ἡττῶνται, γέγονεν αὐτοῖς τὰ ἔσχατα χείρονα τῶν πρώτων. 2:21 κρεῖττον γὰρ ἦν αὐτοῖς μὴ ἐπεγνωκέναι τὴν ὁδὸν τῆς δικαιοσύνης ἢ ἐπιγνοῦσιν ὑποστρέψαι ἐκ τῆς παραδοθείσης αὐτοῖς ἁγίας ἐντολῆς. 2:22 συμβέβηκεν αὐτοῖς τὸ τῆς ἀληθοῦς παροιμίας· Κύων ἐπιστρέψας ἐπὶ τὸ ἴδιον ἐξέραμα, καί· Ὗς λουσαμένη εἰς κυλισμὸν βορβόρου.

In 2:17–22 the author of 2 Peter continues the description of the false teachers begun in vv. 10b–16. In vv. 17–22 the author made highly selective use of Jude 12–16. Jude 12–13 consists of five brief descriptions of the opponents. Second Peter adapted the first of these ("blemishes on your love-feasts, feasting with you without fear, feeding themselves") in 2:13. The remaining four descriptions are metaphors drawn from the natural world.[43] Second Peter 2:17 is an adaptation of the first and fourth; the second and third are completely omitted. Second Peter 2:17 begins with the words "these are," taken from the beginning of Jude 12.

The first of Jude's four metaphors describes the opponents as "waterless clouds carried along by the winds." Second Peter 2:17 changed the

---

43. Bauckham (*Jude, 2 Peter*, 90–91) says that these metaphors may have been suggested by 1 En. 2.1–5.4; 80.2–8.

waterless clouds to "waterless springs" and added "mists driven by a storm." Perhaps the author of 2 Peter thought that waterless springs was better than waterless clouds as a metaphor for lack of productivity.[44] Having changed the clouds into springs, the author of 2 Peter could no longer say that they were carried along by the winds, so he introduced a second metaphor of his own, i.e., mists, and described them as driven by a storm. Jude's image suggests that the opponents have no direction of their own but are moved this way and that by external forces. Second Peter's image suggests that the false teachers are controlled by a powerful external force that directs their actions. This may have conveyed the author's view of the false teachers better than Jude's language did.

Second Peter 2:17 omitted the second, third, and fourth metaphors in Jude 12–13. Either the author of 2 Peter did not find these helpful as a description of the false teachers or he did not think such a multiplication of images was effective.[45] Although 2 Peter did not use the fourth metaphor, i.e., "wandering stars," it did use the description of these wandering stars in Jude 13 as ones "for whom the deepest darkness has been reserved forever." Second Peter 2:17 omitted "forever" but otherwise quoted this verbatim. This is the longest quotation from Jude in 2 Peter thus far.

Jude 14–15 continues to describe the opponents by saying that they are the fulfillment of a passage from 1 Enoch that is cited (i.e., 1 En. 1.9). Second Peter omitted this, perhaps in order to avoid the citation of a writing not found in the Bible. Fornberg argues that 2 Peter omitted this citation because it speaks of a past event and thus "could not be used against those who denied the parousia of Christ."[46] Fornberg also suggests that 1 Enoch may not have been known to the gentile readers of 2 Peter and that it would have been "dangerous" to seek support from it. And the citation mentions only the negative not the positive aspect of judgment; both were of interest to the author of 2 Peter.[47]

---

44. Kelly, *Peter and Jude*, 344–45. According to Watson, "waterless springs" is a traditional metaphor; he cites Jer 2:13 (*Invention, Arrangement, and Style*, 120).

45. According to Bauckham, the author of 2 Peter probably thought these metaphors were redundant (*Jude, 2 Peter*, 272). According to Watson (*Invention, Arrangement, and Style*, 183–84), the author of 2 Peter might not have used the images because he was following rhetorical conventions of not crowding metaphors, avoiding a series of metaphors of the same species, or avoiding use of more than three metaphors in a row. However, the overall style of 2 Peter makes Watson think it unlikely that this was the author's motivation. Second Peter 2:13–22 violates these conventions (*Invention, Arrangement, and Style*, 123–24).

46. Fornberg, *Early Church*, 47.

47. Fornberg, *Early Church*, 56.

Jude 16 continues to describe the opponents in two clauses as "grumblers and malcontents, they indulge their own lusts; they are bombastic in speech, flattering people to their own advantage." Second Peter 2:18 begins with an adaptation of the second clause. The author of 2 Peter transformed Jude's statement that the opponents' mouth speaks bombast into a participial phrase, i.e., "speaking bombast"; he uses a different word meaning "speak," once again displaying a preference for unusual vocabulary. He also added the qualifier "worthless" to make the emptiness of their speech more explicit. He omitted the participial phrase with which the second clause of Jude 16 ends. The author of 2 Peter then adapted the first clause of Jude 16, i.e., the statement that the opponents are grumblers and malcontents who indulge their own desires, into a statement that the false teachers use licentious desires of the flesh to "entice people who have just escaped from those who live in error." The author of 2 Peter took only the word "desires" from Jude. By adding the conjunction "for" at the beginning of 2:18, the author of 2 Peter connected this material to the preceding description of his opponents, so that it became the basis for that description. Second Peter 2:17–19 thus forms an enthymeme,[48] i.e., a syllogism in which one of the premises is implicit.

In 2:19–22 the author of 2 Peter went on to describe the false teachers as ones who tempt Christians to return to the condition from which they have been saved. This material is not found in Jude.

Thus 2 Peter 2:17–22 made use of parts of Jude 12–16. Second Peter 2:17 adapted the first and fourth of four metaphors found in Jude 12–13 but omitted the second and third. Second Peter omitted Jude 14–15 but adapted Jude 16 to serve as the premise for 2:17 and the introduction to a long denunciation of the false teachers for causing Christians to turn back to their pre-Christian state. One element of this is no doubt abandonment of vivid expectation that Jesus will come again.

Jude 17–18/2 Peter 3:1–3

	3:1 Ταύτην ἤδη, <u>ἀγαπητοί</u>, δευτέραν ὑμῖν γράφω ἐπιστολήν, ἐν αἷς διεγείρω ὑμῶν ἐν ὑπομνήσει τὴν εἰλικρινῆ διάνοιαν,
17 Ὑμεῖς δέ, <u>ἀγαπητοί</u>,	

---

48. Watson, *Invention, Arrangement, and Style*, 120.

μνήσθητε τῶν ῥημάτων τῶν προειρημένων ὑπὸ τῶν ἀποστόλων τοῦ κυρίου ἡμῶν Ἰησοῦ Χριστοῦ·	3:2 μνησθῆναι τῶν προειρημένων ῥημάτων ὑπὸ τῶν ἁγίων προφητῶν καὶ τῆς τῶν ἀποστόλων ὑμῶν ἐντολῆς τοῦ κυρίου καὶ σωτῆρος,
18 ὅτι ἔλεγον ὑμῖν·[ὅτι] Ἐπ᾽ ἐσχάτου [του] χρόνου ἔσονται ἐμπαῖκται κατὰ τὰς ἑαυτῶν ἐπιθυμίας πορευόμενοι τῶν ἀσεβειῶν.	3:3 τοῦτο πρῶτον γινώσκοντες ὅτι ἐλεύσονται ἐπ᾽ ἐσχάτων τῶν ἡμερῶν [ἐν] ἐμπαιγμονῇ ἐμπαῖκται κατὰ τὰς ἰδίας ἐπιθυμίας αὐτῶν πορευόμενοι

Second Peter 3:1–3 begins the author's most direct argument against the doctrine of the false teachers. The author has adapted Jude 17–18 for this purpose. This is another point at which 2 Peter has quoted Jude at some length, though with significant changes.

Second Peter 3:1 does not derive from Jude 17–18, except perhaps the address "beloved" from Jude 17.[49] Second Peter 3:1 identifies 2 Peter as a second letter from Peter and begins to state its purpose. This is a transition back to the main argument of the letter, made necessary by the digression in 2:10b–22.[50]

Second Peter 3:2–3 is adapted from Jude 17–18. Jude 17 tells the readers to "remember the predictions of the apostles of our Lord Jesus Christ." In connecting this to 3:1, 2 Peter changed the imperative "remember" to an infinitive. More significantly, 2 Peter changed what the readers should remember from one thing into two things. Jude 17 said that the readers should remember the words spoken in the past by the apostles. Second Peter 3:2 says they should remember "the words spoken in the past by the holy prophets." To this, 2 Peter 3:2 added that they should remember "the commandment of the Lord and savior spoken through your apostles." Second Peter added a reference to the prophets in line with the view, expressed in 1:19–21, that the second coming of Jesus fulfills prophecy. The commandment spoken through the apostles is the same as that mentioned in 2:21,[51] i.e., the commandment that the followers of Jesus live a holy life in expectation of Jesus's return (cf. 2 Peter 3:11–12).

The author of 2 Peter inserted the participle "spoken in the past" between the article and the noun rather than attaching it by repeating the article as Jude had. The author of 2 Peter inserted "the holy prophets" after "by," making them the source of the word spoken in the past instead of the apostles. The author then added a second object of the verb remember, i.e., "the commandment." This made "the apostles" possessors of the

---

49. Kelly, *Peter and Jude*, 354.
50. Watson, *Invention, Arrangement, and Style*, 124–26.
51. Kelly, *Peter and Jude*, 354; Watson, *Invention, Arrangement, and Style*, 126.

commandment; the author of 2 Peter added the specification that they are "your" apostles. The purpose of this—and of attributing the words spoken in the past to prophets rather than apostles—may be to make these words suitable for a letter from the apostle Peter. In Jude 17 the phrase "of our Lord Jesus Christ" modifies "apostles." The author of 2 Peter omitted "our" and "Jesus Christ" and replaced these words with "and savior." "The Lord and savior" then became a second possessor of the commandment. This is awkward. The author of 2 Peter does not seem to have revised Jude thoroughly enough at this point.

Jude 18 contains a direct quotation of the predictions of the apostles, "In the last time there will be scoffers, indulging their own ungodly lusts." Second Peter 3:3 is an adaptation of this. In Jude the quotation spells out what the readers are to remember. Second Peter has transformed it into an additional point made by Peter himself.[52] The author of 2 Peter replaced the formula with which Jude introduced the quotation, i.e., "for they said to you," with the statement that the readers must first know this; what they must know is an adaptation of Jude's quotation.

Second Peter changed the verb from "there will be" to "there will come" and put it first in the sentence. Second Peter changed "in the last time" to "in the last days"; Bauckham observes that the latter is the more familiar expression.[53] Before mentioning the scoffers, 2 Peter inserted the phrase "with scoffing." Bauckham sees this as an imitation of the style of the Septuagint.[54] It is also another example of paronomasia. Second Peter followed Jude 18 closely in describing the scoffers as "indulging their own lusts." However, 2 Peter used a different word for "their own" than Jude 18 did, and 2 Peter omitted "ungodly." All of these changes seem to reflect stylistic preferences on the part of 2 Peter. Second Peter then went on in 3:4 to a direct quotation of the content of the false teaching, after which 2 Peter refuted it.

Thus 2 Peter 3:1–3 is an adaptation of Jude 17–18. Second Peter 3:1 does not derive from Jude. But 2 Peter 3:2–3 is virtually a quotation of Jude 17–18. However, the author of 2 Peter made many small changes in this material to make it better serve his purpose and reflect his stylistic preferences.

---

52. Bauckham (*Jude, 2 Peter*, 283) suggests that the author of 2 Peter here transforms Jude's quotation of the apostles into a direct statement of the apostle Peter. So also Watson, *Invention, Arrangement, and Style*, 127n325.

53. Bauckham, *Jude, 2 Peter*, 288.

54. Bauckham, *Jude, 2 Peter*, 289. So also Watson, *Invention, Arrangement, and Style*, 127.

Conclusion

We began by noting that in adapting Jude, the author of 2 Peter transformed Jude's critique of the behavior of its opponents into a critique of opponents who will not only behave improperly but also teach falsely, i.e., deny that Jesus will come again. Second Peter also transformed Jude's critique of present opponents into a prediction that opponents will arise in the future.

The author of 2 Peter accomplished these transformations partly by incorporating the material taken from Jude into a larger structure, sandwiching it between 2 Peter 1 and 2 Peter 3:4-18. This is part of what gave new meaning to the Jude material. Many of the changes the author of 2 Peter made in the Jude material itself were designed to aid this incorporation. This is especially true in 2 Peter 2:1-3 and 3:1-3, but it can also be seen in such things as the addition of a reference to Noah in 2 Peter 2:5 and the phrase "blots and blemishes" in 2 Peter 2:13, both of which anticipate 2 Peter 3.

The author of 2 Peter also accomplished this transformation by means of other changes in the material he took from Jude. We noted that 2 Peter 2:1 changed the aorist of Jude 4 into future tense. Second Peter 2:1-3 also revised Jude 4 in various ways to make it a critique of false teachers. Second Peter 2:4-10a revised Jude 5-8a into an elaborate refutation of the doctrine of the false teachers. Second Peter 2:10b-22 revised Jude 8b-16, which criticizes the behavior of its opponents, into a critique both of the behavior of the false teachers and of their malign effect on others. Jude 17-18 argues that the rise of its opponents had been predicted; 2 Peter 3:1-3 revised this to make the same point concerning the false teachers.

In addition to adapting the material of Jude 4-18 to a different purpose than it had in Jude, other motives were probably at work in 2 Peter's alteration of this material. The author of 2 Peter may have wanted to eliminate references to extra-biblical literature. The author seems to have wanted to clarify obscurities in the Jude material. He did this both by the addition of words and phrases and by making the connections of the argument more explicit, as he does in 2 Peter 2:10b-11 and 18. However, unsurprisingly, his revision is at times more obscure than the Jude material with which he began. This is especially true in 2:10b-16. The author of 2 Peter also seems to have wanted to revise the Jude material in accordance with his own stylistic preferences, especially the use of unusual vocabulary and the introduction of figures of speech.

It may illuminate 2 Peter's use of Jude to compare it briefly to other instances of literary dependence in early Christian literature.[55] An instance of

---

55. For a discussion of the way Hellenistic authors used predecessors, see Cadbury, *Making of Luke-Acts*, 155-83.

such dependence that at times approximates simple quotation can be seen in Matthew and Luke's use of Q (or Matthew or Luke's use of the other). For example, Matt 4:3-10/Luke 4:3-12 displays a much greater degree of verbatim agreement than does Jude 4-18/2 Peter 2:1-3:3, though there are also many differences between Matthew and Luke at this point. Most of all, they differ in the order of the second and third temptations.

The use of Heb 1:3-13 by 1 Clem. 36.2-5 (or the reverse) is quite similar to the relationship between Jude and 2 Peter. In 36.2 the author of 1 Clement takes the first phrase of Heb 1:3 and joins it to a slightly altered version of Heb 1:4. In 36.3-5 the author of 1 Clement cites Pss 104:4; 2:7; 110:1, which are cited in Heb 1:7, 5, 13 respectively. In this way, the author of 1 Clement uses the material of Hebrews selectively to make a slightly different point than that made by Hebrews.

Literary dependence of 2 Thessalonians on 1 Thessalonians has often been suggested. If this is the case, the relationship between them is more distant than the relationship between Jude and 2 Peter. Second Thessalonians 1:1-2a is almost identical to 1 Thess 1:1; 2 Thess 3:8b is almost identical to 1 Thess 2:9b; and 2 Thess 3:18 is almost identical to 1 Thess 5:28. This is somewhat more verbatim agreement than we find in the relationship between Jude and 2 Peter. What is absent is use of the argument of 1 Thessalonians by 2 Thessalonians. It is sometimes argued that the double thanksgiving in 2 Thess 1:3; 2:13 is based on that of 1 Thess 1:2; 2:13, and that the benediction of 2 Thess 2:16-17 is based on that of 1 Thess 3:11-13. But even if that is the case, it indicates use of the formal elements of 1 Thessalonians by 2 Thessalonians, not use of its content.

2

The Christology of the Second Letter of Peter

The following essay sets forth in systematic form the Christology expressed in the Second Letter of Peter. Despite the relative neglect of 2 Peter in New Testament scholarship, there have been several recent discussions of its theology.[1] However, none discusses 2 Peter's Christology at any length; all focus on its ethics and eschatology. These are clearly the main concerns of 2 Peter. Nevertheless, 2 Peter's presentation of Christ is also significant.[2]

1. Jesus as God

In the first verse of the letter, the author of 2 Peter calls Jesus God. He says that the readers have received faith by the justice τοῦ θεοῦ ἡμῶν καὶ σωτῆρος Ἰησοῦ Χριστοῦ. Because there is only one article, the phrase probably refers to Jesus as both God and savior.[3] Grammatically parallel phrases occur in 2 Peter 1:11; 2:20; 3:18, and unambiguously designate Jesus as both lord and savior.[4]

---

1. Käsemann, "Apologia"; Fornberg, *Early Church*; Bauckham, "2 Peter"; Charles, *Virtue Amidst Vice*. Käsemann is critical of 2 Peter, while Fornberg and Bauckham are more appreciative of it. The present essay is of the appreciative kind.

2. In the terms recently proposed by Vernon K. Robbins, this essay delineates part of the sacred texture of 2 Peter. See Robbins, *Exploring the Texture of Texts*, 120–31.

3. Brown, *Jesus God and Man*, 22; *Introduction to New Testament Christology*, 184; Bigg, *St. Peter and St. Jude*, 250–52; Reicke, *James, Peter, and Jude*, 150; Kelly, *Peter and Jude*, 297–98; Fornberg, *Early Church*, 142; Bauckham, *Jude, 2 Peter*, 168–69; Harris, *Jesus as God*, 229–38. Harris lists others who hold this view as well as those who disagree with it (238). The former is by far the majority position.

4. Against this, it might be argued that a grammatically parallel phrase (i.e., article–noun–possessive pronoun–καὶ–noun–noun–noun) in 2 Thess 1:12 is to be interpreted

This is the only place where 2 Peter explicitly calls Jesus God. However, other things 2 Peter says about Jesus more or less clearly imply this same understanding. One of the clearest instances is 1:3, where the author of 2 Peter speaks of τῆς θείας δυνάμεως αὐτοῦ, and the antecedent of αὐτοῦ is probably Jesus, the last named substantive (in v. 2).[5] Because the author of 2 Peter sees Jesus as God, he also believes that Jesus possesses divine power.[6] Another clear instance is 1:4, where the author of 2 Peter says that those he addresses are destined to become θείας κοινωνοὶ φύσεως. If divinity is the destiny of those who follow Jesus, Jesus himself is surely divine.

a) Lord

The view that Jesus is divine is probably also implied by 2 Peter's use of Lord as a title both for Jesus and for God. In itself, "Lord" does not imply divinity. Use of this title indicates a relationship between the one who uses the title and the one to whom it is applied. Calling someone "Lord" indicates recognition of that person as a superior to whom one gives respect and even obedience. "Lord" was widely used as a title for God but also as a title for any other superior.[7] Nevertheless, 2 Peter's use of the title both for Jesus and for God suggests that they are Lord in the same sense of the word, as does the ambiguity of some of 2 Peter's uses of the title; at times it is not clear whether the title refers to Jesus or to God.

Second Peter uses the title Lord fourteen times. Seven times Jesus is explicitly said to be the Lord (1:2, 8, 11, 14, 16; 2:20; 3:18). In addition, the Lord and savior in 3:2 is very likely to be Jesus; elsewhere in 2 Peter Jesus is explicitly said to be the Lord and savior (1:11; 2:20; 3:18) or God and savior (1:1). The remaining six occurrences of "Lord" probably refer to God.

In 2:9 "Lord" is the subject of the apodosis of the long conditional sentence that begins in 2:4. The subject of the protasis is "God." It would

---

as referring to God and Jesus as distinct from one another (Brown, *Jesus God and Man*, 15–16; *Introduction to New Testament Christology*, 180; Harris, *Jesus as God*, 265–66). However, in this verse the construction pairs the nouns "God" and "Lord" in that order. These are not as easily understood as applying to one person as either "God" and "savior" or "Lord" and "savior." Note, however, the use of the titles "Lord" and "God" (reversing the order of 2 Thess 1:12) for a single person in John 20:28; Suetonius, *Domit.* 13.2.

5. So Fornberg, *Early Church*, 144; Bauckham, *Jude, 2 Peter*, 177. Kelly disagrees (*Peter and Jude*, 300).

6. Bigg, *St. Peter and St. Jude*, 253. 1:16 implies that Jesus's power was revealed at the transfiguration and that it is connected with his παρουσία.

7. On this, see Cullmann, *Christology*, 195–203; Hahn, *Titles of Jesus*, 68–73.

be most natural to understand "Lord" as another name for "God" in this sentence. Thus the sentence would say that if God did not spare the sinful angels, etc., then God knows how to punish and save. It is possible that "Lord" refers to Jesus here, and the sentence says that if God did not spare the sinful angels, etc., then Jesus knows how to punish and save. However, this would be comprehensible only if "Lord" were so strongly connected with Jesus, that the title alone meant Jesus; this does not seem to be true for 2 Peter. 2:10 says that those whom the Lord will punish especially include those who despise κυριότητος. This refers back to "Lord" in v. 9 and takes its meaning from that.

In 2:11 the meaning of "Lord" is ambiguous. I will suggest below that the slander of the glorious ones mentioned in 2:10 refers to the false teachers' slander of God and Jesus. 2:11 contrasts this behavior with that of the angels. Though greater in might and power than the false teachers, the angels do not bring against them a slanderous judgment from the Lord. If it refers to the glorious ones, "Lord" might mean either God or Jesus. Or it may refer back to κυριότητος in v. 10. If so, it most likely refers to God.

3:8 immediately follows a reference to the present heavens and earth's being treasured up for fire by the word of God (3:7). This makes it likely that "Lord" in 3:8 refers to God. Likewise, since 3:8 quotes Ps 90:4, it would be most natural to understand "Lord" as a reference to God. However, it is possible that the author of 2 Peter sees this as a passage that refers to the Lord Jesus. "Lord" in 3:9 and 15 must refer to the same person as "Lord" in 3:8. 3:9 says that the Lord is not slow about the promise but is patient; 3:15 refers again to the patience of the Lord.

Finally, 3:10 refers to the day of the Lord. The parallel with "day of God" in 3:12 suggests that "Lord" here means God. On the other hand, 3:10 quotes 1 Thess 5:2, where "day of the Lord" is probably understood as the day of the Lord Jesus.

If these six occurrences of "Lord" refer to God, then 2 Peter uses "Lord" about half of the time to mean Jesus and the other half to mean God. This suggests that 2 Peter sees God and Jesus as the same kind of Lord. In addition, we have just seen that the occurrences of "Lord" that probably refer to God are themselves ambiguous and might be seen as referring to Jesus. This also indicates that God and Jesus are Lord in the same sense of the word in 2 Peter.

In 1:11 the author refers to the eternal kingdom of our Lord and savior Jesus Christ. This suggests that, as Lord, Jesus is an eternal king, like God. In 1:14 the author says that our Lord Jesus Christ has revealed to him that he will die soon. This probably refers to John 21:18-19[8] and thus to a revelation given by Jesus to Peter before Jesus's definitive return to the Father. It might also refer to a revelation subsequent to that.[9] If so, the verse implies that Jesus continues to guide his followers from heaven, again like God.

b) Other Passages Implying the Divinity of Jesus

In 1:16 the author of 2 Peter says that he and others were eyewitnesses (ἐπόπται) of Jesus's majesty. Since this term was used to designate the highest level of initiate into the Eleusinian mysteries, it implies that the vision of Jesus transfigured was comparable to that. And if the highest level of initiation involved a vision of the goddess,[10] the word may also suggest that the transfiguration was a vision of Jesus's divinity.

The transfiguration was an occasion on which God, the μεγαλοπρεποῦς δόξης, gave τιμὴν καὶ δόξαν to Jesus. This suggests that Jesus's glory is the same as God's and that Jesus is divine. Thus in 3:18 the author of 2 Peter praises Jesus with the kind of doxology usually reserved for God. According to Bauckham, the phrase δόξῃ καὶ ἀρετῇ in 1:3 is synonymous with divine power.[11]

In 2:10, using language borrowed from the Letter of Jude, the author criticizes the false teachers for slandering the δόξας. This is usually understood to refer to church[12] or secular[13] leaders or to angels, either good[14] or evil.[15] These interpretations may be too much influenced by Jude's use of the word. In the context of 2 Peter, it is most likely that the δόξας are God and Jesus, since they are the ones said in 2 Peter to have glory—God in 1:17; Jesus in 1:3, 17; 3:18. The false teachers' slander of God and Jesus is their skepticism about Jesus's return and all that will accompany it.

The description of Jesus in 2:1 as the master who has purchased his followers might allude to the practice of sacral manumission at Delphi.[16]

---

8. Bigg, *St. Peter and St. Jude*, 264; Reicke, *James, Peter, and Jude*, 155; Bauckham, *Jude, 2 Peter*, 200-201; Neyrey, *2 Peter, Jude*, 167.

9. Kelly, *Peter and Jude*, 313-14.

10. Fornberg, *Early Church*, 123.

11. Bauckham, *Jude, 2 Peter*, 179.

12. Bigg, *St. Peter and St. Jude*, 279-80.

13. Reicke, *James, Peter and Jude*, 167.

14. Neyrey, *2 Peter, Jude*, 213-14.

15. Kelly, *Peter and Jude*, 337; Bauckham, *Jude, 2 Peter*, 261.

16. Neyrey, *2 Peter, Jude*, 191-92. According to Dale B. Martin, however, this thesis, first proposed by Deissmann, is now generally rejected because of differences in

This involved sale of slaves to a god in order to free them. If this is what the author of 2 Peter has in mind, he thinks of those purchased by Jesus as effectively freed and only nominally transferred to another owner. This would be another instance of 2 Peter's presentation of Jesus as divine.

2. Jesus as Distinct From God

Although 2 Peter calls Jesus God and consistently presents him as divine, God and Jesus are clearly distinguished in 2 Peter. They are first distinguished from one another in 1:2, where the author wishes that peace might be multiplied for the readers by the knowledge of both God and Jesus our Lord. Because this phrase closely follows and parallels the phrase in 1:1 that refers to Jesus as God, it is sometimes used to argue that Jesus is not being called God in 1:1.[17] However, we see a similar alternation between identifying Jesus with and distinguishing him from God in the first verses of the Gospel according to John. In John 1:1-2 the author first says that the Word was with God, then that the Word was God, then (again) that the Word was with God.[18] It seems most likely that both 2 Peter and John consciously intend to identify Jesus with God and to distinguish him from God.

In addition to the two occurrences of "God" in 1:1-2, 2 Peter uses the word five other times. These five uses of "God" present the following picture of God:

1. There were of old heavens and earth created by the word of God (3:5). Second Peter does not say explicitly that God created the present heavens and earth, but this can probably be assumed.

2. God did not spare the angels who sinned but sent them to hell (2:4).

3. God did not spare the ancient world (cf. 3:6) but preserved Noah (2:5).

---

terminology between the inscriptions that speak of sacral manumission and the New Testament (*Slavery as Salvation*, xvi).

17. Neyrey, *2 Peter, Jude*, 148.

18. Harris, *Jesus as God*, 275. Another parallel to the way 2 Peter both identifies Jesus with and distinguishes him from God may be seen in 2 Peter's one reference to the Holy Spirit. In 1:21 the author says that in prophecy, "moved by the Holy Spirit men spoke from God." Prophecy is said to derive both from the Holy Spirit and from God. This suggests an identity between the two, but the use of two different names suggests that they are distinct.

4. God condemned Sodom and Gomorrah, reducing them to ashes and establishing them as a sign of what will happen to the ungodly (2:6), but saved Lot (2:7-8).
5. The prophets were men who spoke from God (1:21).
6. God the father gave Jesus honor and glory when a voice was conveyed to him by the majestic glory, "This is my beloved son in whom I am well pleased" (1:17).
7. The present heavens and earth have been treasured up by the word of God for fire on the day of judgment (3:7); this is also the day of God (3:12).

The six occurrences of "Lord" that probably refer to God add the following items to the depiction of God in 2 Peter:

8. God knows how to save the pious and punish the wicked (2:9), a general conclusion from the specific cases mentioned in 2:4-8.
9. Time is different for God than for humans (3:8).
10. God is not slow to keep the promise of Jesus's return and all that will accompany it, but is patient, wanting all to repent (3:9, 15).

God and Jesus are most explicitly distinguished in item 6. However, items 1-5, 8-9 describe God in terms drawn from the Hebrew scriptures. This is a figure distinct from Jesus unless the author of 2 Peter thinks Jesus is the God revealed by the Hebrew scriptures. Nothing suggests this.

God's creation of the first heavens and earth by means of the word probably refers to the depiction of creation in Genesis 1 as produced by God's speech, which is also summed up as by the word in Ps 33:6.[19] God created the first heavens and earth ἐξ ὕδατος καὶ δι' ὕδατος. This refers to Gen 1:2, 6-9 and indicates that God created by first separating the primeval waters with the dome of the heavens and then gathering them together below the heavens so that earth might appear.[20]

God's punishment of the sinful angels refers to Gen 6:1-4, but presumes an understanding of it that is only explicit in extra-biblical literature. God's destruction of the ancient world and preservation of Noah are drawn from Gen 6:5-8:19. If δι' ὧν in 2 Peter 3:6 refers to water and the word of God,[21] then God destroyed the first heavens and earth by means of both

---

19. Bauckham, *Jude, 2 Peter*, 298.
20. Kelly, *Peter and Jude*, 358-59; Bauckham, *Jude, 2 Peter*, 297.
21. Bigg, *St. Peter and St. Jude*, 293-94; Kelly, *Peter and Jude*, 359-60; Bauckham, *Jude, 2 Peter*, 298.

water and the word. The former means that God ceased to restrain the primeval waters, and creation was undone (cf. Gen 7:11).

God's destruction of Sodom and Gomorrah and salvation of Lot come from Gen 19:1–29. Prophets sent by God appear very frequently in the Bible. We have already noted that the different meaning of time for God than for humans derives from Ps 90:4.

Although 2 Peter's presentation of God is clearly drawn from the Hebrew scriptures, the author does not say anything about God's election of and subsequent dealings with Israel. Second Peter presents God as God of the whole world and has little to say about the relationship of God to Israel. This probably indicates that the author writes for gentiles, for whom God's dealing with people in general is more meaningful than is God's involvement with Israel.

It is noteworthy that 2 Peter often avoids making "God" the subject of sentences. The main exception to this is 2:4–8, where the author speaks about God's punishment of sinners and salvation of the righteous. Elsewhere, the author is respectfully indirect, making "God" the object of a preposition, to indicate that God is the source of something (1:17, 21), or putting "God" in the genitive case (1:2; 3:12). The author also refers to God by speaking of the majestic glory (1:17) and the word of God (3:5).

Even more striking is the emphasis on the word of God in 2 Peter's references to God. This is explicit in the statements, mentioned above, that God created the first heavens and earth by the word, then destroyed them through the word, and has treasured up the present heavens and earth for destruction by the same word.[22] It is implicit in the statement that prophets spoke from God, i.e., they spoke the word of God, and in the story of the transfiguration, when God spoke words concerning Jesus. It may even be implicit in the examples of God's saving the pious and punishing the wicked that are cited in 2:4–8, if they are seen as examples of prophecy that point to the end of the world.

3. Jesus and God

Second Peter sees Jesus as God, yet distinct from God. How can this be? Despite the emphasis on the word of God noted above, the author of 2 Peter does not explain the relationship between Jesus and God by saying that Jesus is the Word of God. The Gospel of John first proposed this explanation, and it has been very important in subsequent Christian theology. However, 2 Peter does not seem to identify Jesus and the word of God.

22. Reicke, *James, Peter and Jude*, 175.

Second Peter explains the relationship between Jesus and God by saying that Jesus is the Son of God. This occurs in 1:16–18, 2 Peter's account of the transfiguration. In v. 16 the author says that he did not make known to the readers the δύναμιν καὶ παρουσίαν of Jesus by following myths but as a result of having been an eyewitness of Jesus's majesty. In v. 17 he goes on to say that Jesus received τιμὴν καὶ δόξαν from God the Father and that a voice was conveyed to him from the μεγαλοπρεποῦς δόξης, saying, "This is my son, my beloved, with whom I am well pleased."

Jesus's reception of τιμὴν καὶ δόξαν from God probably refers to his being transfigured, as is narrated in the accounts of the transfiguration in the Synoptic Gospels (Mark 9:2–8 and parallels).[23] The voice identifies Jesus as the beloved son of God the Father.

In the Hebrew scriptures, "son of God" does not imply a special ontological relationship with God. "Son of" is an idiom in Semitic languages that expresses a range of relationships in addition to that of biological descent. "Son of God" indicates a relationship with God shared by many people, including the people of Israel as a whole, the king of Israel, and the Messiah. However, in the Hellenistic world, "son of God" designated divinities who were seen as literal offspring of the gods.[24]

Since 2 Peter regards Jesus as God, it is very likely that 2 Peter understands the phrase on Hellenistic lines. Bauckham argues persuasively that the reference to the "holy mountain" in v. 18 indicates that the author sees the words of v. 17 as an allusion to Ps 2:7.[25] Nevertheless, he may understand them in a Hellenistic sense. This would be consistent with the presentation of Jesus as God, yet distinct from God described above. Jesus is God in the sense that he was revealed to be son of God at his transfiguration. He is distinct from God because he is the son, not God himself.

4. The Background and Foreground of 2 Peter's Christology

Jesus is the son of God the father. If the author of 2 Peter understands this as an ontological relationship, it is easy to understand why he calls Jesus God and sees Jesus as having divine power, sharing divine nature, possessing

---

23. Bigg, *St. Peter and St. Jude*, 267; Bauckham, *Jude, 2 Peter*, 217–18. Kelly suggests that only the reception of δόξαν refers to the transfiguration (*Peter and Jude*, 319).

24. On this, see Cullmann, *Christology*, 271–75; Hahn, *Titles of Jesus*, 279–84; Hengel, *Son of God*, 21–56; Young, "Two Roots," 87–121; Dunn, *Christology in the Making*, 13–22, esp. 18–19.

25. Bauckham, *Jude, 2 Peter*, 219–21.

God's glory. It is also easy to see why both Jesus and God are properly called Lord. What is not easy to understand is why the author of 2 Peter does not think there are two Gods.

Calling Jesus God would most naturally mean either that he is identical with God or that there are two Gods. Because early Christians did not wish to assert either of these things, use of the title "God" for Jesus is rare in the New Testament, though more common in post-New Testament Christian literature.[26] Jesus is clearly called God only in John 1:1; 20:28; Heb 1:8, though there are several other passages (in addition to 2 Peter 1:1) that are probably to be interpreted this way.[27] The adjective θεῖος is used elsewhere in the New Testament only in Acts 17:29, where it refers to God.

Jesus is frequently called son of God in the New Testament. In the Synoptic Gospels the title is likely to be used as it is in the Hebrew scriptures. In the Gospel and letters of John and the letter to the Hebrews, the title is likely to have a more Hellenistic sense, as I have argued it does in 2 Peter. Like 2 Peter, these writings also call Jesus God. The meaning of the title in the letters of Paul is uncertain.[28]

The use of "God" and related titles for Jesus in 2 Peter and elsewhere in the New Testament, probably reflects theological developments among Jews influenced by Hellenistic culture. In its early history the people of Israel seem to have given exclusive allegiance to one God without denying the existence of others. Because of this, the Hebrew Bible often refers to gods alongside the God of Israel (e.g., Exod 2:2-3; Ps 82:1, 6) and even occasionally uses "God" as a title for human beings.[29] For example, Moses is called god (אלוהים) in Exod 7:1; cf. 4:16, and the king is called god in Ps 45:6 (אלוהים) and Isa 9:6 (אל). From at least the sixth century BCE onward, Israel was monotheistic in the strict sense, denying the existence of other gods.

Greco-Roman religion was polytheistic, recognizing the existence of many gods and rather readily speaking of human beings, especially rulers, as gods.[30] In contact with this culture, Hellenistic Jews adopted this usage

---

26. See early examples in Ignatius of Antioch, *Smyrn.* 1.1; *Eph.* 1.1; 7.2; 15.3; 19.3. Cf. also Pliny's statement that early Christians chant in honor of Christ as if to God (*Ep.* 10.96.7).

27. On this, see Cullmann, *Christology*, 306-14; Brown, *Jesus God and Man*, 1-38; *Introduction to New Testament Christology*, 171-95; Harris, *Jesus as God*. Brown considers this interpretation probable in the case of John 1:18; Titus 2:13; Rom 9:5; 1 John 5:20.

28. See Cullmann, *Christology*, 290-305; Dunn, *Christology in the Making*, 33-60.

29. Harris, *Jesus as God*, 22-26.

30. Harris, *Jesus as God*, 27-28. Note, for example, recognition of Herod Agrippa as god in Acts 12:22; Josephus, *Ant.* 19.345, 347.

to some extent, in part reviving the similar language of the Bible.³¹ Philo of Alexandria once refers to God as supreme father of gods and humans (*Spec.* 2.165). He distinguishes between God and God's two highest powers, the creative and the kingly.³² God is most properly called the one who is (ὁ ὤν), while the creative power is called God and the kingly power is called Lord.³³ Standing between God and these two powers is the Word of God (*Cher.* 28; *Fug.* 95). In *QG* 2.62 Philo calls the Word a second God. Depending on Exod 7:1, Philo often refers to Moses as God.³⁴ At one point, Philo observes that the passage does not mean that Moses actually was God (*Det.* 161-62; cf. also *Prob.* 43). However, at another point, he simply says that Moses was named God (*Mos.* 1.158).³⁵

Even more strikingly, Hellenistic Jews made abundant use of θεῖος.³⁶ In view of Philo's references to Moses as God, it is not surprising that he also calls Moses divine. For example, in *QE* 2.29 Philo says that when Moses, the prophetic mind, becomes divinely inspired and led by God, he becomes kin to God and truly divine.³⁷ Philo also speaks of the high priest as divine.³⁸ Although Philo most often uses divine power as a synonym for God,³⁹ in *Mos.* 1.94 he implies that Aaron exercised divine power in performing signs

---

31. On this, see Holladay, *Theios Aner*. Holladay argues that Hellenistic Jews were very restrained with regard to divinizing human beings. On use of "God" as a title by Hellenistic gentiles and Jews, see Dunn, *Christology in the Making*, 16-17.

32. *Cher.* 27-28; *Sacr.* 59; *Fug.* 95. Alan F. Segal discusses this and other themes in Philo, suggesting that there were two Gods (*Two Powers in Heaven*, 159-81).

33. *Plant.* 86-87; *Her.* 166; *Abr.* 121; 124-25; *Mos.* 2.99; *QG* 2.51; 4.2; *QE* 2.62. In *Conf.* 137; *Mut.* 29 Philo mentions only that the creative power is called God.

34. *Leg.* 1.40; *Sacr.* 9-10; *Migr.* 84; *Mut.* 19, 125-29, 208; *Somn.* 2.189; *QE* 2.6 (Greek fragment). Artapanus says that the Egyptian priests considered Moses worthy to be honored like a God and that he was called Hermes (in Eusebius, *Praep. ev.* 9.27.6). On rabbinic and Samaritan interpretation of Exod 7:1, see Meeks, *Prophet-King*, 192-95, 234-37.

35. Holladay (*Theios Aner*, 108-55) argues that all of these passages must be understood in light of *Det.* 161-62. Hurtado agrees (*One God, One Lord*, 62-63). Meeks thinks that at least in *Sacr.* 9-10 Philo calls Moses God in the proper sense (*Prophet-King*, 103-7, esp. 104-5).

36. Kelly, *Peter and Jude*, 302; Bauckham, *Jude, 2 Peter*, 177; Holladay, *Theios Aner*. Holladay points out that θεῖος has at least four meanings: (1) literally divine, (2) inspired, (3) in some sense related to God, and (4) extraordinary (57-58, 237). Holladay discusses Philo's use of θεῖος in *Theios Aner*, 177-83.

37. On this passage, see Holladay, *Theios Aner*, 155-60. Cf. also *Mos.* 1.27; 2.188; *QE* 2.40, 54.

38. Holladay, *Theios Aner*, 170-73. He cites *Spec.* 1.116; *Fug.* 108; *Somn.* 2.188-89, 231; *Her.* 84.

39. Cf. *Abr.* 26; *Post.* 27; *Det.* 83; *Conf.* 115; *Spec.* 2.2; *Virt.* 54.

before Pharoah. Philo also uses divine nature as a synonym for God (*Abr.* 144). However, he speaks of the planets as sharing divine nature (*Decal.* 104) and refers to the divine natures in heaven (*Conf.* 154). And in *Post.* 28 he says that God shares his own nature with the one who is eager, i.e., in the first instance Moses.[40]

Josephus refers to Moses as a divine man in *Ant.* 3.180. Josephus uses divine power as a synonym for God[41] but also speaks of the prophet Elisha as having divine power in *Ant.* 9.183. Josephus also uses divine nature as a synonym for God in *Ant.* 8.107.[42]

Hellenistic Jews also made abundant use of the title son of God. In part, this was simply a continuation of the usage of the Hebrew Bible. However, they also used son of God in a more Hellenistic sense. For example, Philo calls the Word of God God's firstborn son (*Agr.* 51) or simply God's firstborn (*Conf.* 146; *Somn.* 1.215).

This combination of monotheism with a broad understanding of divinity to encompass not only God in the strictest sense but also others, even human beings, closely related to God, forms the background for early Christian use of "God" and related titles for Jesus.

In *One God, One Lord* Larry Hurtado argues that there was no erosion of monotheism among Hellenistic Jews because none of the divine agents about whom they spoke was worshipped alongside God.[43] Early Christian reflection on the risen and exalted Jesus viewed him as a divine agent, but introduced the novel idea that Jesus should share the devotion and cultic attention usually reserved for God. This correctly identifies the starting point for the view that Jesus is divine, but does not in itself fully account for the language we find in 2 Peter and elsewhere, i.e., calling Jesus God and speaking of his divine power. In order to do this, we must reckon with the influence of Greek thought on Jewish monotheism.

Richard Bauckham argues that the monotheism of Second Temple Judaism was a matter of believing in one God, identified by several features, and of offering worship to that God alone. Bauckham groups the features

---

40. Philo makes this comment in interpreting Deut 5:31. His other treatments of this passage imply something very similar but do not say explicitly that God shares his divine nature with Moses. See *Sacr.* 8; *Gig.* 48–49; *Deus* 22–23; *Conf.* 30–31; *Somn.* 2.227–28.

41. Cf. *Ant.* 4.318; 9.58; 19.69.

42. Josephus quotes Manetho as speaking of someone thought to share in divine nature (*Ag. Ap.* 1.232). According to Origen (*Commentary on John* 13.25), Heracleon said that pneumatics receive a share in divine nature when they are given knowledge.

43. Note, however, as Hurtado does (*One God, One Lord*, 67), that Philo addresses a prayer to Moses in *Somn.* 1.164–65.

that identify God into two categories, those identifying God in relationship to Israel and those identifying God in relationship to all reality. The latter are that God is sole Creator of all things and sole Ruler of all things. Bauckham then argues that there was no ambiguity about this monotheism. Whatever did not share the identifying features of God and receive the worship accorded to God was not God; whatever did share these features and receive this worship was God. However, this monotheism was not simple but allowed for "real distinction within the unique identity of the one God."[44]

Bauckham presents this as an alternative to the view that intermediary figures blurred the boundary between God and all other reality. However, Bauckham's perspective could also be seen as explaining how such blurring occurred. If an intermediary figure gradually shared the identifying features of God and was worshipped along with God, the figure would be seen as sharing the identity of God.

Perhaps we can understand this development in Hellenistic Judaism and early Christianity as follows. When Jewish monotheists encountered Hellenistic polytheism, they began to use the word "god" in two different ways. They continued to use "god" as a proper noun to refer to the one God who revealed himself in the Hebrew scriptures. However, they also began to use "god" occasionally as polytheists did, as a common noun that designated any one of a class of beings. This usage was simply part of the Greek language. When Jews and early Christians used "god" in this second sense, they were neither identifying this "god" with the God who revealed himself in the Bible nor seriously affirming the existence of more than one god. Rather they were locating this "god" in the category of the divine.[45] We do something similar when we speak of the gods and goddesses of ancient Greece or modern India. These two uses of "god" were logically incompatible. Eventually, Jews eliminated this inconsistency by abandoning the second use of "god," and Christians did so by developing the doctrine of the Trinity.

The existence of this second significance of "god" among Hellenistic Jews and early Christians is confirmed by Justin Martyr's *Dialogue with Trypho*. In sections 55–62, 126–29 Justin argues that the Bible speaks of another god besides the Maker of all things (55). In the course of his argument he appeals in passing to Ps 45:6–7 (56). Trypho resists the argument at first but is eventually persuaded to accept it rather easily.

---

44. Bauckham, *God Crucified*, 1–22 (quotation from 22).

45. In "Theos in the New Testament," Karl Rahner argues that the referent of θεός in the New Testament is God the Father. When Jesus is called θεός, the word is used generically (136–38). Rahner discusses the Greek conception of God on 90–92.

In making this argument Justin seems little concerned to avoid affirming the existence of more than one god. He rejects the gods of the Greco-Roman world (*Apology* 6, 25) but not because there is only one god. Justin's main concern was to show that Jesus was God. The problem this presented for monotheism was not foremost in his mind, perhaps because as a gentile, polytheism seemed natural to him. However, Justin emphasizes the unity between Jesus and the Maker of all things by saying that Jesus is the son of God and Word of God. Although Jesus and the Father are numerically distinct, they are not separate, just as reason and speech are not separate.[46]

Using similar terms, Tertullian explained the relationship between Jesus and the Father in a way eventually adopted by the whole church. In *Apology* 21 he says that the Word, who became flesh in Jesus, proceeded from God and was generated by God, and so is called the Son of God, but is called God because of unity of substance with God. The relationship of God and the Word is like that of the sun and a ray of light going forth from it, no division of substance, but merely an extension.[47] Tertullian used this account of the relationship between Jesus and God to refute the charge that he believed in two Gods in *Praxeas* 13.[48]

There is no indication that the author of 2 Peter has anything like this in mind. He has probably not reflected systematically on the relationship between God and Jesus. He speaks of Jesus as God, yet regards Jesus as distinct from God and does not seem to think there is more than one God. When he speaks of the Lord, it might mean either God or Jesus, and sometimes it is not clear which. He stands near the beginning of early Christian use of "god" in two senses. Most of the time, he uses "god" as a proper noun, designating the one who revealed himself in the Hebrew Bible. But he can also call Jesus "god" in a more general sense, meaning that he belongs to the category of the divine. However, he does not mean either that Jesus is the God who revealed himself in the Hebrew Bible or that there is more than one God.

---

46. *Dial.* 61; cf. 128. Earlier, Ignatius of Antioch had also explained the unity of Jesus and the Father by saying that Jesus was son of God and Word of God (*Magn.* 8.2). On Ignatius and Justin, see Kelly, *Early Christian Doctrines*, 92–93, 96–98.

47. See Kelly, *Early Christian Doctrines*, 112–14; Grillmeier, *From the Apostolic Age*, 118–21.

48. See also Novatian, *On the Trinity* 30–31.

Conclusion

The Christology of 2 Peter is very exalted. The author calls Jesus God and speaks of his divine power. He uses the title "Lord" both for Jesus and for God; in the latter cases, there is usually some ambiguity about which of them is meant. However, the author presents God as a person distinct from Jesus, and there is no suggestion that the author would affirm the existence of two Gods. The transfiguration revealed Jesus as the son of God. It may be understood as an epiphany of the divine Jesus. It was a moment when Jesus received glory from God, in virtue of which he is praised like God.

Second Peter reflects a stage in early Christian thinking when the word "god" was used in two ways. Usually it was a proper noun that designated the one who revealed himself in the Hebrew scriptures. Occasionally, it was used as a common noun that designated those who belonged to the category of the divine. In this way 2 Peter can call Jesus God without either identifying Jesus with God or seriously affirming the existence of two Gods. Eventually these uses were related in the doctrine of the Trinity.

3

The Soteriology of the Second Letter of Peter

Discussion of the theology of the Second Letter of Peter has focused mainly on its ethics and eschatology.[1] The following essay proposes that the ethics and eschatology of 2 Peter are best understood in the context of its presentation of Jesus Christ as savior.

The author of 2 Peter explicitly calls Jesus savior four times[2] and probably refers to Jesus when he speaks of the savior a fifth time in 3:2. This is the principal role played by Jesus in the letter. It is implicit in the designation of Jesus as Christ, i.e., Messiah,[3] though there is no indication that the author of 2 Peter is aware of this; he seems to use Christ simply as a name for Jesus.

How Jesus Saves

The designation of Jesus as Lord is also related to the presentation of Jesus as savior. This is suggested by the linking of the titles "Lord" and "savior" in several passages.[4] It is most explicit in 2:1, where the false teachers opposed by 2 Peter are described as τὸν ἀγοράσαντα αὐτοὺς δεσπότην ἀρνούμενοι. The author of 2 Peter is adapting Jude 4 at this point, specifically the phrase τὸν μόνον δεσπότην καὶ κύριον ἡμῶν Ἰησοῦν Χριστὸν ἀρνούμενοι. In Jude it is clear that "Master" is synonymous with "Lord," and both probably

---

1. Käsemann, "Apologia"; Fornberg, *Early Church*; Bauckham, "2 Peter"; Charles, *Virtue Amidst Vice*.
2. 2 Pet 1:1, 11; 2:20; 3:18.
3. 2 Pet 1:1, 8, 11, 14, 16; 2:20; 3:18.
4. 2 Pet 1:11; 2:20; 3:2, 18.

38

refer to Jesus.[5] The same is probably true for 2 Peter, but the author of 2 Peter has replaced "Lord" and the explicit reference to Jesus with the description of the Master as the one who purchased them. This implies an understanding of how Jesus saves, i.e., by purchasing his followers from those to whom they are enslaved.

This might refer to setting free enslaved persons by purchase, something known both from the Old Testament (cf. Lev 25:47–55) and Greek literature.[6] A particular form of this that might underlie 2 Peter is the sacral manumission practiced at Delphi; here, Apollo purchased slaves for freedom.[7] However, two things make it more likely that 2 Peter 2:1 refers to transferring ownership of slaves from one master to another. One is the use of the term "Master" for Jesus; it suggests that Jesus is the new owner of his followers. The other is the verb ἀγοράζω, which connotes purchase in the market.[8] Jesus has purchased his followers from their previous owner, and they have become Jesus's slaves. Thus the author of 2 Peter refers to himself as slave and apostle of Jesus Christ in 1:1.[9] Like Paul, the author presumes that it is better to be Jesus's slave than that of any other master.[10]

Second Peter says nothing about how Jesus made this purchase. The language of purchase is also used in Rev 14:4, without explanation of how the purchase was made, and in 1 Cor 6:20; 7:23, where it is only said that a price was paid. Rev 5:9 says that the purchase price was the blood of Jesus. This may be presumed wherever the language of purchase is used. If so, the author of 2 Peter regards Jesus's death as the price he paid to transfer his followers from their previous owner to his ownership.

---

5. So Bigg, *St. Peter and St. Jude*, 327; Bauckham, *Jude, 2 Peter*, 39–40. Kelly disagrees (*Peter and Jude*, 252). A grammatically similar phrase (i.e., article–pronoun–noun–καί–noun–pronoun–noun–noun) is found in Titus 2:13. This phrase probably refers to Jesus as both God and savior (Brown, *Introduction to New Testament Christology*, 181–82). This is the most common interpretation of the passage (Harris, *Jesus as God*, 185).

6. Cf. Diodorus Siculus, *Hist.* 15.7.1; 36.2.2. This is clearly the idea in 1 Pet 1:18–19 where λυτρόω is used as in the LXX of Lev 25:47–55.

7. On manumission of slaves, see Bartchy, *Mallon Chresai*, 87–125.

8. Paul uses this term in a similar way in 1 Cor 6:19–20. On the other hand, when Paul speaks of manumission in Gal 3:13; 4:5, he uses ἐξαγοράζω. On this, see Marshall, "Development of the Concept of Redemption," 156–57, esp. n8. Diodorus Siculus also uses ἐξαγοράζω in 15.7.1; 36.2.2.

9. Cf. Rom 1:1; Gal 1:10; Phil 1:1; Jas 1:1; Jude 1.

10. Cf. Rom 6:16–23; 1 Cor 7:22–23.

From What Jesus Saves

Second Peter 2:1 does not specify the previous owner from whom Jesus purchased his followers. However, 2:19-20 strongly suggests that before being purchased by Jesus, his followers were slaves of corruption and the defilements of the world.[11] In this passage the author describes the false teachers he opposes as promising freedom while they themselves are slaves of corruption (φθορᾶς). He then explains that someone is enslaved by whatever overcomes that person (v. 19), clearly presuming that the false teachers have been overcome by corruption. The author says this more directly in 2:12. The false teachers are like irrational animals, born for capture and corruption. In the corruption of the animals, the false teachers will also undergo corruption (φθαρήσονται).[12] In 2:20 the author says, referring to the false teachers and any who might follow them, that if those who have escaped the defilements (μιάσματα) of the world by recognizing Jesus are again overcome by them, their last state is worse than the first.

What does it mean to be a slave of corruption? The basic meaning of φθορά is destruction, with a strong implication that the destruction is caused by the kind of disintegration that occurs in decay or even when something is eaten (see Philo, *Aet.* 5). Thus φθορά is often seen as the negative counterpart of γένεσις,[13] and it is often paired with sickness (νόσος)[14] and pestilence (λοιμός).[15] It is also used to mean the sexual corruption of an unmarried woman.[16] When the connotation of disintegration is less prominent, φθορά is synonymous with ἀπώλεια.[17]

In addition to its use to mean physical destruction/disintegration, φθορά can also be used to mean metaphorical destruction/disintegration (like the English word "corruption"). Thus Philo uses φθορά to mean the corruption of virtue (*Leg.* 1.105), even though virtues are intrinsically

---

11. Philo uses σωτηρία as the opposite of φθορά in *Mos.* 1.146; *Praem.* 22; *Aet.* 37; *QG* 2.22.

12. The antecedent of αὐτῶν in 2:12 is unclear. I take it to refer to the irrational animals. According to Bauckham (*Jude, 2 Peter*, 264), this is the view of most modern commentators.

13. Cf. Philo, *Opif.* 58; *Leg.* 1.7; *Cher.* 51, 62; *Her.* 209, 247; *Somn.* 1.253; *Decal.* 58; *Spec.* 1.27; 2.154; 3.178; *Virt.* 132; *Praem.* 68; *Aet.* 8, 27, 117, 137; *QG* 4.8b.

14. Cf. Philo, *Deus* 124; *Plant.* 114; *Ebr.* 12, 141; *Spec.* 3.28; *Aet.* 37, 67, 126; Josephus, *Ant.* 6.3.

15. Cf. Josephus, *Ant.* 7.324; 8.115; 10.116; *J.W.* 6.421.

16. Cf. Philo, *Det.* 102; *Conf.* 117; *Mos.* 1.300; *Spec.* 2.13; 3.65, 72; 4.84; Josephus, *Ant.* 1.339; 4.251; 5.339; 17.309; *Ag. Ap.* 2.276.

17. Cf. Philo, *Congr.* 119; *Mos.* 1.145; *Aet.* 20.

ἀφθάρτων (*Somn.* 2.258). Likewise, he uses it to mean corruption of the soul[18] and other immaterial entities, especially passion.[19]

Second Peter 2:12 clearly shows that the author of 2 Peter uses φθορά to mean physical corruption. Two things suggest that the author uses the term to mean metaphorical as well as physical corruption in 2:19. First, in 2:20 he implies that enslavement to φθορά is equivalent to being overcome by the defilements of the world. The basic meaning of μίασμα is "stain," e.g., a color imparted to a fabric. However, it is used almost exclusively in a figurative and pejorative sense to mean wrongful behavior of various kinds. It is used particularly to mean bodily wrongdoing,[20] especially various kinds of killing,[21] sexual misconduct,[22] and idolatry.[23] Other defilements include drunkenness, gluttony, etc.[24] μίασμα can designate not only bodily wrongdoing but also defects of mind (cf. Philo, *Cher.* 16) or soul.[25] These defects may especially consist of inner states that lead to bodily wrongdoing. Thus Philo refers to defilement of the minds of those who premeditate murder (*Spec.* 3.92) and speaks of love of money, reputation, and pleasure as defilement (*Spec.* 1.281).

Second, in 2 Peter 2:18 the author implies that enslavement to φθορά is equivalent to living in error (πλάνη) and involvement in licentious desires of the flesh.[26] Philo also connects error and corruption in various ways. Thus he says that those who listen neither to right reason nor to education will receive corruption (*Ebr.* 35).[27] Destruction of the reasoning principle causes

18. *Leg.* 2.77; *Plant.* 114; *Ebr.* 23; *QG* 2.22.

19. *Leg.* 2.102; *Agr.* 109; *Somn.* 2.270.

20. Cf. Philo's association of lawlessness with the soul, defilement with the body, and blasphemy with the tongue in *Decal.* 93.

21. Philo mentions the following as defilements: child sacrifice (*Abr.* 181), fratricide (*Jos.* 13; *Praem.* 68), capital punishment (*Mos.* 2.214), murder (*Spec.* 3.89, 92), manslaughter (*Spec.* 3.121), and sacrifice of a pregnant animal (*Virt.* 138). Josephus treats killing as defilement in *Ant.* 2.33; *J.W.* 2.455, 473; 6.110.

22. Philo mentions adultery (*Jos.* 45), the Israelites' consorting with the Moabite women in Numbers 25 (*Mos.* 1.303–304), prostitution (*Spec.* 1.102; 3.51), pederasty (*Spec.* 3.42), and bestiality (*Spec.* 3.49).

23. Cf. Josephus, *Ant.* 9.262, 263, 272; 12.286.

24. Cf. Philo, *Spec.* 1.206, 281. Josephus also mentions secretions and contact with the dead as defilement (*Ant.* 3.262), as well as theft of something consecrated to God (*Ant.* 5.42).

25. Cf. Philo, *Det.* 133, 170; *Deus* 126; Josephus, *J.W.* 6.48.

26. Corruption and desire are also connected in 1:4. Desire is also presented negatively in 2:10; 3:3.

27. Philo also says that lack of education causes corruption in *Ebr.* 141. In *Plant.* 114 he says that improper education leads to corruption.

corruption (*Deus* 16); one who will not listen will receive corruption (*Deus* 183). Those who lack knowledge receive corruption.[28] In *Deus* 15 Philo links desire and corruption.

The author of 2 Peter may understand enslavement to corruption to mean "subject to corruption," i.e., mortal. This seems to be the meaning of slavery to corruption in Rom 8:21. In line with this, the author of 2 Peter mentions frequently that destruction (ἀπώλεια) is the end of those enslaved to corruption. The false teachers introduce heresies of destruction and by denying the Master who bought them, bring destruction on themselves (2:1). Their destruction does not sleep (2:3). Just as the former world was destroyed (3:6), so the present heavens and earth are treasured up for the destruction of the impious (3:7). Because God does not wish that any be destroyed, God gives time for repentance (3:9). The ignorant and unstable twist the letters of Paul to their own destruction (3:16).[29]

However, the author of 2 Peter also understands enslavement to corruption as meaning being overcome by the defilements of the world, living in error and being subject to licentious desires. In 2:10 the author describes those whom the Lord will punish as going after the flesh in the desire for defilement (μιασμοῦ). Cf. also 3:3. Enslavement to this metaphorical corruption leads to literal corruption.

Origin of Predicament

The followers of Jesus were previously enslaved to corruption and the defilements of the world, and they have escaped this enslavement through recognition of Jesus as savior. Second Peter does not explain how this enslavement to corruption and the defilements of the world came to be; however, several passages hint at an explanation that seems to be presupposed. 2:18 says that the false teachers tempt those who have escaped those who live in error, by speaking bombast of futility (ματαιότητος) and appealing to licentious desires of the flesh. Having escaped those who live in error is probably another description of freedom from slavery to corruption. Since the false teachers tempt them with futile speech and an appeal to desire, it seems likely that this is how they originally became slaves to corruption. Since futility is the opposite of knowledge (see Philo, *Conf.* 141, esp. 159), it is easy to see how futile speech would lead people into error and thus into

---

28. *Her.* 204; cf. *Leg.* 3.52; *Post.* 164.

29. Cf. Paul's designation of unbelievers as "those who are being destroyed" in 1 Cor 1:18; 2 Cor 2:15; 4:3; 2 Thess 2:10. A similar idea is expressed in a different way in Phil 1:28; 3:19; 2 Thess 2:3; 1 Tim 6:9.

slavery to corruption. The causal role of desire is confirmed by 1:4, which refers to the author and readers of 2 Peter as ones who have escaped the corruption in the world by desire. Thus the author of 2 Peter sees enslavement to corruption not as intrinsic to the human condition but rather as due to error, futility, and the desires of the flesh.[30] We can probably see yet another reference to Jesus's followers' having escaped slavery in 1:9, which mentions the cleansing of past sins. This suggests that enslavement to corruption derives from sin.

We find a similar constellation of ideas in the letter of Paul to the Romans. In Rom 8:20 Paul says that all creation was subjected to futility by God; in the following verse this futility is equated with slavery to corruption. In saying this Paul refers back to 1:18-32, where he explains how this happened. Although God revealed himself to humans (v. 19), they did not glorify God or give thanks to him but became futile in their thinking (v. 21) and exchanged the glory of the incorruptible God for an image resembling a corruptible human being (v. 23). Therefore God gave them up to the desires of their hearts (v. 24). The desires of their hearts led human beings into the futility of offering the worship proper to God to images of corruptible human beings. When God gave them over to these desires of their hearts, the desires of their hearts made them slaves to corruption. In 5:12 Paul speaks of the same thing as sin.

Subjective Appropriation of Salvation

I suggested above that the author of 2 Peter understands Jesus as having purchased his followers from enslavement to corruption by his death, even though the author does not say explicitly that Jesus's death was the purchase price. However, the author does speak explicitly about the way followers of Jesus appropriate this salvation. In 1:3 the author says that Jesus's divine power has given them everything pertaining to life and piety through recognition of the one who called them by his own glory and excellence (v. 3), i.e., Jesus.[31] Jesus has done this by first calling them and then having them answer the call by recognizing him as savior.

The first verse of 2 Peter says that the readers have received faith from Jesus. Faith is a synonym for recognition of Jesus. Specifically, they have received faith equal in honor to that of Peter and others, through the justice of Jesus.

---

30. Bauckham, *Jude, 2 Peter*, 182-84.

31. Bigg, *St. Peter and St. Jude*, 253-54; Kelly, *Peter and Jude*, 300-301; Bauckham, *Jude, 2 Peter*, 178.

The author presupposes that Jesus's death has transferred human beings from enslavement to corruption to his own service. However, this transfer does not take effect until it is known to have occurred. Prior to such knowledge, human beings continue to serve their previous master because they do not know they have a new one. For the author of 2 Peter, faith, i.e., recognition of Jesus, is absolutely crucial.

The author and readers have received faith (1:1, 5) and have recognized Jesus as their new Master (1:3; 2:20). However, as 2:20 implies, it is possible to have escaped slavery to the defilements of the world by recognizing Jesus and then return to one's former master. Jesus's purchase of human beings from their former master and their recognition of him as their new master does not eliminate the possibility that they serve their old master. They can undo their salvation. To avoid this, their recognition of Jesus must be ongoing. This is why ethics is necessary.

In 1:5–8 the author urges the readers to progress in virtue (vv. 5–7) because having and increasing in these things makes them fruitful for recognition of Jesus. Those who have been set free from sin by recognizing Jesus need to persist in that freedom from sin, which is an ongoing recognition of Jesus. This is how they make secure their call and election (1:10), which is the starting point of their salvation (cf. v. 3). Those who do this will receive entrance into the eternal kingdom of Jesus (1:11). For 2 Peter ethics is a matter of continuing in the recognition of Jesus, which is the appropriation of the salvation Jesus accomplished. Thus the author wishes that the readers continue their recognition of Jesus in 1:2 and 3:18. An immoral life is a denial of Jesus and a return to slavery. On the other hand, persisting in lives of holiness and piety is salvation.

Ethics

Käsemann criticizes the ethical teaching of 2 Peter, saying that it is not linked with justification.[32] However, as we have just seen, 2 Peter presents Jesus as having saved his followers from slavery to corruption and defilement and argues that the readers must continue in this freedom.[33] Jesus's followers accept salvation from him by faith (1:1), which is equivalent to recognition of God and/or Jesus (1:3; 2:20–21); this recognition is the source of peace

---

32. Käsemann, "Apologia," 184.

33. Bauckham says that for 2 Peter, the saving action of God in the past is the basis for ethical life in the present. He also observes that the emphasis on ethics in 2 Peter is elicited by the need to counteract the ethical laxity of the false teachers it opposes (Bauckham, "2 Peter," 53–60).

(1:2). This recognition must continue and develop through a life of virtue (1:8; 3:18). Likewise, faith must lead to virtue (1:5–7).[34]

One general name for this life of virtue is justice. This is the virtue that characterizes our God and savior Jesus Christ (1:2). Jesus's justice is manifested in giving everyone faith equal in honor, i.e., treating them fairly and without favoritism.[35] It is the virtue of which Noah, saved from the flood, was herald (2:5).[36] Christian life can be called the way of justice (2:21). The new heavens and earth that the followers of Jesus await will be a world in which justice dwells (3:13). In 1:13 the author describes his behavior as just, and in 2:7–8 he refers to Lot as just. The author seems to see Lot as a type of his readers. Just as Lot was saved from Sodom and Gomorrah when they were destroyed by fire, the readers will be saved when the present heavens and earth are destroyed by fire. Like them, Lot was a just man living among those engaged in licentiousness and lawless deeds.

The most specific information about the virtue to which 2 Peter calls the reader is found in 1:5–7. Here the author first of all urges the readers to be eager to grow in virtue (v. 5). The admonition to eagerness is repeated in 1:10 and 3:14. The author himself manifests this eagerness in 1:15. The author then continues to specify the virtues in which the readers should be eager to grow.

The readers begin with faith (cf. 1:1). By their faith, they should add excellence (v. 5). This is a virtue attributed to Jesus in 1:3 and seems to be a general term for the virtue to which the author calls the readers here.[37] By their excellence, the readers should add knowledge (v. 5). This is another indication that the recognition or knowledge of God and Jesus that the readers have in faith must grow. Many see a difference between γνῶσις and ἐπίγνωσις.[38] However, the parallel between 2:20 and 3:18 suggests that there is little difference in meaning between the two words.

We have already seen that recognition of Jesus is the way that his followers appropriate the salvation Jesus accomplished. The importance of knowledge for the author of 2 Peter is also indicated by his frequent

---

34. According to Philo (*Ebr.* 23), those who act against virtue bring their souls to utter corruption.

35. Bigg, *St. Peter and St. Jude*, 250; Kelly, *Peter and Jude*, 297; Bauckham, *Jude, 2 Peter*, 168.

36. Philo says that Noah was saved from the destruction of the deluge because of his justice (*Abr.* 56; *Praem.* 22).

37. Bauckham, *Jude, 2 Peter*, 185–86; Neyrey, *2 Peter, Jude*, 156.

38. Bigg, *St. Peter and St. Jude*, 253; Bauckham, *Jude, 2 Peter*, 186; Neyrey, *2 Peter, Jude*, 149.

references to it.[39] In addition, the author speaks of forgetfulness as the opposite of virtue (1:9),[40] and speaks of his purpose as reminding the readers.[41] He says that the readers are established in the truth (1:12) and calls Christianity the way of truth (2:2).

In 1:6 the author says that by their knowledge, the readers should add self-control. Self-control is the opposite of both desire and pursuit of pleasure on the one hand, and greed on the other.[42] The readers have escaped the corruption in the world by desire (1:4). The Lord will punish those going after the flesh in desire of defilement (2:10), who will appear in the last days (3:2). They use desires of the flesh to entice those who have escaped them (2:18). The false teachers also pursue pleasure (2:13). They are characterized by greed (2:3,14).

Licentiousness is equated with desire in 2:18. The false teachers are also said to be licentious in 2:2. In 2:7 licentiousness characterizes Sodom and Gomorrah. In 2:14 the false teachers are described as having eyes full of adultery. These are other references to the desire that is the opposite of self-control.

By their self-control, the readers should add endurance (1:6), perhaps specifically of any delay in the return of Jesus.[43] This is synonymous with being established in the truth (1:12) and having stability (3:17). The opposite is the instability that characterizes the author's opponents (3:16) and those who follow them (2:14).

By their endurance, the readers should add piety (1:6). This is the opposite of the slander that characterizes the false teachers. In 2:10 the false teachers are said to slander the glorious ones. In 2:12 the false teachers are said to slander what they do not understand, probably expressing in different words the same idea as 2:10. By contrast, in 2:11 the angels are said to refrain from slanderous judgment of the false teachers. According to 2:2, because many will follow the false teachers, the way of truth will be slandered.

Second Peter 1:3 says that Jesus's divine power has given the author and readers everything pertaining to piety. 3:11 says that in view of the coming end the readers should live in holiness and piety. 2:9 says that the Lord knows how to save the pious. On the other hand, 2:5 says that God

39. Cf. 2 Pet 1:12, 14, 16, 20; 2:9; 3:3, 17.

40. Cf. 2 Pet 3:5, 8.

41. 2 Pet 1:12, 13, 15; 3:1.

42. Neyrey, *2 Peter, Jude*, 159–60. Bigg sees it only as opposite to greed (*St. Peter and St. Jude*, 258), Kelly (*Peter and Jude*, 306) and Bauckham (*Jude, 2 Peter*, 186) as opposite to licentiousness.

43. Bigg, *St. Peter and St. Jude*, 258; Kelly, *Peter and Jude*, 307.

destroyed the world of the impious by the flood. 2:6 says that Sodom and Gomorrah are a sign of things that are going to happen to the impious. And 3:7 says that the present heavens and earth are treasured up for the day of destruction of impious human beings.

The virtues of self-control and piety are the principal antidotes to the problem presented by the false teachers. Piety is the opposite of their false teaching about eschatological matters; self-control is the opposite of the moral laxity that flows from this teaching.

By their piety, the readers should add brotherly love, and by their brotherly love, love (1:7). These are the pinnacle of Christian virtue.

The Completion of Salvation

Jesus's salvation of his followers from slavery to corruption is a present reality but not a final one. At present it is always possible to return to slavery; hence the need for ethics. Salvation only becomes final when this world is destroyed at the end of time. Those enslaved to corruption will be destroyed along with it. Those who have been freed from slavery to corruption will then be definitively free.

The end of the world not only completes salvation in this negative sense, it also completes the life of freedom begun through recognition of Jesus. This positive dimension is indicated in 1:3, where the author says that Jesus's divine power has given them everything pertaining to life and piety. By setting them free from impiety, Jesus has given them what they need for piety. And this piety will bring them to life.

In 1:4 the author says that Jesus has given promises in order that through these promises the readers might be θείας κοινωνοὶ φύσεως. Not only do they look forward to life as a result of piety, they are also destined to share divine nature.[44] The most salient characteristic of divine nature is incorruptibility; the immediately following reference to having escaped the corruption in the world makes it very likely that the author equates sharing divine nature with becoming incorruptible.[45] If so, the hope of shar-

---

44. Like the idea that followers of Jesus escape the corruption in the world, the idea that they become sharers of divine nature expresses the meaning of Christianity in terms taken from dualistic Greek philosophical and religious thought. However, these terms are given new meaning (Bigg, *St. Peter and St. Jude*, 255–56; Kelly, *Peter and Jude*, 302–4; Käsemann does not think the terms have been given new meaning ["Apologia," 184]). Just as for 2 Peter the corruption in the world derives from desire, not from the nature of the world, so the followers of Jesus do not share divine nature by essence but rather receive a share in divine nature as a gift.

45. Fornberg, *Early Church*, 86–88; Bauckham, *Jude, 2 Peter*, 180–81; Neyrey, *2*

ing divine nature is equivalent to that of putting on incorruptibility and immortality in 1 Cor 15:50–55. This will occur when they enter the eternal kingdom of Jesus (2 Peter 1:11).

The promises of definitive freedom from corruption and entry into Jesus's eternal kingdom are part of the prophetic word that points forward to the end of the world (1:19), which is found in scripture (1:20). Specifically, they are found in the letters of Paul (3:15–16). What is promised includes the return of Jesus (3:4) and the establishment of new heavens and earth (3:13). The author of 2 Peter emphasizes that the future completion of salvation has been promised by Jesus in order to convince his readers to maintain this expectation.

Eschatology

Käsemann criticizes 2 Peter for not making eschatology central to its theology but using it merely to solve the problem of theodicy and to encourage morality.[46] Eschatology, however, is central to the theology of 2 Peter in that it functions as the completion of the salvation God has begun in Jesus.[47] We have seen that ethics for 2 Peter, as for Paul, is a matter of behaving so as not to undo salvation. Second Peter's eschatological expectations present the ultimate consequences of one's ethical choices. As a warrant for ethics, the eschatology of 2 Peter is soteriological because ethics is soteriological.

One element of 2 Peter's beliefs about the end of the world, and the first mentioned in the letter, is that Jesus will come again at the end. In 1:16 the author says that his teaching about the δύναμις καὶ παρουσία of Jesus did not derive from myths. There is another reference to this in 3:4, where the author quotes his opponents as asking, "Where is the promise of his παρουσία?" It is clear that the author, like other early Christians, expected the return of Jesus at the end of the world. However, the author does not say why Jesus will return or what he will do at his return; the author simply says that Jesus will return. Perhaps the author presumes that at his παρουσία Jesus's kingdom will be fully established (cf. 1:11), as Paul says explicitly in 1 Cor 15:23–25.

In 3:12 the author speaks of the παρουσίαν τῆς τοῦ θεοῦ ἡμέρας, another way of referring to the events of the end. This is apparently the same as the day of the Lord (3:10). This is the day on which the heavens and earth will

---

Peter, Jude, 157–58.
46. Käsemann, "Apologia," 185.
47. Cf. Bauckham, "2 Peter," 59–66.

be destroyed by fire and replaced by new heavens and a new earth in which justice dwells (3:13). The author has much more to say about this.

The present heavens and earth have been treasured up by the word of God for fire, held for the day of judgment and destruction of impious people (3:7). The destruction of Sodom and Gomorrah by fire was a sign of what was going to happen to the impious (2:6). The idea that the present heavens and earth have been treasured up for fire by the word of God probably implies that this is based on prophecy. Several passages might have been understood to predict this.[48] The idea that the eschatological fire destroys the present heavens and earth might have been seen as implied in the prediction of new heavens and earth in Isa 66:22, following upon vv. 15-16. However, this idea also has significant parallels in Iranian and especially Stoic ideas about a conflagration that ends the world.[49]

On the day of the Lord, the heavens will pass away with a loud noise and the elements, burning, will be dissolved, and the earth and the works in it will be disclosed (3:10). The physical universe will be dismantled. At the same time, the truth about the earth and its works will be made known. The slavery to corruption of the earth and some of its inhabitants will be clear when they undergo corruption. Likewise, the freedom from corruption of those who do not will be clear. The dissolution of the universe at the end is thus a motive for living virtuously (3:11). On the day of God, the heavens, burning, will be dissolved, and the elements, burning, will melt (3:12).

The return of Jesus, the destruction of the present heavens and earth in fire, and their replacement with new heavens and a new earth, will happen unexpectedly, like the coming of a thief (3:10, quoting 1 Thess 5:2). Moreover, it is impossible to tell even approximately when this will happen because time is not the same for God as for humans (3:8, quoting Ps 90:4). Further, God is patient because God wants everyone to repent and be found among the pious at the end of the world (3:9, 15).

In 2 Peter 1:19 the author pictures the coming of the day of the Lord, foretold in scripture, as the dawning of day and the rising of the morning

---

48. Deut 32:22; Mal 3:19; Isa 66:15-16; Zeph 1:18. Justin understands Deut 32:22 this way in *1 Apol.* 60.8. Bauckham argues that 2 Peter is immediately dependent on a Jewish apocalypse that in turn depended on these passages (*Jude, 2 Peter*, 301). The idea of an eschatological conflagration can be seen in many Jewish and Christian writings, such as 1 QH iii 19-36 (*Jude, 2 Peter*, 300). Josephus says that Adam predicted destruction of the universe, at one time by fire, at another by water (*Ant.* 1.70).

49. Bauckham, *Jude, 2 Peter*, 300-301; Neyrey, *2 Peter, Jude*, 240-41. In the Stoic view, the conflagration is followed by regeneration of the world. Bauckham also mentions an idea found in Plato (*Timaeus* 22C-E) and elsewhere that the world undergoes recurrent destructions by flood and fire alternately (*Jude, 2 Peter*, 301).

star.⁵⁰ The image of the morning star may allude simultaneously to Num 24:17 and to Hellenistic astrological interests.⁵¹ Expectation of the end of the world does provide a negative incentive to virtue, namely to avoid being destroyed with the impious. However, the expectation also provides a positive incentive; it will be the dawning of day after a dark night.

The return of Jesus and the end of the world are mainly presented as God's final punishment of the impious. However, insofar as the situation of the pious is like that of Lot, distressed by the behavior of the impious (2:7–8), the punishment of the impious will benefit the pious. The punishment of the impious will also eliminate their temptation of the pious (2:18). In addition, righteousness will dwell in the new heavens and earth that will replace the present heavens and earth when they are brought to an end (3:13, alluding to Isa 32:16).

Summary

Second Peter presents Jesus as savior in that he purchased his followers from slavery to corruption and the defilements of the world. Human beings became slaves of corruption through erroneous thinking and following the desires of the flesh, i.e., sin. Jesus's followers have been released from this servitude by their recognition that Jesus has purchased them from their previous owner and is now their master. The ethical teaching of 2 Peter is based on continuing in the freedom from slavery to sin that has come through Jesus. The eschatological teaching of 2 Peter describes the completion of salvation, the culmination of both slavery to sin and following Jesus.

The Pauline character of the soteriology of 2 Peter is very marked. In view of the author's claim (in 2 Peter 3:16) that Paul agrees with what the author has said, this is not surprising.

---

50. Contra Kelly, *Peter and Jude,* 322, the final phrase of 1:19, i.e., ἐν ταῖς καρδίαις ὑμῶν, should be taken with the following verse to indicate where the understanding of the readers occurs, not where the morning star rises.

51. Bauckham, *Jude, 2 Peter,* 226; Neyrey, *2 Peter, Jude,* 183–84.

4

The Style of the Second Letter of Peter

1. Introduction

Those who have studied the second letter of Peter have often commented on its style. Most frequently noted are the numerous rare words in 2 Peter[1] and its penchant for repetition of words.[2] Commentators also offer more general impressions of 2 Peter's style, usually critical ones.[3] The

---

1. Bauckham, *Jude, 2 Peter*, 135–37; Bigg, *St. Peter and St. Jude*, 224; Chase, "Peter," 3:807; Mayor, *St. Jude and St. Peter*, lx–lxiv; Turner, *Grammar*, 4:142.

2. Bauckham, *Jude, 2 Peter*, 137; Bigg, *St. Peter and St. Jude*, 225–26; Chase, "Peter," 3:808; Mayor, *St. Jude and St. Peter*, lvii–lviii; Turner, *Grammar*, 4:142. Note, however, that 2 Peter does not seem to repeat words to an unusual degree. Second Peter repeats 38 percent of its vocabulary (151 out of 401 words). Six NT writings repeat a smaller percentage of their vocabulary: Jude (26 percent), Titus (28 percent), 1 Peter (34 percent), 1 Timothy (36 percent), and James (37 percent). All others repeat an equal or greater percentage: Philemon (38 percent), Philippians (38 percent), Colossians (38 percent), 2 Thessalonians (40 percent), Ephesians (41 percent), 1 Thessalonians (43 percent), Galatians (43 percent), Hebrews (45 percent), Romans (46 percent), 2 Corinthians (49 percent), Mark (53 percent), Luke (53 percent), Acts (54 percent), 1 Corinthians (55 percent), 1–3 John (60 percent), Matthew (60 percent), John (63 percent), and Revelations (66 percent). The NT as a whole repeats 64 percent of its vocabulary (statistics based on Morgenthaler, *Statistik*).

There is obviously some relationship between the length of a text and the degree to which it repeats its vocabulary. This may partly explain why Jude and Titus, both shorter than 2 Peter, are less repetitive. On the other hand, Philemon, the shortest NT text, is just as repetitive as 2 Peter, and 2 Thessalonians, which is shorter than 2 Peter, is more repetitive. It seems clear that 2 Peter is not exceptionally repetitive in the context of the NT.

3. Abbott, "Second Epistle of St. Peter III"; Bauckham, *Jude, 2 Peter*, 137–38; Chase, "Peter," 3:807–9; Kelly, *Peter and Jude*, 228; Mayor, *St. Jude and St. Peter*, xxvi–lxvii; Turner, *Grammar*, 4:140–44; and most recently Gerdmar, *Rethinking the Judaism-Hellenism*

most extensive discussion of style in 2 Peter is that of Duane F. Watson.[4] Watson's work is basic to any further discussion of the style of 2 Peter. One such further discussion is that of Lauri Thurén.[5] Thurén says that style is not currently studied as part of rhetorical analysis and argues that it should be.

The following essay is an attempt to advance description and analysis of the style of 2 Peter. I will do this by making use of Cicero's discussion of the virtues of style, especially as developed by Quintilian, and supplemented by the discussions of others.[6] Watson has discussed tropes and figures of speech and thought almost exhaustively. However, he has discussed other aspects of style less thoroughly. A full catalog of stylistic ornament in 2 Peter should deepen our understanding of its style.

In *De oratore* 3.37 Cicero, in the person of Crassus, identifies four virtues of style: correct diction, lucidity, ornament, and appropriateness to the matter under consideration.[7] He discusses the first two and the last one very briefly in 3.38-39 and 3.210-12 respectively.[8] Cicero discusses ornament at some length in 3.96-208.[9] He discusses ornament under two general head-

---

Dichotomy, 30-63. Reicke also disparages the style of 2 Peter but suggests that it can be seen more positively (*James, Peter, and Jude*, 146-47). So also Green, *Peter and Jude*, 18.

4. Watson, *Invention, Arrangement, and Style*. Watson describes ancient thinking about style on 22-26; he then discusses the style of 2 Peter (along with invention and arrangement in the letter) on 81-141; he lists the topics of 2 Peter on 192-93 and the tropes and figures he has detected on 195-97; and he summarizes his analysis of the style of 2 Peter on 144-46.

5. Thurén, "Style Never Goes out of Fashion."

6. On this subject, see Leeman, *Orationis Ratio*; Russell, *Criticism in Antiquity*, 129-47; and Rowe, "Style." Cicero is explicitly dependent on Aristotle's discussion of style in *Rhetoric* 3.1-12, but he presents the subject more systematically than does Aristotle. Other discussions of style, in addition to Quintilian's, are found in *Ad Herennium* 4.10-69; Demetrius, *On Style*; Dionysius of Halicarnassus, *On Literary Composition*; and "Longinus," *On the Sublime*.

7. *Latine, plane, ornate, apte congruenterque dicere*. In *Rhetoric* 3.2 Aristotle mentions only two virtues—clarity and appropriateness. This list of four virtues was apparently developed by Theophrastus. *Ad Herennium* 4.17 gives a list of three virtues of style: *elegantiam, compositionem, dignitatem*. The first of these includes the first two on Cicero's list; the second is one element of the third on Cicero's list; the third corresponds to *ornate*; Cicero's fourth virtue is omitted. Quintilian follows Cicero, as is indicated by the citations that follow.

8. Cf. Quintilian, *Institutio Oratoria* 8.1-2; 11.1. Diction and lucidity are often seen as problematic in 2 Peter (see, e.g., Bauckham, *Jude, 2 Peter* 137-38). The following essay will not address this issue at length, but some of the problems are mentioned in the discussion of 2 Peter's sentence structure below. I am inclined to see 2 Peter as exhibiting correct diction and lucidity.

9. Cf. Quintilian, *Institutio Oratoria* 8.3-9.4.

ings—vocabulary (3.149-70) and syntax (3.171-208).[10] He interrupts the latter to describe briefly three styles of oratory, namely the full, plain, and middle styles (3.199-200).[11] Elsewhere, Cicero describes another threefold typology of styles, namely the Attic, Asian, and Rhodian.[12]

With regard to vocabulary, Cicero argues that there are three kinds of ornament: (1) rare, usually archaic, words (3.153); (2) new coinages (3.154); and (3) metaphors and other tropes (3.155-98). The first should be used rarely, the second occasionally, and the third frequently (3.201). With regard to syntax, Cicero discusses: (1) avoidance of a harsh clash of consonants or hiatus of vowels (3.171-72);[13] (2) the use of rhythm (3.173-98);[14] and (3) the figures of thought and speech that can be used for ornament (3.200-208).[15] Elsewhere, Cicero discusses the distinction between continuous and periodic style and the special importance of rhythm in the latter.[16]

2. Stylistic Ornament in 2 Peter

a) Vocabulary

One indication that the author of 2 Peter has tried to embellish its vocabulary is that it contains fifty-seven words not found elsewhere in the NT. According to Bauckham, twenty-five of these words are found in the Septuagint; another seventeen are found in other contemporary Jewish literature; and one more is found in the Apostolic Fathers. Thus, these words are not unique in the context of Hellenistic Jewish and early Christian literature.

---

10. Dionysius of Halicarnassus, *On Literary Composition* is a treatment of syntax.

11. Cicero discusses Cotta and Sulpicius as representative of the plain and full styles respectively in *Brutus* 201-3 and discusses all three of these styles in *Orator* 20-23, 69-111. Cf. *Ad Herennium* 4.11-16; Dionysius of Halicarnassus, *Demosthenes* 1-3; Quintilian, *Institutio Oratoria* 12.10.58-68. Dionysius of Halicarnassus gives a different set of three styles in *Demosthenes*, 35-end and *On Literary Composition*, 21-24. Demetrius, *On Style*, 36 distinguishes four styles: plain, grand, elegant, and forceful. The first three seem to correspond to Cicero's plain, full, and middle styles respectively. "Longinus," *On the Sublime* can be seen as a treatment of the full or grand style.

12. Cf. *Brutus* 51; *Orator* 23-27. See also Dionysius of Halicarnassus, *Ancient Orators* 1-3; Quintilian, *Institutio Oratoria* 12.10.16-26. On Attic and Asian in Cicero, see Leeman, *Orationis Ratio*, 91-111, 136-67.

13. Cf. *Orator* 150-52.

14. Cf. *Orator* 168-236.

15. Cf. *Orator* 135-39.

16. *Orator* 204, 208, 211, 221, etc. Cf. Aristotle, *Rhetoric* 3.9; Demetrius, *On Style* 1-35; Quintilian, *Institutio Oratoria* 9.4.19-22, 122-30.

However, most of the remaining fourteen words are very rare.[17] These words are: ἀκατάπαστος (2:14), ἀστήρικτος (2:14; 3:16), αὐχμηρός (1:19), ἑκάστοτε (1:15), ἐμπαιγμονή (3:3), ἐξέραμα (2:22), καυσόω (3:10, 12), μυωπάζω (1:9), παραφρονία (2:16), παρεισφέρω (1:5), ῥοιζηδόν (3:10), στηριγμός (3:17), ταρταρόω (2:4), and ψευδοδιδάσκαλος (2:1).

Three of these words—ἀκατάπαστος, ἐμπαιγμονή, and παραφρονία—are found nowhere else in Greek literature. However, ἀκατάπαστος is probably a mistake for ἀκατάπαυστος, which is found elsewhere.[18] In addition to the other two words, found nowhere else, two more are found for the first time in 2 Peter—μυωπάζω and ψευδοδιδάσκαλος. These four words are likely to be new coinages, i.e., examples of Cicero's second kind of embellishment of vocabulary. The remaining ten words (including ἀκατάπαυστος) are rare words, i.e., examples of Cicero's first kind of ornamentation of vocabulary. For the most part, they do not seem to be archaic. However, ἑκάστοτε, found only in Plato and earlier writers, may be an archaism.

καυσόω may be used metaphorically in 3:10, 12. According to Bauckham, this verb is "elsewhere used only of fever by medical writers."[19] In 2 Peter it is used for the heat that dissolves the universe. This is metaphorical if the author thinks of this heat as a kind of fever that brings about the dissolution of the universe. Watson has identified twenty-five additional metaphors.[20] Watson has also identified the following tropes in 2 Peter: metonymy, antonomasia, synecdoche, hyperbole, onomatopoeia, periphrasis, and epithet.[21] These are examples of Cicero's third kind of verbal ornamentation.

Although the author of 2 Peter has used at least ten rare words and four new coinages, he has used at least twenty-seven metaphors as well as a number of other tropes. Thus he is in accord with Cicero's advice to use metaphor and other tropes more frequently than the other two kinds of verbal embellishment. However, he may use rare words more frequently than Cicero recommends. Watson thinks that the eleven metaphors in 2:13–21

---

17. Bauckham, *Jude, 2 Peter*, 135–36.
18. Bauckham, *Jude, 2 Peter*, 136.
19. Bauckham, *Jude, 2 Peter*, 136.
20. In 2 Pet 1:8, 9, 10, 12, 13, 14 (two metaphors), 15; 2:1, 2, 4, 13, 14 (two metaphors), 15 (four metaphors), 17 (two metaphors), 18, 21; 3:4, 14, 17 (Watson, *Invention, Arrangement, and Style*, 195–97).
21. Metonymy in 2 Pet 1:17; 2:14; 3:16; antonomasia in 1:3, 19; 2:1; synecdoche in 1:3, 11; 2:8, 21; hyperbole in 2:14 (twice); onomatopoeia in 3:10; periphrasis in 1:9, 12, 13 (twice), 14, 15, 17 (twice); 2:14, 16; 3:1, 7; and epithet in 1:1, 2, 11; 2:20; 3:18 (Watson, *Invention, Arrangement, and Style*, 195–97).

constitute too frequent use of metaphors of the same kind, something condemned by Quintilian (*Institutio Oratoria* 8.6.14–16).²²

b) Syntax

Cicero does not specify what constitutes a harsh clash of consonants or hiatus of vowels. Quintilian says that for successive words to end and begin with two long vowels, especially when they are the same, and most especially the vowels "o" and "a," constitutes the worst problem. But he also says that he is not sure whether too little or too much care to avoid hiatus is the worse (*Institutio Oratoria* 9.4.33–37). Quintilian says that for successive words to end and begin with "s" or "x" is jarring (*Institutio Oratoria* 9.4.37–38).

There seems to be little indication that the author of 2 Peter has made any great effort to avoid these problems. In the first five verses of the letter, I count seventeen instances of hiatus. However, none of these is an instance of successive words ending and beginning with the long vowels "o" or "a." Likewise the first five verses of the letter include no instance of successive words ending and beginning with "s" or "x."

1) Rhythm

With regard to rhythm, Cicero approvingly quotes Aristotle as prohibiting frequent use of iamb (short—long) and tribrach (short—short—short) and recommending primary use of the heroic foot, i.e., the dactyl (long—short—short).²³ Aristotle also especially approves of the paean (either long—short—short—short, or short—short—short—long), the former kind at the beginning of a sentence, and the latter at the end. Cicero comments that the latter kind of paean is almost the same as the cretic (long—short—long) (3.182–83). Sentences should end with either the trochee (long—short) or dactyl or either of them alternating with the second kind of paean or the cretic (3.193).

Dionysius of Halicarnassus describes the twelve possible two- and three-syllable feet and evaluates each (*On Literary Composition* 17). The

---

22. Watson, *Invention, Arrangement, and Style*, 123–24.

23. Aristotle, *Rhetoric* 3.8. Aristotle speaks of the iamb and the trochee, and these are the words Cicero uses. However, Cicero understands trochee to mean what is commonly called tribrach and so misunderstands Aristotle, who does not use trochee in this sense. Aristotle's heroic foot may include spondee and anapest, as well as dactyl. Cicero summarizes the views of Aristotle somewhat differently, and less accurately, in *Orator* 191–96.

pyrrhic (short—short) is not impressive or solemn, while the spondee (long—long) is. The iamb is not ignoble, but the trochee is. The tribrach is a mean foot, but the molossus (long—long—long) is elevated. The amphibrach (short—long—short) is effeminate and ignoble. The anapest (short—short—long) and the dactyl are both very beautiful. The cretic is not ignoble. Both the bacchius (long—long—short) and hypobacchius (short—long—long) have dignity and grandeur.

Quintilian's discussion of rhythm (in *Institutio Oratoria* 9.4.45–120) is less prescriptive. He too describes the twelve possible two- and three-syllable feet (79–82) and argues that each has its proper use in prose (83, 87–89). He says that one should be concerned about no more than the last three feet of a sentence, nor fewer than two (95), and illustrates the effect of using various feet to conclude a sentence (95–111). He notes that Asian writers frequently end a sentence with two trochees (103).

Charles Bigg finds in 2 Peter a "tendency to fall into iambic rhythm."[24] He explains that "many sentences can be turned into tragic senarii with very little alteration."[25] Bigg illustrates this assertion by citing portions of 2 Peter 2:1, 3, 4 that he has altered by omitting or rearranging words. He says that the cadence and color of 1:19 are the same but does not provide a citation. He says that in the third chapter "there is a perceptible approach to the movement of blank verse"[26] and illustrates this by citing portions of 3:10 and 12, in this case without alteration. Finally, Bigg says that 2 Peter 2:22 "falls very readily into iambics"[27] and cites the παροιμία from the verse in altered form.

However, contrary to Bigg's suggestion, the unaltered text of 2 Peter is not particularly characterized by iambic rhythm, especially not at the ends of its sentences. Of course, iambic feet are found in 2 Peter, and by my estimate, an iambic foot ends a sentence four times.[28] However, other rhythms are much more common at the ends of sentences.

The most common foot at the end of the sentences in 2 Peter is the spondee; it is found at the end of eighteen sentences.[29] This foot is praised

---

24. Bigg, *St. Peter and St. Jude*, 227. Mayor comments on the fine rhythm of sections of 2 Peter but does not describe the rhythm more precisely except to refer to iambic fragments in 1:19; 2:4, 8, 22 (*St. Jude and St. Peter*, lviii–lix).

25. Bigg, *St. Peter and St. Jude*, 227. Tragic senarii are lines of poetry consisting of six iambic feet, characteristic of tragedies.

26. Bigg, *St. Peter and St. Jude*, 227.

27. Bigg, *St. Peter and St. Jude*, 228.

28. At the ends of 2 Pet 1:7, 18, 20; 3:4b.

29. At the ends of 2 Pet 1:2, 10a, 11, 12, 14, 15, 21; 2:3, 17, 19b, 20; 3:4a, 7, 9, 13, 14, 16, 18a.

by Dionysius of Halicarnassus. Quintilian says that the spondee is best preceded by a cretic (*Institutio Oratoria* 9.4.97), as it is at the ends of seven of these sentences.[30] However, Quintilian says that two spondees should not end a sentence (*Institutio Oratoria* 9.4.97, 101). This is the case nine times in 2 Peter;[31] twice this is because the sentence ends with Ἰησοῦ Χριστοῦ (1:11; 3:18a).

The second most common foot at the end of 2 Peter's sentences is the cretic. It is found eleven times.[32] This is in accord with the recommendation of Cicero. This foot is also praised by Dionysius of Halicarnassus. Quintilian says that the cretic makes an excellent ending, but disapproves preceding it with a trochee (*Institutio Oratoria* 9.4.107). This happens four times in 2 Peter.[33]

The third most common foot at the end of 2 Peter's sentences is the trochee, found seven times.[34] This also accords with the recommendation of Cicero, but Dionysius of Halicarnassus says this foot is ignoble. Quintilian approves having two trochees end a sentence (*Institutio Oratoria* 9.4.103). This happens three times in 2 Peter (i.e., 1:16, 17; 2:15).

Second Peter's sentences also end with paean (1:10b; 2:16a and b) and dactyl (3:6). As noted above, Cicero commends both; Dionysus of Halicarnassus commends the dactyl. Quintilian approves ending with a dactyl (*Institutio Oratoria* 9.4.104) but not a paean (9.4.110-11). Cicero thinks the first kind of paean should be used at the beginning of a sentence (cf. also Quintilian *Institutio Oratoria* 9.4.111); however, it is used at the end of 2 Peter 1:10b. Quintilian cautions that he does not recommend too great attention to rhythm (*Institutio Oratoria* 9.4.112-16; cf. Cicero, *De oratore* 3.193).

2) Figures of Speech and Thought

We earlier noted that 2 Peter frequently repeats words. Often words are repeated in close proximity, producing the figures of speech called paronomasia and transplacement, which are included among the figures mentioned by Cicero (*De oratore* 3.206) and Quintilian (*Institutio Oratoria* 9.3.41-44, 66-74) as means of ornamentation.[35] Watson has identified many instances

---

30. 2 Pet 1:2, 12; 2:17, 19b; 3:4a, 14, 16.
31. At the end of 2 Pet 1:10a, 11, 14, 15, 21; 2:3; 3:7, 9, 18a.
32. At the ends of 2 Pet 1:9; 2:2, 11, 14, 19a, 21, 22; 3:8, 10, 12, 17.
33. At the ends of 2 Pet 1:9; 2:19a; 3:8, 10.
34. At the ends of 2 Pet 1:8, 16, 17; 2:1, 10a, 15; 3:18b.
35. Cf. *Ad Herennium* 4.20, 29-31.

of transplacement[36] and paronomasia.[37] To Watson's list, we can add several additional transplacements.[38]

Other instances of repetition of words in 2 Peter are a means of developing certain topics. Watson has discussed the development of many of these topics, including: righteousness; knowledge; power; piety; glory; promises; escaping corruption; desire; eagerness; the reminder topic; being established; the metaphor of the day; eschatological destruction; the way; and keeping.[39]

---

36. 2 Pet 1:3-4 δεδωρημένης—δεδώρηται, 1:5-7 the word for each virtue (except the first and last) is repeated, 1:10 ποιεῖσθαι—ποιοῦντες, 1:13-14 σκηνώματι—σκηνώματος, 1:17 δόξαν—δόξης, 1:17-18 φωνῆς ἐνεχθείσης—φωνὴν . . . ἐνεχθεῖσαν, 1:21 ἠνέχθη—φερόμενοι cf. use of same verb in vv. 17-18; 2:1 παρεισάξουσιν αἱρέσεις ἀπωλείας—ἐπάγοντες . . . ταχινὴν ἀπώλειαν, 2:1-3 repetition of ἀπώλεια (?), 2:5-6 ἀσεβῶν—ἀσεβέ[σ]ιν, 2:7-9 δίκαιον—ἐρρύσατο, δίκαιος—ἡμέραν—ἡμέρας—δικαίαν, ῥύεσθαι—ἀδίκους, 2:10-12 βλασφημοῦντες—βλάσφημον—βλασφημοῦντες, 2:12 φθοράν—φθορᾷ—φθαρήσονται, 2:13 ἀδικούμενοι—ἀδικίας, 2:15 ὁδὸν—ὁδῷ (?), 2:16-18 φθεγξάμενον—φθεγγόμενοι (?), 2:21 ἐπεγνωκέναι—ἐπιγνοῦσιν; 3:5-7 οὐρανοὶ—γῆ—ὕδατος—ὕδατος—λόγῳ, ὕδατι—ἀπώλετο, οὐρανοὶ—γῆ—λόγῳ—ἀπωλείας, 3:10-12 λυθήσεται—λυομένων—λυθήσονται, 3:12-14 προσδοκῶντας—προσδοκῶμεν—προσδοκῶντες (Watson, *Invention, Arrangement, and Style*, 195-97). On 195 Watson indicates a transplacement in 1:18 that does not seem to be there.

37. 2 Pet 1:10 ποιεῖσθαι—ποιοῦντες, 1:12-15 ὑπομιμνῄσκειν—ὑπομνήσει—μνήμην ποιεῖσθαι, 1:16-17 μεγαλειότητος—μεγαλοπρεποῦς, 1:19-21 προφητικὸν—προφητεία (?); 2:1 ψευδοπροφῆται—ψευδοδιδάσκαλοι and παρεισάξουσιν αἱρέσεις ἀπωλείας—ἐπάγοντες . . . ταχινὴν ἀπώλειαν, 2:6-7 κατακλυσμὸν—[καταστροφῇ]—κατέκρινεν—καταπονούμενον . . . ἀναστροφῆς and ἀσεβέ[σ]ιν—ἀθέσμων—ἀσελγείᾳ, 2:8-9 δίκαιος—ἀδίκους, 2:12 φθοράν—φθορᾷ—φθαρήσονται, 2:13 τρυφήν—ἐντρυφῶντες, 2:16 παρανομίας—παραφρονίαν and ἄφωνον—φωνῇ, 2:19 δοῦλοι—δεδούλωται; 3:1-2 ὑπομνήσει—μνησθῆναι, 3:2 προειρημένων ῥημάτων (?), 3:3 ἐμπαιγμονῇ ἐμπαῖκται, 3:9 βραδύνει—βραδύτητα, 3:16-17 ἀστήρικτοι—στηριγμοῦ (Watson, *Invention, Arrangement, and Style*, 195-97). On 114 and 196 he speaks of paronomasia in 2:6-7 as including the word κατακλυσμὸν, but this word is found in 2:5.

38. 2 Pet 1:2-3 ἐπιγνώσει—ἐπιγνώσεως, 1:3-4 repetition of θείας, 1:3-5 ἀρετῇ—ἀρετήν, 1:12-14 εἰδότας—εἰδώς, 2:4-5 repetition of οὐκ ἐφείσατο, 2:9-11 κρίσεως—κρίσιν, 3:7-8 ἡμέραν—μία ἡμέρα—ἡμέρα μία, 3:10-13 ἡμέρα—οὐρανοὶ—στοιχεῖα . . . καυσούμενα—γῆ—ἡμέρας—οὐρανοὶ—στοιχεῖα καυσούμενα—οὐρανοὺς—γῆν.

39. According to Watson, the topic of righteousness (δικαιοσύνη) is introduced in 1:1 and further developed in 2:5, 7, 8, 9, 15, 21; 3:13. Likewise, the topic of knowledge (ἐπίγνωσις) is introduced in 1:2 and developed in 1:3, 5, 6, 8, 9, 12, 16, 20; 2:12, 20, 21; 3:5, 8, 16, 18. The topic of power (δύναμις) is introduced in 1:3 and developed in 1:16; 2:11. The topic of piety (εὐσέβεια) is introduced in 1:3, 6, 7 and developed in 2:5, 6, 9, 13; 3:7, 11, 14. The topic of glory (δόξα) is introduced in 1:3 and developed in 1:17; 3:18. The topic of promises (ἐπαγγέλματα) is introduced in 1:4 and developed in 2:19; 3:4, 9, 13. The topic of escaping corruption (ἀποφυγόντες φθορά) is also introduced in 1:4 and developed in 1:9; 2:12, 18-22. The topic of desire (ἐπιθυμία) is introduced in 1:4 and developed in 2:10, 18; 3:3. The topic of eagerness (σπουδή) is introduced in 1:5 and developed in 1:10; 3:14. The reminder topic occurs three times in 1:12-15 and is

Second Peter also develops topics not discussed by Watson. The παρουσία topic is introduced in 1:16 and developed in 3:4, 12. The topic of holiness (ἅγιος) is introduced in 1:18 and developed in several passages.[40] The related topics of prophecy (προφητεία) and scripture (γραφή) are introduced in 1:20. The former is developed in 1:21; 2:16; 3:2, the latter in 3:16.

The development of some of these topics constitutes inclusio, i.e., the repetition at the end of a section, of a word or phrase used at its beginning. Thus the topic of knowledge is mentioned in 1:2 and 3:18, and the topic of glory is mentioned in 1:3 and 3:18. In addition, grace (χάρις) is mentioned in 1:2 and 3:18; and peace (εἰρήνη) is mentioned in 1:2 and 3:14. All of these serve to end the letter by returning to items mentioned at the beginning. On a smaller scale, supplying abundantly (ἐπιχορηγέω) is mentioned in 1:5 and 11, tying that section together.

Thus most repetition of words in 2 Peter can be seen as an effort to produce the artistic and other effects described above.[41] Watson has catalogued many other figures of speech and thought that serve to ornament 2 Peter.[42]

---

repeated in 3:1-2. The topic of being established (στηρίζω) is introduced in 1:12 and developed in 2:14; 3:16, 17. The metaphor of the day (ἡμέρα) is first used in 1:19 and then used again in 3:7, 10, 12, 18. The topic of eschatological destruction is introduced in 2:1 and developed in 2:3, 12; 3:6, 7, 9, 16. The topic of the way (ὁδός) is discussed in 2:2, 15, 21. The topic of keeping is found in 2:4, 9, 17; 3:7 (Watson, *Invention, Arrangment, and Style*, 192-93. This is Watson's summary of topics in 2 Peter; he also discusses most of them earlier as he analyzes the letter.)

The topic of knowledge is also developed in several other passages not mentioned by Watson, i.e., 2 Pet 1:14; 2:9; 3:3. Watson does not mention the presence of the topic of glory in 2:10, eagerness in 1:15, or use of the day metaphor in 2:9; however, he does list 3:3 and 8, where "day" is not used metaphorically. The topic of being established might be seen as introduced in 1:10 rather than 1:12 and also developed in 1:19.

40. 2 Pet 1:21; 2:21; 3:2, 11.

41. Contra Bauckham (*Jude, 2 Peter*, 137) "often there seems to be no literary intention in the repetition."

42. Watson, *Invention, Arrangement, and Style*, 97-99, 100, 103, 104-5, 107-9, 114, 115-24, 132-35, 195-97. A number of these are listed in the following sections of this paper.

3) Sentence Structure

Many of the sentences of 2 Peter are relatively short and simple. However, 2 Peter also contains several long, complex sentences.[43] These are instances in which the periodic style is used for ornament.[44]

The first and most elaborate of these periods is 1:3–7. This is a complex sentence, of which vv. 3–4 form the protasis and vv. 5–7 the apodosis.[45] Vv. 3–4 are a genitive absolute introduced by ὡς, on which depend a relative clause and a purpose clause. The main verb of vv. 5–7 is an imperative. If vv. 5–7 are taken as a single clause, the sentence consists of four clauses, which is the maximum length of a period according to Demetrius.[46] The last clause is also the longest, as Demetrius recommends (*On Style* 18). This period forms the introduction to the message of 2 Peter, a good place to use a period according to Quintilian (*Institutio Oratoria* 9.4.128). This sentence is not only grammatically complex, it is also ornamented with many figures of speech and thought. According to Watson, vv. 3–4 exhibit two figures of speech in addition to the tropes and transplacement already noted above—personification and hendiadys.[47] Vv. 5–7 constitute the figure of speech called climax and also exhibit the following figures of speech in addition to transplacement: homoeoptoton, isocolon, polysyndeton, and reduplication.[48]

Another somewhat elaborate sentence is found in 2 Peter 1:19–20. The main clause is v. 19a. On this depends a relative clause (v. 19b). A temporal clause (v. 19c) depends on the relative clause, as does a participial phrase (v. 19d–20a). A noun clause (v. 20b) depends on the participial phrase. Like 1:3–7, 1:19–20 consists of four clauses, of which the last is the longest. Once again, the sentence is not only grammatically complex but also exhibits many tropes and figures. In addition to the antonomasia and paronomasia

---

43. Cicero recommends such use of different sentence types in *Orator* 211; cf. also Demetrius, *On Style* 15.

44. *Ad Herennium* lists the period among the figures of speech that can be used for ornament (4.27).

45. For this analysis, see Reicke, *James, Peter and Jude*, 152; Danker, "2 Peter 1"; and most recently Starr, *Sharers in Divine Nature*, 24–26. Bigg (*St. Peter and St. Jude*, 253), Kelly (*Peter and Jude*, 299), and Gerdmar (*Rethinking the Judaism-Hellenism Dichotomy*, 33) disagree.

46. Demetrius, *On Style* 16. Quintilian says that an average number of clauses in a period is four, but it often allows more (*Institutio Oratoria* 9.4.125).

47. Watson, *Invention, Arrangement, and Style*, 97–98; on 195 he adds polyptoton.

48. Watson, *Invention, Arrangement, and Style*, 98. Gerdmar is critical of Watson's identification of figures of speech in 1:4–5 and elsewhere (*Rethinking the Judaism-Hellenism Dichotomy*, 99n35).

already noted, in this passage we find a striking similitude, likening the prophetic word to a lamp shining in a dark place. We also find a metaphor in which the παρουσία of Jesus is presented as the dawn of day and rising of the morning star. Use of the latter two terms for one reality constitutes hendiadys. This passage also exhibits antithesis.[49]

After 1:3–7 the most polished sentence in 2 Peter is 2:4–10a. This is another conditional sentence, of which vv. 4–8 form the protasis and vv. 9–10a the apodosis.[50] Vv. 4–7 consist of three parallel conditional clauses; the last is followed by a parenthetical explanatory clause in v. 8. The first two conditional clauses, in vv. 4 and 5, each have two main verbs coordinated by ἀλλά. The third conditional clause, in vv. 6–7, also has two main verbs coordinated by καί. The second and third conditional clauses are linked to the first with καί. In vv. 9–10a two infinitives depend on the main verb; the object of the second infinitive is modified by two participial phrases. If the parenthetical clause in v. 8 is not counted, 2:4–10a consists of four clauses, of which the last is the longest. Each of the four clauses presents an antithesis, something especially appropriate for a period.[51] In addition to the tropes, transplacement and paronomasia already noted, this passage exhibits epiphora, homoeoptoton, regressio, polyptoton (4), antithesis (3), adjunction (2), and parenthesis.[52]

Another elaborate sentence is found in 2:12–14. The subject is οὗτοι; the verb is φθαρήσονται. The subject is modified by one participial phrase in v. 12 and two more in v. 13a. A relative clause depends on the first of these three. In v. 13b–14 two nouns in apposition to the subject are modified by five more participial phrases. V. 14 ends with a phrase in apposition to the subject. This period consists of two clauses. In it we find—in addition to tropes, paronomasia, and transplacement—another similitude, asyndeton, ellipsis, polyptoton, regressio, homoeoprophoron, irony, emphasis (2), and exclamation.[53]

3:1–4a is another elaborate sentence. The main clause is 3:1a. A relative clause (3:1b) depends on it, and an infinitive phrase (3:2) depends on the relative clause. In 3:3a a participial phrase, modifying the vocative ἀγαπητοί in 3:1,[54] introduces a noun clause (3:3b), whose subject

---

49. Watson, *Invention, Arrangement, and Style*, 104–5; on 195 he adds ellipsis.

50. Gerdmar sees 2:4–7 as a protasis that lacks an apodosis (*Rethinking the Judaism-Hellenism Dichotomy*, 33).

51. Cf. Aristotle, *Rhetoric* 3.9.7–8; Demetrius, *On Style* 22–24.

52. Watson, *Invention, Arrangement, and Style*, 196.

53. Watson, *Invention, Arrangement, and Style*, 196.

54. Mayor (*St. Jude and St. Peter*, liv–lv) analyzes 3:2 as an accusative-infinitive construction, and the participle in 3:3a as modifying the implied subject. On this analysis

ἐμπαῖκται is modified by two participles, the second of which introduces a direct quotation in 3:4a. This period consists of four clauses. In addition to tropes, paronomasia, and transplacement, 3:1–4a exhibits aphodos, transitio, ellipsis (2), irony, pleonasm, dialogue, and rhetorical question.[55]

3. The Grand Style

Especially the ornamentation of 2 Peter probably makes it an example of the full or grand style.[56] Watson draws upon a number of sources to describe the grand style as follows:

> The Grand Style is a "smooth and ornate arrangement of impressive words" and is characterized by a "power of thought and majesty of diction." It is forceful, yet stately and opulent. It is the most ornamented style, using the most ornate words available and all figures of speech and thought, particularly hyperbole. Amplification is found throughout.[57]

This description applies to 2 Peter in every respect except that 2 Peter does not make much use of hyperbole. Watson identifies only two instances, both in 2:14. Nevertheless, the other correspondences between this description and 2 Peter strongly indicate that 2 Peter was written in the grand style.

The most extensive discussion of the grand style is found in Demetrius, *On Style* 38–124; he calls it the elevated (μεγαλοπρεπής) style. According to Demetrius, elevation comes from thought, vocabulary, and syntax.

With regard to vocabulary, Demetrius says that elevation results from the use of unusual words (77), new coinages (95–98), including compound words (91–93) and onomatopoeia (94), and metaphors (78–90) and other tropes, especially epithet, which may be combined with metaphor (85), and allegory (99–102). Poetic vocabulary adds elevation (112–13).

With regard to syntax, Demetrius says that hiatus should neither be ignored nor avoided completely. Hiatus, especially between the same long vowels and diphthongs, produces grandeur (68–74). Although Aristotle does not discuss full, plain, and middle styles, Demetrius seems to understand Aristotle as describing the full or elevated style. Therefore, Demetrius

---

the case of the participle is wrong, nominative instead of accusative. Gerdmar agrees (*Rethinking the Judaism-Hellenism Dichotomy*, 34–35).

55. Watson, *Invention, Arrangement, and Style*, 196.
56. So Watson, *Invention, Arrangement, and Style*, 144.
57. Watson, *Invention, Arrangement, and Style*, 24–25, references omitted. On the grand style in *Ad Herennium*, see Leeman, *Orationis Ratio*, 29–32; on the grand style in Cicero, see Leeman, *Orationis Ratio*, 145–49.

regards Aristotle's comments on rhythm as referring to the elevated style. Thus use of the paean is elevated, but heroic rhythm (i.e., dactyl, spondee, and possibly anapest) is too solemn,[58] and the iamb too ordinary (38–43). Demetrius identifies the following figures of speech as appropriate to the elevated style: repetition (59, 61, 66, 103), anthypallage, or substitution of one grammatical case for another (60), asyndeton, though polysyndeton can also increase elevation (61–63, 54–58), variety in the use of cases (65). Crowding figures together should be avoided (67). Long clauses produce grandeur (44), as does composition in periods (45–47). Other syntactical features that produce elevation are: a series of ugly sounds (48–49, 105), putting less vivid words before the more vivid (50–52), not having connectives correspond too precisely (53), aposiopesis (103), indirect construction (104), and use of the epiphoneme (106–11).

The faulty style corresponding to the elevated is the frigid. It arises particularly from speaking too grandly of small things (119–23). Hyperbole is the most frigid of all figures (124–27).

To a considerable extent, Demetrius's description of the grand style resembles Cicero's description of stylistic ornament in general. We have already observed that the style of 2 Peter largely conforms to the latter. However, Demetrius adds some items. Demetrius says that the new coinages that produce elevation include compound words and onomatopoeia. All four of 2 Peter's new coinages are compound words. None is an example of onomatopoeia, but one of 2 Peter's rare words is, i.e., ῥοιζηδόν. According to Demetrius, allegory produces elevation, but there is no allegory in 2 Peter. F. H. Chase and Richard J. Bauckham describe the vocabulary of 2 Peter as poetic.[59]

Of the figures of speech Demetrius says are appropriate to the elevated style, various kinds of repetition are particularly characteristic of 2 Peter, as we have seen. Watson has detected asyndeton in 2 Peter 2:10 and 12–15, and polysyndeton in 2 Peter 1:5–7.[60] And, as we have seen, 2 Peter does have a number of complex sentences. We may see instances of putting the less vivid word before the more vivid in 2 Peter 1:9 and 19. Τυφλός is less vivid than μυωπάζων (1:9); ἡμέρα διαυγάσῃ is less vivid than φωσφόρος ἀνατείλῃ (1:19). The other syntactical elements that Demetrius thinks produce elevation do not seem to occur in 2 Peter. Second Peter's subject matter is not too mundane for appropriate use of the elevated style, and its limited use of hyperbole is consistent with avoidance of frigidity.

58. This does not seem to be Aristotle's view in *Rhetoric* 3.8.
59. Chase, "Peter," 3:807–9; Bauckham, *Jude, 2 Peter*, 136.
60. Watson, *Invention, Arrangement, and Style*, 195–97.

"Longinus," *On the Sublime* can also be seen as a discussion of the grand style, which the author calls the sublime (ὕψος). According to the author, sublimity comes from great thoughts, strong emotion, certain figures of thought and speech, noble diction, and dignified word arrangement (8). Noble diction consists of metaphors (32) and other tropes, including hyperbole (38). Use of trivial words should be avoided (43).

Dignified word arrangement makes use of dactyls (39); the pyrrhic, tribrach, and combination of two trochees all detract from sublimity (41).[61] Composition in periods rather than short sentences produces sublimity (40, 42). Figures of thought and speech that produce sublimity are: adjuration (16), rhetorical question and answer (18), asyndeton (19), combination of figures, e.g., asyndeton combined with repetition and vivid presentation (20–21), hyperbaton (22), polyptoton (23–24), historical present (25), change of person (26–27), and periphrasis (28–29).

The diction of 2 Peter is in line with "Longinus"'s description of noble diction. With regard to rhythm, 2 Peter departs from "Longinus"'s prescriptions mainly by making use of the combination of two trochees. We have already noted that 2 Peter includes some complex sentences and uses some of the figures "Longinus" says produce sublimity, namely, asyndeton and repetition, as well as the trope periphrasis. Watson has also noted rhetorical question in 3:4 and polyptoton in many passages.[62]

4. Asian Style

More often than 2 Peter has been identified as an example of the grand style, it has been identified as an example of Asian rhetoric.[63] The relationship between the two typologies of style, grand—middle—plain, and Attic—Asian—Rhodian is not clear. It is tempting to see them alternative names for

---

61. In this passage, as in Cicero, the tribrach is called the trochee, and the combination of two trochees is called the dichoree.

62. 2 Pet 1:4, 10, 13, 14, 17, 18, 21; 2:1, 5, 6, 7, 8, 9, 12, 15; 3:5, 6, 7, 10–12, 12–14 (Watson, *Invention, Arrangement, and Style*, 195–97).

63. Reicke, *James, Peter and Jude*, 146–47; Green, *Peter and Jude*, 18, 41; Kelly, *Peter and Jude*, 228; Bauckham, *Jude, 2 Peter*, 137; Watson, *Invention, Arrangement, and Style*, 145–46; Thurén, "Style Never Goes Out of Fashion," 340. Gerdmar contests this (*Rethinking the Judaism-Hellenism Dichotomy*, 60–62). Moulton describes 2 Peter as Attic (*Grammar*, 2:5–6, 27–28), but by this he means that it is written in an "artificial literary dialect" (5), not that it is Attic as opposed to Asian. The contrast between Asian and Attic styles seems to have arisen at Rome, see Wilamowitz-Moellendorff, "Asianismus und Atticismus"; Russell, *Criticism in Antiquity*, 48–50; Wisse, "Greeks, Romans and the Rise of Atticism"; Swain, *Hellenism and Empire*, 22–26, 39. However, the style labeled "Asian" by Roman authors was widespread.

the same thing: grand = Asian, middle = Rhodian, plain = Attic. However, since Cicero and Quintilian discuss both but do not relate them in this way, there is little basis for this equation of the two. Most likely, there are Attic, Asian, and Rhodian versions of each of the grand, middle, and plain styles.

Unfortunately, few examples of Asian style survive, and our understanding of it mainly derives from somewhat critical references to it. Following Cicero (in *Brutus* 325), Eduard Norden distinguished two kinds of Asianism—the refined and the bombastic. Norden presents Hegesias of Magnesia as an example of the former. His style was characterized by (1) replacement of the period with short, choppy sentences; (2) each of which had a marked rhythm; and (3) unusual usage, e.g., nonsensical metaphors and absurd paraphrases (cf. Cicero, *Orator* 230–31). Norden presents the Nemrud Dagh inscription as an example of the bombastic style. It shared the second and third characteristics with the refined Asian style but used long instead of short sentences. Norden describes the style of the inscription as passionately elevated, making use of highly poetic words and new coinages, avoiding hiatus, freely altering word order for the sake of rhythm, and making use of stilted, bombastic, and refined expression.[64] These two kinds of Asianism can be seen as the middle and grand Asian styles.

H. J. Rose describes Asianism as follows, apparently referring mainly to the first, the middle Asian style:

> It would seem to have abandoned the use of the period to a considerable extent and made up its compositions mostly of short sentences, ending with a marked, almost a versified rhythm. The wording was often very artificial, and on occasion normal word-order . . . was sacrificed and even meaningless words inserted to get the desired sound-effects. The Georgian figures seem also, from the specimens we have, to have been used to excess, and poetical ornaments to have abounded.[65]

Bo Reicke describes Asianism as "characterized by a loaded, verbose, high-sounding manner of expression leaning toward the novel and bizarre, and careless about violating classic ideals of simplicity";[66] he is apparently referring mainly to the second, grand Asian style. Second Peter is an example of this kind of Asian style.[67]

---

64. Norden, *Die antike Kunstprosa*, 134–47. On Cicero and Asianism, see Leeman, *Orationis Ratio*, 91–111. Leeman discusses *Brutus* 325 on 94–95.

65. Rose, *Outlines of Classical Literature*, 146.

66. Reicke, *James, Peter and Jude*, 147.

67. Thurén also sees 2 Peter as exhibiting grand Asian style ("General New Testament Writings," 600).

5. Second Peter and the Nemrud Dagh Inscription

If we take the Nemrud Dagh inscription as typical of this style, the similarities between it and 2 Peter confirm that 2 Peter is written in the grand Asian style. Of course, the two are different as well as similar.[68] The style of the inscription has been studied most thoroughly by Joseph Waldis.[69] His work is basic to the following discussion.

a) Vocabulary

They are similar in vocabulary. The inscription does not seem to use as many rare words as does 2 Peter, but it contains more new coinages. Waldis lists six—ἀνειλάτος in sentences 14 and 25; ἐνθρόνισμα in sentence 5; ἐπίθυσις in sentence 18; ἱεροθέσιον in sentences 5 and 17; μεταδιατάττω in sentence 23; and προσκαθοσιόω in sentence 11.[70] To this can be added ὀπισθοβαρής in sentence 15 and ὑπολήνιος in sentence 19, for a total of eight new coinages. As we have seen above, 2 Peter contains four. The inscription uses somewhat more metaphors than 2 Peter. Waldis lists thirty-three metaphors in the inscription;[71] as we have seen above 2 Peter uses twenty-seven. Waldis also identifies the following tropes in the inscription: metonymy (in sentences 7 and 17), hyperbole (in sentence 5), periphrasis[72] and synecdoche (in sentence 5). As is true of 2 Peter, the most common trope in the inscription, after metaphor, is periphrasis. Waldis notes that this is characteristic of Asian style.[73]

---

68. Reicke (*James, Peter and Jude*, 184) and Green (*Peter and Jude*, 18) mention that there are similarities but do not describe them in detail. Gerdmar (*Rethinking the Judaism-Hellenism Dichotomy*, 62) denies that the inscription and 2 Peter are similar.

69. Waldis, *Sprache und Stil*. References to the inscription make use of Waldis's division of it into sentences on 3–11.

70. Waldis, *Sprache und Stil*, 27.

71. In sentences 1, 2 (four metaphors), 3 (three metaphors), 4 (two metaphors), 5 (five metaphors), 6, 7 (four metaphors), 10, 14 (three metaphors), 15, 16, 18, 19, 22, 25 (two metaphors), 26, 27 (Waldis, *Sprache und Stil*, 65–66).

72. In sentences 1, 2, 4 (twice), 5 (five times), 7, 8, 9, 10, 12, 17, 18, 19 (three times), 22 (twice), 23, 25, 26.

73. Waldis, *Sprache und Stil*, 66.

b) Syntax

The inscription makes efforts to avoid hiatus;[74] as was noted above, 2 Peter does not seem to do so. In the opening lines of the inscription (i.e., sentences 1–3), hiatus occurs five times. In the opening lines of 2 Peter (i.e., 1:1–5) hiatus occurs seventeen times.

1) Rhythm

The rhythm of the two texts is similar, though there are differences between them. As is true for 2 Peter, the most common foot at the end of sentences in the inscription is the spondee; it is found at the end of eleven sentences.[75] Also like 2 Peter, the spondee is preceded by a cretic four times.[76] Unlike 2 Peter, the sentences of the inscription do not frequently end with two spondees; this happens only at the end of sentence 21.

Unlike 2 Peter, the second most common foot at the end of the inscription's sentences is not the cretic. It is found only twice, at the ends of sentences 6 and 17. In the latter case it is preceded by a trochee.

The second most common foot at the end of the inscription's sentences is the trochee, the third most common foot at the end of 2 Peter's sentences. A trochee is found at the end of nine of the inscription's sentences.[77] Two trochees end a sentence five of these times.[78]

Like 2 Peter, the inscription's sentences also end with iambs (at the end of sentence 4), dactyls (at the ends of 1, 5, 12) and paeans (at the end of 26). The last is of the kind best used at the end of a sentence.

According to Waldis, Asian style allowed four possible sentence endings:[79]

1. Cretic—trochee/spondee, which may also take the forms paean—trochee/spondee, molossus (long—long—long)—cretic, and paean—trochee—iamb, among others. Twelve of the inscription's sentences end in one of these ways.[80]

---

74. Waldis, *Sprache und Stil*, 62–63.
75. At the ends of sentences 3, 9, 10, 11, 14, 15, 18, 19, 21, 24, 25.
76. In sentences 3, 10, 14, 19.
77. At the ends of sentences 2, 7, 8, 13, 16, 20, 22, 23, 27.
78. In sentences 8, 20, 22, 23, 27.
79. Waldis, *Sprache und Stil*, 58–60.
80. Sentences 2, 3, 4, 7, 9, 11, 12, 13, 14, 16, 19, 21. Although Waldis does not include them in this category, it seems that sentences 10 and 18 also belong here. If these sentences are included, Waldis's four categories include all of the inscription's sentences.

2. Cretic—cretic/dactyl, which may also take the forms cretic—paean and paean—cretic, among others. Four of the inscription's sentences end in one of these ways.[81]

3. Trochee—trochee, which may also take the form trochee—spondee. Eight of the inscription's sentences end in one of these ways.[82]

4. Cretic—iamb. One of the inscription's sentences ends this way, namely 17.

Sixteen of 2 Peter's sentences end in the first of the ways listed above.[83] Fourteen of 2 Peter's sentences end in the third way listed above.[84] None of 2 Peter's sentences ends in the second or fourth ways listed above; these are also less frequent in the inscription than the first and third sentence endings. While all of the inscription's sentences end in one of these four ways, fifteen of the sentences in 2 Peter end in some way other than these four.

2) *Figures of Speech and Thought*

Both 2 Peter and the inscription repeat words frequently. Both texts repeat about 38 percent of the words in their vocabulary.[85] As we have seen, 2 Peter often repeats words for artistic effect. This is also the case for the inscription.

---

81. Sentences 1, 5, 6, 26.

82. Sentences 8, 15, 20, 22, 23, 24, 25, 27.

83. 2 Pet 1:2, 7, 8, 12, 20; 2:1, 10a, 17, 19b, 20, 21; 3:4a and b, 14, 16, 17. Other forms of this sentence ending that are found in 2 Peter are cretic—trochee—iamb, trochee—iamb—spondee, and trochee—iamb—cretic.

84. 2 Pet 1:10a, 11, 14, 15, 16, 17, 21; 2:3, 15; 3:7, 9, 13, 18a and b. Other forms of this sentence ending that are found in 2 Peter are spondee—spondee and spondee—trochee.

85. Second Peter repeats 151 of a total vocabulary of 401 words; the inscription repeats 165 of a total of 436. Since the total number of different words in the inscription is somewhat larger than in 2 Peter, although the latter is slightly longer than the former, we can see that 2 Peter repeats its words somewhat more frequently than does the inscription.

THE STYLE OF THE SECOND LETTER OF PETER   69

As in 2 Peter, the inscription's repetition of words can often be seen as transplacement[86] or paronomasia.[87]

Also as in 2 Peter, other instances of repetition of words in the inscription can be seen as developing certain topics. Such topics include: being just; piety; establishing; sanctification; race; being common; honor; favor; time; and law.[88] Note that several of these have counterparts in 2 Peter, namely, being just; piety; establishing; sanctification; and favor.

As is the case in 2 Peter, the development of some of these topics in the inscription constitutes inclusio. The topic of sanctification is mentioned in sentences 1 and 26, as are the topics of favor and time. The topic of piety is mentioned in sentences 2 and 26. The topic of race is mentioned in 4 and 26; the topics of honor and law are mentioned in 4 and 27.

Waldis lists other figures in the inscription on pages 67–71.

---

86. Sentence 1 βασιλεύς—βασιλέως, ἐπιφανής—ἐπιφανοῦς, repetition of καλλινίκου; 2–3 μακαριστῆς . . . βίον—βίου μακαριστῶς; 4 κοινήν—κοινόν; 5 οὐρανίων . . . θρόνων—οὐρανίους . . . θρόνους, ὑπάρξαν—ὑπάρχῃ; 5–6 repetition of ὁρᾷς, καθιδρυμένος—καθιδρυσάμην; 8–9 πρεπούσαις—πρέπουσαν, θυσιῶν—θυσίας; 11–12 θυσιῶν πλήθους—πλῆθος . . . θυσίας; 14 repetition of τηρεῖν, ἰδίας—ἰδίαι, καθοσιώσας—καθωσιωμένων, ἀσύλοις—ἄσυλον; 14–15 ἀσέβειαν—ἀσεβείας; 14–16 νόμον—νόμος—νόμον; 16–17 repetition of θεῶν; 17 repetition of ἱεροθεσίωι; 17–18 κόσμου—κόσμον; 18 πᾶν—πάντας, χάρις—χάρισιν, τιμαῖς—τιμάς; 18–19 ἱεραῖς—ἱεράς; 20–21 repetition of καθείρωσα; 21 συνόδοις—σύνοδος; 23 κώμας . . . δαίμοσιν—κώμας . . . δαιμόνων; 24–25 τιμῆς—τιμήν; 25 ἁπάντων—ἅπασαν; 25–26 θεῶν—θεοῖς, γένει—γένους; 26 πολλῶν—πολλά; 26–27 εἴλεως . . . πᾶσαν—ἵλεως . . . πάντας . . . πάντα; 27 τιμάς—τιμῆς, δαίμονας . . . θεούς—δαιμόνων . . . θεῶν.

87. Sentence 1 βασιλεύς—βασιλίσσης, φιλορώμαιος—φιλέλλην—φιλαδέλφου—φιλομήτορος, θεός—θεᾶς; 18 καθιέρωσα—καθωσίωσα; 21 καθειέρωσα—καθοσιωθῇ, ἀφείσθωσαν—προσκαρτερείτωσαν—ποιείσθωσαν; 26 προγόνοις—ἐκγόνοις—γένους—συγγενεῖς, ἅπαντας—πᾶσαν.

88. The topic of being just (δίκαιος) is introduced in sentence 1 and developed in 4, 7, 25. The topic of piety (εὐσέβεια, εὐσεβής) is introduced in sentence 2 and developed in 4, 5, 14, 18, 22, 26. Impiety (ἀσέβεια) is mentioned in 14, 15. The topic of establishing (ἀνατίθημι, καθίστημι) is introduced in sentence 5 and developed in 8 (twice), 10, 14, 17, 22, 23. The topic of sanctification (καθιδρύω, καθιερόω, καθοσιόω, προσκαθοσιόω) is introduced in sentence 1 and developed in 5 (twice), 6, 11, 14 (twice), 17, 18 (twice), 20, 21 (twice), 23. Being holy (ἅγιος, ὅσιος) is mentioned in 5, 15, 22, 23, 26; holiness (ὁσιότης) is mentioned in 2. The topic of race (γένος, ἔκγονος, πρόγονος, γενεά, συγγενής) is introduced in sentence 4 and developed in 5, 8, 14, 18, 21, 22 (twice), 25, 26 (four times). Sons and daughters (υἱός, θυγάτηρ) are mentioned in 21; children (παῖς) are mentioned in 22, 26. The topic of being common (κοινός) is introduced in sentence 4 (twice) and developed in 5, 9, 10, 19, 20. The topic of honor (τιμή) is introduced in sentence 4 and developed in 7, 9, 14, 18 (twice), 19, 22, 24, 25, 26, 27 (twice). The topic of favor (χάρις) is introduced in sentence 1 and developed in 18 (twice), 19, 22, 26. The topic of time (χρόνος) is introduced in sentence 1 and developed in 5, 13, 14, 17, 21, 22, 26. The topic of law (νόμος) is introduced in sentence 4 and developed in 9, 14 (twice), 16, 18, 27. Being illegal (παράνομος) is mentioned in 27.

70 A VOYAGE AROUND THE SECOND LETTER OF PETER

3) Sentence Structure

One of the most obvious ways the inscription and 2 Peter differ is in the average length—and thus complexity—of their sentences. The two texts are approximately equal in length: 2 Peter contains 1103 words; the inscription consists of 1065 words. However, I count 44 sentences in 2 Peter, and Waldis counts 27 in the inscription. Both texts include both long and short sentences, but average sentence length in 2 Peter is approximately 25 words, while average sentence length in the inscription is approximately 39 words. In this respect, 2 Peter is less grand than the inscription and may be seen as falling between the grand and middle Asian styles.[89]

One of the inscription's elaborate sentences is sentence 5. This is a complex sentence with the protasis introduced by ἐπεί, and the apodosis by τότε. A relative clause is dependent on the main clause of the protasis, and a participial phrase modifies the subject of the relative clause. A compound purpose clause, introduced by ὅπως, is dependent on the apodosis. This purpose clause consists of two clauses introduced by μὴ μόνον, ἀλλὰ καί. A brief relative clause is dependent on the first of these. This period consists of five clauses, of which the last is the longest. According to Waldis, this sentence exhibits the following figures in addition to the tropes and transplacements listed above: litotes, isocolon, homoioteleuton, and alliteration.[90]

Another elaborate sentence is sentence 19. The main clause of the sentence is the imperative clause that the priest should afford common enjoyment of the festival for the gatherings of the crowds. This clause is preceded by three participial phrases, each modifying the implied subject of the imperative. The main clause is then followed by two more participial phrases also modifying the subject of the imperative. A brief clause is dependent on the first of these phrases. A purpose clause, introduced by ὅπως, is dependent on the second. The purpose clause includes a participial phrase modifying the subject of the clause, and a second participle introducing a dependent adverbial clause. This period consists of four clauses; in its abundant use of participial phrases, it is similar to 2 Peter 2:12–14. According to Waldis, this sentence of the inscription exhibits hendiadys, homoioteleuton, alliteration, and antithesis in addition to the tropes and transplacement listed above.

A third elaborate sentence is sentence 22. This is a compound sentence consisting of three independent clauses, all with imperative verbs. The first

---

89. See Watson, *Invention, Arrangement, and Style*, 145–46.

90. For grammatical analysis of this and the other sentences of the inscription, see Waldis, *Sprache und Stil*, 3–11, 71–74. For tropes and figures in the inscription, see Waldis, *Sprache und Stil*, 66–71.

clause states that no one should enslave the sacred slaves of the sanctuary or their descendants or interfere with them in other ways. Two relative clauses are dependent on this clause, the first modifying the sacred slaves, the second their descendants. The second independent clause, introduced by ἀλλ᾽, states that the priests should take care of the sacred slaves, and the third, introduced by δέ, states that various people should aid them. A relative clause depends on this third independent clause; it modifies the subject of the independent clause. This period consists of six clauses, and there is an antithetical relationship between the first independent clause on one hand and the second and third independent clauses on the other. According to Waldis, this sentence exhibits anaphora, polysyndeton, homoioteleuton, alliteration (twice), and antithesis in addition to the tropes listed above.

6. Conclusion

We have seen that the vocabulary and syntax of 2 Peter display the kinds of ornamentation recommended by Cicero, Quintilian, and others. We have also seen that the quantity and quality of this stylistic ornamentation indicate that 2 Peter is written in the grand style. Finally, we have seen that the similarity between 2 Peter and the Nemrud Dagh inscription, taken as representative of the grand Asian style, indicates that 2 Peter is written in that style.

This understanding of the style of 2 Peter can help us to see what the author intended to achieve and estimate his degree of success in doing so. We can also see that many negative assessments of the style of 2 Peter are not evaluations of it according to the canons of style recognized by its author and readers. Instead, they are implicitly expressions of preference for a different style, like the criticism of Asian style in its own time. Recognition of this may open the way to greater appreciation of this style on its own terms. Reicke compares Asian style to European art and literature of the baroque period, a parallel that may allow us to be more appreciative of this style.[91]

Writing in the grand style implies that the author of 2 Peter sees himself as expressing powerful and impressive thoughts. The author summarizes these thoughts in 2 Peter 1:3–11: since Jesus's divine power has given us everything needed for life and piety, including the hope of participating in divine nature (vv. 3–4), it is necessary to confirm this call and election (v. 10) by striving to grow in virtue (vv. 5–9) so as to enter the eternal kingdom

---

91. Reicke, *James, Peter, and Jude*, 146–47. Wilamowitz-Moellendorff had earlier compared Asian style to baroque style ("Asianismus und Atticismus," 400–401, cf. 374).

of our Lord and Savior Jesus Christ (v. 11). We may readily agree that these are indeed powerful and impressive thoughts.

Writing in the grand style also implies that the author is primarily attempting to appeal to the emotions of his audience, not to inform or please them.[92] The author's principal aim is to arouse his readers to strive for growth in virtue in order to be suited for the new heavens and earth that are coming. It is necessary to pursue this aim because the readers are being exposed to other teachers who seem to doubt that new heavens and earth are coming and thus doubt that efforts to grow in virtue are needed. The author tries to prevent his readers from accepting this teaching. He does so by offering various arguments for his position. However, they are presented in a highly ornate way so that they appeal to emotion as well as to reason.

Writing in the Asian style implies that the author stood outside the mainstream of literary development in the first and second centuries, which was flowing in the direction of Attic style. It would have been possible to write in this style anywhere, even in Rome, by imitating writers like Demosthenes or Cicero. However, the author's Asian style may imply that 2 Peter was not written in Rome or in any other cultural center, but rather somewhere like Commagene, the location of the Nemrud Dagh inscription.

The author of 2 Peter was rather adept in the rhetoric of his time. He had surely received at least an elementary education in a Greek school or in a Jewish school modeled on Greek schools. This is indicated by his literacy in Greek and the literary level of the letter. His rhetorical skill might have been acquired without higher education. For example, Frederick W. Danker suggests that inscriptions would have provided rhetorical formation for those who could read them or heard them read.[93] However, it seems more likely that the author had received higher education in rhetoric.

---

92. Cf. Cicero, *Orator*, 69; Quintilian, *Institutio Oratoria*, 12.10.59.
93. Danker, "2 Peter 1," 64–65.

5

The Syntax of 2 Peter 1:1–7

Commentators disagree concerning the syntax of 2 Peter 1:1–7, especially that of vv. 3–4. Some understand vv. 3–4 as a continuation of the letter salutation (vv. 1–2).[1] Others view vv. 3–4 as the beginning of a sentence that continues in vv. 5–7.[2] Still others interpret vv. 3–4 as an independent sentence standing between vv. 1–2 and vv. 5–7.[3] Not only do commentators disagree about the syntax of 2 Peter 1:1–7, many do not espouse any definite analysis of it. With the exception of Robert H. Mounce and Anton Vögtle, the commentators listed in note 3 above indicate that vv. 3–4 are an independent sentence simply by putting periods after vv. 2 and 4 without explaining the syntactical basis on which they do so.[4] Half of them say nothing about syntax.[5] Richard J. Bauckham and Karl H. Schelkle discuss the syntactical uncertainty of vv. 3–4 without arguing that any of the

---

1. Bigg, *St. Peter and St. Jude*, 253; Fornberg, *Early Church*, 86; James, *Peter and Jude*, 10–11; Kelly, *Peter and Jude*, 299; Kraus, *Sprache, Stil*, 401, cf. 403, 247–48; Spitta, *Petrus und Judas*, 26–30, 58–61; Windisch, *Katholische Briefe*, 84–85; Wohlenberg, *Petrusbrief und Judasbrief*, 172.

2. Danker, "2 Peter 1"; Engberg-Pedersen, "Not an Iota, Not a Dot?"; Hofmann, *Der zweite Brief Petri*, 6; Reicke, *James, Peter, and Jude*, 152; Starr, *Sharers in Divine Nature*, 24–26.

3. Bauckham, *Jude, 2 Peter*, 173; Harrington, "Jude and 2 Peter," 243, cf. 247; Mounce, *Living Hope*, 105; Neyrey, *2 Peter, Jude*, 106, 111, 150; Paulsen, *Der Zweite Petrusbrief*, 106–7; Perkins, *First and Second Peter*, 168–69; Schelkle, *Petrusbriefe*, 186–87; Senior, *1 and 2 Peter*, 106–9; Sidebottom, *James, Jude, and 2 Peter*, 105–8; Spicq, *Épîtres de Saint Pierre*, 208–13; Vögtle, *Der Judasbrief/Der 2. Petrusbrief*, 137.

4. Schelkle and Spicq also put a period after v. 3. Neyrey (111) and Perkins treat vv. 3–4 as equivalent to a Thanksgiving section of 2 Peter; Senior treats these verses as an independent section of the letter.

5. This is true of Harrington, Neyrey, Perkins, Sidebottom, and Spicq.

possible construals of these verses is correct.[6] Henning Paulsen and Donald Senior discuss the syntax of vv. 3–4 and seem to indicate some preference for seeing them as a continuation of vv. 1–2, but they do not divide the text in a way that is consistent with this preference.[7]

The uncertain syntax of 2 Peter 1:1–7 causes Troels Engberg-Pedersen to suggest that the text requires emendation. Alternatively, Anders Gerdmar argues that this uncertainty reveals the ineptitude of the author of 2 Peter.[8]

Obviously, there is need for a clear and convincing analysis of the syntax of 2 Peter 1:1–7. I hope to provide such an analysis in what follows by arguing that vv. 3–4 should be understood as the beginning of a sentence that continues in vv. 5–7. More specifically, I will argue that vv. 3–4 should be understood as the protasis of a conditional sentence of which vv. 5–7 are the apodosis.[9]

Grammatically, vv. 3–4 consist of a genitive absolute (τῆς θείας δυνάμεως αὐτοῦ . . . δεδωρημένης) on which depend a relative clause and a purpose clause. Thus interpreting vv. 3–4 as an independent sentence requires understanding it as an anacolouthon (so J. N. D. Kelly, Mounce, and Vögtle). Examples of letters in which an anacolouthon follows the salutation include 1 Timothy (vv. 3–4) and probably the letters of Ignatius of Antioch to the Ephesians and Romans. However, none of these is very similar to 2 Peter 1:3–4 in its grammar.[10] While it is possible to understand 2 Peter 1:3–4 as an anacolouthon, an interpretation according to which it is syntactically complete is preferable.[11]

---

6. Schelkle, *Petrusbriefe*, 187n1. Gerdmar (*Rethinking the Judaism-Hellenism Dichotomy*, 33) similarly emphasizes the ambiguity of vv. 3–4. He seems inclined to view them as an independent sentence but does not clearly say so.

7. Senior, *1 and 2 Peter*, 107. Mayor (*St. Jude and St. Peter*, 83) similarly discusses the syntax of vv. 3–4 and seems inclined to see them as a continuation of vv. 1–2 but does not clearly argue for this or any other construal of the verses.

8. Gerdmar, *Rethinking the Judaism-Hellenism Dichotomy*, 34.

9. Hofmann (*Der zweite Brief Petri* 6, 10–14) argues that the apodosis begins with the purpose clause in v. 4b, which is dependent on the imperative in v. 5, rather than the genitive absolute in v. 3. The main argument for this construal is that direct address to the recipients of 2 Peter begins with v. 4b rather than v. 5. However, the author of 2 Peter alternates rather readily between speaking of "us" and "you," and beginning an apodosis with a purpose clause would be very unusual.

10. 1 Tim 1:3–4 is a subordinate clause introduced by καθώς, on which depend a purpose clause and a relative clause. The salutation of Ignatius's letter *To the Ephesians* is followed by a simple participial phrase on which depends a relative clause. The salutation of Ignatius's letter *To the Romans* is followed by the protasis of a conditional sentence that lacks an apodosis. It is introduced by ἐπεί; on it depends a result clause introduced by ὡς.

11. Kelly and Windisch also make this point.

The genitive absolute of vv. 3-4 is introduced by ὡς. This particle can be used with a genitive absolute to indicate the basis for something. It is thus equivalent to the protasis of a conditional sentence. Since the protasis of a conditional sentence can either precede or follow the apodosis, understanding vv. 3-4 as the protasis of a conditional sentence underlies both seeing the passage as the continuation of vv. 1-2 and seeing it as continued by vv. 5-7.

In 2 Cor 5:20 we find an instance in which a genitive absolute introduced by ὡς serves as the protasis of a simple conditional sentence and follows its apodosis.[12]

> ὑπὲρ Χριστοῦ οὖν πρεσβεύομεν ὡς τοῦ θεοῦ παρακαλοῦντος δι' ἡμῶν.
>
> So we are ambassadors for Christ, since God is making his appeal through us.

Charles Bigg seems to see 2 Peter 1:2-4 as a parallel construction in which vv. 3-4 indicate the basis for the wish expressed in v. 2. Vv. 3-4 are the protasis and v. 2 the apodosis of a simple conditional sentence, thus vv. 3-4 continue the salutation of 2 Peter. In support of this construal Kelly, James M. Starr, and others have observed that vv. 3-4 are closely related to v. 2b. Vv. 3-4 elaborate the topic of recognition (ἐπίγνωσις) introduced in v. 2b, and the antecedent of αὐτοῦ in v. 3 is Ἰησοῦ in v. 2b.

Kelly, Paulsen, Friedrich Spitta, and Hans Windisch suggest that there is a parallel to such a grammatical extension of the letter salutation into the body of the letter in Ignatius of Antioch's letter *To the Philadelphians*.[13]

> Ἰγνάτιος, ὁ καὶ Θεοφόρος, ἐκκλησίᾳ θεοῦ πατρὸς καὶ κυρίου Ἰησοῦ Χριστοῦ τῇ οὔσῃ ἐν Φιλαδελφίᾳ τῆς Ἀσίας, . . . ἣν ἀσπάζομαι ἐν αἵματι Ἰησοῦ Χριστοῦ, ἥτις ἐστὶν χαρὰ αἰώνιος καὶ παράμονος, μάλιστα ἐὰν ἐν ἑνὶ ὦσιν σὺν τῷ ἐπισκόπῳ καῖ τοῖς σὺν αὐτῷ πρεσβυτέροις καὶ διακόνοις ἀποδεδειγμένοις ἐν γνώμῃ Ἰησοῦ Χριστοῦ, οὓς κατὰ τὸ ἴδιον θέλημα ἐστήριξεν ἐν βεβαιωσύνῃ τῷ ἁγίῳ αὐτοῦ πνεύματι.
>
> Ὃν ἐπίσκοπόν ἔγνων οὐκ ἀφ' ἑαυτοῦ οὐδὲ δι' ἀνθρώπων κεκτῆσθαι τὴν διακονίαν τὴν εἰς τὸ κοινὸν ἀνήκουσαν οὐδὲ κατὰ κενοδοξίαν, ἀλλ' ἐν ἀγάπῃ θεοῦ πατρὸς καὶ κυρίου Ἰησοῦ Χριστοῦ

---

12. See also 1 Pet 4:12. Other conditional sentences in which the protasis is a genitive absolute and follows its apodosis can be found in John 5:13; Acts 18:21; 19:40; Rom 2:15; 9:1; 2 Cor 4:17-18a; Heb 8:4; 11:4, 39-40; 3 John 3.

13. Fornberg suggests that there is a parallel to the salutations of Ignatius's letters to the Ephesians and Romans.

> Ignatius, who is also called Theophorus, to the Church of God the Father, and our Lord Jesus Christ, which is at Philadelphia, in Asia ... which I salute in the blood of Jesus Christ, who is our eternal and enduring joy, especially if [men] are in unity with the bishop, the presbyters, and the deacons, who have been appointed according to the mind of Jesus Christ, whom He has established in security, after His own will, and by His Holy Spirit,
>
> Which bishop I know obtained the ministry for the common good not from himself, nor through men, nor for vainglory, but in the love of God the Father and the Lord Jesus Christ.

Although the salutation of this letter is grammatically linked to what follows it, the connection is different from that proposed to exist between 2 Peter 1:1-2 and 3-4. What follows the salutation of Ignatius's letter is a relative clause that modifies the bishop mentioned in the salutation. This is entirely unlike the genitive absolute introduced by ὡς found in 2 Peter 1:3-4. None of Ignatius's other letters has any greater resemblance to the proposed construal of 2 Peter 1:1-4.[14]

Spitta finds other instances of the grammatical extension of a letter saluation into the body of the letter in the third and eighth letters of Plato, James 1:1-2, and 3 John 2-3. Immediately after their salutations, the third and eighth letters of Plato comment on the salutation, but this comment is not grammatically connected to the salutation. Likewise, there is no grammatical connection between the salutations of James, 3 John, and what follows them. And even if any of these were instances of such a grammatical connection, the grammar would be very different from that of 2 Peter 1:3-4. There is thus no close parallel to the interpretation of 2 Peter 1:3-4 as the continuation of the letter salutation in vv. 1-2.

---

14. The beginnings of Ignatius's letters vary in their syntax but in no case is there much resemblance to the proposed interpretation of 2 Pet 1:1-4. The salutations of his letters to the Magnesians, Trallians, and Polycarp are not grammatically connected with what follows. The salutation of his letter *To the Smyrnaeans* is grammatically connected with what follows if the word that follows the salutation is a participle (δοξάζων), but not if it is a finite verb (δοξάζω), which is what I read. It is possible to understand the salutations of his letters to the Ephesians and Romans as grammatically connected with what follows. The participle (ἀποδεξάμενος) that follows the salutation of *To the Ephesians* can be understood as modifying Ignatius, who is named in the salutation; the protasis of a conditional sentence that follows the salutation of *To the Romans* can be understood as its continuation. However, as I have mentioned above, it is more likely that both should be understood as anacolouthons. Engberg-Pedersen and Starr also observe that the salutations of Ignatius's letters have a different grammatical structure than that of 2 Pet 1:1-4; Starr mentions explicitly the letters to the Ephesians, Romans, and Smyrnaeans.

While it is possible to understand vv. 3–4 as a protasis whose apodosis is found in v. 2, it seems better to understand the verses as a protasis whose apodosis is found in vv. 5–7. There is no close parallel to the former construal, but parallels to the latter are abundant. Also supportive of the latter is the observation that in fact vv. 3–4 do provide the basis for the exhortation in vv. 5–7. Starr, who adopts this construal, says that vv. 3–4 would be an incomplete protasis because it lacks a main verb (cf. also G. Wohlenberg). However, in saying this, Starr seems to misunderstand the genitive absolute. In itself, the genitive absolute is equivalent to a subordinate clause and needs no further verb. However, it does require a main clause on which it depends. Vv. 5–7 constitute that main clause.

We find a comparable use of the genitive absolute in 2 Peter 3:11:

Τούτων οὕτως πάντων λυομένων ποταποὺς δεῖ ὑπάρχειν ὑμᾶς ἐν ἁγίαις ἀναστροφαῖς καὶ εὐσεβείαις, κτλ.

Since all these things are to be dissolved in this way, what sort of persons ought you to be in leading lives of holiness and godliness, etc.

As is the case with the proposed interpretation of 1:3–7, 3:11 is a conditional sentence whose protasis is a genitive absolute, and the protasis precedes the apodosis. Such a construction is found rather frequently in the New Testament.[15]

This construction is also found in the prologue to the Book of Sirach, where it is used in a long, complex sentence like that found in 2 Peter 1:3–7. The first 14 verses of Sirach's prologue are a conditional sentence; vv. 1–6 are the protasis and vv. 7–14 the apodosis. The protasis consists of a genitive absolute (πολλῶν καὶ μεγάλων . . . δεδομένων) on which depends a compound relative clause.

We find a shorter, but in some ways closer, parallel to 2 Peter 1:3–7 in 1 Cor 4:18:

ὡς μὴ ἐρχομένου δέ μου πρὸς ὑμᾶς ἐφυσιώθησάν τινες·

Since I am not coming to you, some have become arrogant.

Here the protasis is a genitive absolute introduced by ὡς as in 2 Peter 1:3–7. However, in 1 Cor 4:18 the protasis is contrary to fact; in 2 Peter 1:3–7 it is not.

---

15. See Matt 18:25; 25:5; John 2:5; 8:30; 18:22; Acts 5:15; 6:1; 7:21; 9:38; 15:2; 18:6, 27; 19:36; 20:3; 21:14, 34, 40a; 22:23–24; 23:7, 10, 30; 24:2–3, 25; 25:21, 25; 27:7, 9, 12, 13, 15, 18, 20, 21; 28:6, 9, 13, 19; Heb 7:12; 9:15; 10:26–27. In John 6:18 and 1 Pet 4:4 the genitive absolute is found in the middle of the main clause.

First Peter 4:1 is another instance of this construction that is parallel to 2 Peter 1:3-7 in a different way:

Χριστοῦ οὖν παθόντος σαρκὶ καὶ ὑμεῖς τὴν αὐτὴν ἔννοιαν ὁπλίσασθε, κτλ.

Since therefore Christ suffered in the flesh, arm yourselves also with the same intention etc.

In this passage, the genitive absolute is not introduced by ὡς, but the main verb of the apodosis is an imperative as is the case in 2 Peter 1:5.[16] The apodosis is also introduced by καί as in 2 Peter 1:5.

We find yet another instance of this construction that is parallel to 2 Peter 1:3-7 in 1 Thess 3:6-8. The protasis of this conditional sentence is found in v. 6. It consists of a genitive absolute (ἐλθόντος Τιμοθέου ... καὶ εὐαγγελισαμένου) on which depends a noun clause modified by a participial phrase. Vv. 7-8 form the apodosis, which is introduced by the phrase διὰ τοῦτο. This phrase somewhat resembles the phrase that introduces 2 Peter 1:5-7, i.e., καὶ αὐτὸ τοῦτο δέ.

The interpretation of καὶ αὐτὸ τοῦτο δέ presents a problem for any interpretation of 2 Peter 1:3-7. The phrase is apparently unique in Greek literature. There are thus neither parallels to its use in 2 Peter nor any alternative uses of the phrase. However, there are partial parallels. I will discuss four categories of such partial parallels.

1. First of all, it should be noted that δέ alone is often used to introduce the apodosis of a conditional sentence.[17]
2. Secondly, the combination καὶ ... δέ is a common one.[18] When the two words are combined, καί is often the conjunction, while δέ means "on the other hand" or "also."[19] This seems to be the meaning of καὶ ... δέ in 2 Peter 1:5. καὶ αὐτὸ τοῦτο δέ means "and for this very reason also."[20] We find an example of καὶ ... δέ used to begin the apodosis of a conditional sentence in Plato, *Crito* 51A.

---

16. In Matt 6:3 and Luke 21:28 genitive absolutes are used as the equivalent of circumstantial clauses, and the verb of the main clause is an imperative.
17. See Denniston, *Greek Particles*, 177-81. Denniston calls this usage "apodotic."
18. Denniston, *Greek Particles*, 199-203.
19. Denniston, *Greek Particles*, 199n1. See also Mayor, *St. Jude and St. Peter*, 89.
20. Hofmann (*Der zweite Brief Petri* 15-17) understands the phrase in the same way I do here, but sees it as linking the participial phrases in vv. 4b and 5a, not as the introduction to vv. 5-7.

> ἐάν σε ἐπιχειρῶμεν ἡμεῖς ἀπολλύναι δίκαιον ἡγούμενοι εἶναι, καὶ σὺ δὲ ἡμᾶς τοὺς νόμους καὶ τὴν πατρίδα καθ' ὅσον δύνασαι ἐπιχειρήσεις ἀνταπολλύναι,

> if we [laws] undertake to destroy you, thinking it is right, you will undertake in return to destroy us laws and your country, so far as you are able.

3. Thirdly, αὐτὸ τοῦτο occurs rather frequently and is sometimes used as an adverbial accusative with the meaning "for this very reason," as is the case in in 2 Peter 1:5. One example of this usage is found in Plato, *Symposium* 204A

> οὐδ' αὖ οἱ ἀμαθεῖς φιλοσοφοῦσιν οὐδ' ἐπιθυμοῦσι σοφοὶ γενέσθαι· αὐτὸ γὰρ τοῦτό ἐστι χαλεπὸν ἀμαθία, τὸ μὴ ὄντα καλὸν κἀγαθὸν μηδὲ φρόνιμον δοκεῖν αὑτῷ εἶναι ἱκανόν. οὔκουν ἐπιθυμεῖ ὁ μὴ οἰόμενος ἐνδεὴς εἶναι οὗ ἂν μὴ οἴηται ἐπιδεῖσθαι.

> Neither do the ignorant pursue wisdom, nor desire to be made wise: for this very reason is ignorance distressing, when a person who is not comely or worthy or intelligent is satisfied with himself. The man who does not feel himself defective has no desire for that whereof he feels no defect.

We find another example of this usage in Xenophon, *Anabasis* 1.9.21. In Plato *Protagoras* 310E αὐτὰ ταῦτα is used with the same meaning.

Engberg-Pedersen has observed that in all of these examples αὐτὸ τοῦτο refers to something that follows it in the text, not to something that precedes it as is the case in 2 Peter 1:5, where καὶ αὐτὸ τοῦτο δέ refers to vv. 3–4. This is true of the Xenophon passage, but only partly true of the passages from Plato. Thus in the passage from the *Symposium* quoted above, αὐτὸ τοῦτο refers both to what precedes and to what follows. The reason ignorance is distressing is both the previously mentioned behavior of the ignorant and the explanation of that behavior that follows. The same is true in the other passage from Plato.[21]

In replying to Engberg-Pedersen's observation, Starr argues that αὐτὸ τοῦτο is used in Rom 13:6; 2 Cor 5:5, 7:11 and Gal 2:10 to refer to what precedes, and he concludes that the phrase can refer either to what precedes or to what follows. This is correct. However, only in 2

---

21. αὐτὸ τοῦτο also seems to refer both to what precedes and to what follows it in the text in Phil 1:6. τοῦτο αὐτό is used the same way in 2 Cor 2:3.

Cor 7:11 is the phrase used as an adverbial accusative; in Rom 13:6 and 2 Cor 5:5 the phrase is used as the object of the preposition εἰς,[22] while in Gal 2:10 it is the direct object of the verb.

4. Fourthly, I have been unable to find any examples of the phrase αὐτὸ τοῦτο δέ apart from 2 Peter 1:5. However, the phrase καὶ αὐτὸ τοῦτο occurs rather frequently. καὶ γὰρ αὐτὸ τοῦτο is found in the Xenophon passage mentioned above. But precisely καὶ αὐτὸ τοῦτο is also rather common. However, in only a few cases is it used as an adverbial accusative meaning "and for this very reason" as it is in 2 Peter 1:5.

One example of this usage is Xenophon, *Cyropaideia* 8.3.39.

καὶ ὁ Σάκας εἶπεν· ὦ μακάριε σὺ τά τε ἄλλα καὶ αὐτὸ τοῦτο ὅτι ἐκ πένητος πλούσιος γεγένησαι· πολὺ γὰρ οἴομαί σε καὶ διὰ τοῦτο ἥδιον πλουτεῖν ὅτι πεινήσας χρημάτων ἐπλούτησας.

"What a happy fellow you must be," said the Sacian, "for every reason, but particularly for this very reason that from being poor you have become rich. For you must enjoy your riches much more, I think, because of this that it was only after being hungry for wealth that you became rich."

In this passage καὶ αὐτὸ τοῦτο refers to a reason that is specified in what follows, namely that he was poor before becoming rich. We find a similar use of the phrase to refer to a reason that follows in a number of passages.[23]

One place where the phrase is used to refer to a reason mentioned previously is Josephus, *Ant.* 10.11.6 §257.

ἀπὸ γὰρ μείζονος ἧς προσεδόκων εὐνοίας τοῦτο ποιεῖν τὸν Δαρεῖον ὑπολαμβάνοντες, ὡς καὶ καταφρονήσαντι τῶν ἐκείωου προσταγμάτων συγγνώμην ἑτοίμως νέμειν, καὶ αὐτὸ τοῦτο βασκαίνοντες τῷ Δανιήλῳ, οὔτε μετεβάλλοντο πρὸς τὸ ἡμερώτερον, ῥίπτειν δ' αὐτὸν ἠξίουν κατὰ τὸν νόμον εἰς τὸν λάκκον τῶν λεόντων.

For supposing that Darius did this out of a greater kindness to him than they expected, and that he was ready to grant him pardon for this contempt of his injunctions, and for this very reason envying Daniel, they did not become more

---

22. αὐτὸ τοῦτο is also used as the object of the preposition εἰς, but in reference to something that follows it in the text, in Rom 9:17, quoting Exod 9:16.

23. See Demosthenes, *Philippic* 4.57; Cassius Dio, *Roman History* 2.11.5; 36.27.1; 50.6.1; 52.26.5.

honorable to him, but desired he might be cast into the den of lions according to the law.

Here, the phrase introduces a participial phrase and refers to the preceding description of Darius's favorable attitude toward Daniel. Another example of this usage is Aelius Aristides, *To Plato: In Defense of Oratory* 455–56:

> οὐκοῦν οὐδὲ ἐνταῦθα ἀμφότερα ἐᾶν ὁ λόγος φαίνεται· ἐπεὶ καὶ αὐτὸ τοῦτο ὑπὲρ αὐτοῦ Πλάτωνος ἡμεῖς νῦν ποιοῦμεν.

> (455) So even here the argument does not appear to allow both things to be said of oratory. (456) Indeed, for this very reason we act now on Plato's behalf.

In this passage καὶ αὐτὸ τοῦτο refers to the previously stated argument. Yet another example of this usage is Cassius Dio, *Roman History* 78.25.3:

> οὐδὲ ἐπαρκέσαι αὐτῷ οὔτε ἀνθρωπίνη ἐπικουρία, καίπερ παντὸς ὡς εἰπεῖν ὕδατος ῥέοντος, οὔθ' ἡ τοῦ οὐρανίου ἐπίρροια πλείστη τε καὶ σφοδροτάτη γενομένη ἠδυνήθη· οὕτω που καὶ τὸ ὕδωρ ἑκάτερον ὑπὸ τῆς τῶν σκηπτῶν δυνάμεως ἀνηλίσκετο, καὶ ἐν μέρει καὶ αὐτὸ τοῦτο προσεσίνετο, ὅθεν ἡ θέα τῶν μονομαχιῶν ἐν τῷ σταιδίῳ ἐπὶ πολλὰ ἔτη ἐτελέσθη.

> Neither human aid could avail against the conflagration, though practically every aqueduct was emptied, nor could the downpour from the sky, which was most heavy and violent, accomplish anything—to such an extent was the water from both sources consumed by the power of the thunderbolts, and, for this very reason contributed in a measure to the damage done. In consequence of this disaster the gladiatorial show was held in the stadium for many years.

Here καὶ αὐτὸ τοῦτο refers to the previously mentioned consumption of water by the thunderbolts as the reason why it contributed to the damage rather than mitigating it.

The closest parallel to the use of this phrase in 2 Peter 1:5 is found in Lucian, *Icaromenippus* 2:

> Εἰ δὲ ἀπιστεῖς, καὶ αὐτὸ τοῦτο ὑπερευφραίνομαι τὸ πέρα πίστεως εὐτυχεῖν.

> If you do not believe, for this very reason I rejoice exceedingly to have seen what is past belief.

Here as in 2 Peter 1:5, καὶ αὐτὸ τοῦτο introduces the apodosis of a conditional sentence and refers back to the protasis.

✳ ✳ ✳

Although καὶ αὐτὸ τοῦτο δέ is unique in Greek literature, these partial parallels, particularly the last, show that it is possible to interpret it as the introduction to the apodosis of the conditional sentence in 2 Peter 1:3-7, referring to vv. 3-4 as the reason for what the addressees are urged to do in vv. 5-7. In 2 Peter 1:3-7 it is not possible to understand καὶ αὐτὸ τοῦτο δέ as a reference to what follows, as Engberg-Pedersen has observed. Thus even those who see v. 5 as the beginning of a new section understand καὶ αὐτὸ τοῦτο δέ in the way I suggest here. However, I hope to have shown that there is no obstacle to interpreting vv. 3-7 as a conditional sentence, and that this is the most probable interpretation of these verses.

6

A Note on 2 Peter 1:19–20

19 καὶ ἔχομεν βεβαιότερον τὸν προφητικὸν λόγον, ᾧ καλῶς ποιεῖτε προσέχοντες ὡς λύχνῳ φαίνοντι ἐν αὐχμηρῷ τόπῳ, ἕως οὗ ἡμέρα διαυγάσῃ καὶ φωσφόρος ἀνατείλῃ ἐν ταῖς καρδίαις ὑμῶν 20 τοῦτο πρῶτον γινώσκοντες ὅτι πᾶσα προφητεία γραφῆς ἰδίας ἐπιλύσεως οὐ γίνεται,

Virtually all recent commentators interpret the prepositional phrase at the end of 2 Peter 1:19 (ἐν ταῖς καρδίαις ὑμῶν) as modifying the immediately preceding verb (ἀνατείλῃ).[1] A few commentators consider—and reject—two other possible construals. First, Julius Boehmer, D. Edmond Hiebert, J. N. D. Kelly, and G. Wohlenberg say that the prepositional phrase does not modify the participle προσέχοντες found earlier in 1:19; the last three correctly argue that the prepositional phrase is too distant from this

1. Bauckham, *Jude, 2 Peter*, 226; Bigg, *St. Peter and St. Jude*, 269; Boehmer, "Tag und Morgenstern?," 231; Harrington, "Jude and 2 Peter," 257; Hiebert, "Prophetic Foundation of Christian Life," 162–63; Kelly, *Peter and Jude*, 322–23; Mayor, *St. Jude and St. Peter*, 109–11; Mounce, *Living Hope*, 120; Neyrey, *2 Peter, Jude*, 178; Paulsen, *Der Zweite Petrusbrief*, 121–22; Perkins, *First and Second Peter*, 177; Reicke, *James, Peter, and Jude*, 158; Schelkle, *Petrusbriefe*, 200; Senior, *1 and 2 Peter*, 115–16; Sidebottom, *James, Jude, and 2 Peter*, 111; Spicq, *Épitres de Saint Pierre*, 224; Vögtle, *Der Judasbrief/ Der 2. Petrusbrief*, 170–71; Windisch, *Katholische Briefe*, 90; Wohlenberg, *Petrusbrief und Judasbrief*, 202–5.

The earliest patristic commentators also interpret the prepositional phrase at the end of v. 19 as modifying the preceding verb. See, for example, the Latin commentary attributed to Hilary of Arles (401–49) PL Supp 3:110; the Latin commentary of Bede (673–735) PL 93:73; and the Greek commentary of Oecumenius (c. 990) PG 119:589.

participle.² Second, E. M. Sidebottom observes, "Commentators have sometimes sought to alter the implications of 'in your hearts' in this context by taking it as the beginning of the next verse."³ J. Chr. K. V. Hofmann is one of these, and Karl M. Schmidt is another.⁴ Boehmer mentions and rejects this possibility; Kelly discusses and rejects it because "the balance of the sentence" and "the stereotype expression" that begins 1:20 are against this.⁵ However, Kelly does not explain why he thinks "the balance of the sentence" and "the stereotype expression" make this construal unlikely.⁶

Wohlenberg rejects both construals for three reasons.⁷ First, προσέχοντες and γινώσκοντες can only refer to something that happens in one's heart; it would only be necessary to make this explicit for some special reason, but none is given. Second, the placement of the prepositional phrase is not consistent with its modifying either participle. And third, the parallel between ὡς λύχνῳ φαίνοντι ἐν αὐχμηρῷ τόπῳ, and ἕως οὗ ἡμέρα διαυγάσῃ καὶ φωσφόρος ἀνατείλῃ ἐν ταῖς καρδίαις ὑμῶν implies that ἐν ταῖς καρδίαις ὑμῶν modifies ἀνατείλῃ. The first of these points overlooks the possibility that specifying ἐν ταῖς καρδίαις ὑμῶν might be an instance of the figure of speech pleonasm, i.e., language fuller than absolutely required.⁸ I will address the second point, the placement of the prepositional

---

2. Friedrich Spitta also makes this point, but he concludes that the words intervening between προσέχοντες and ἐν ταῖς καρδίαις ὑμῶν are a gloss that has become part of the text; originally ἐν ταῖς καρδίαις ὑμῶν did modify προσέχοντες (*Petrus und Judas*, 112).

3. Sidebottom, *James, Jude, and 2 Peter*, 111. Sidebottom does not name any of these commentators.

4. Hofmann, *Der zweite Brief Petri*, 41-42; Schmidt, *Mahnung und Erinnerung*, 300-301, 359-61.

5. Kelly, *Peter and Jude*, 322. Spitta also mentions the first of these objections (*Petrus und Judas*, 111-12).

6. Schmidt says that the stereotyped expression found in 2 Pet 1:20 and 3:3 is reminiscent of a "Kundgabeformel" that he finds in Ezra 4:12, 13; 5:8; 2 Bar 79:1; 82:2; 85:1 (*Mahnung und Erinnerung*, 300). None of these passages contains a formula identical to the one found in 2 Peter, and in any case Schmidt sees no obstacle to its being modified by ἐν ταῖς καρδίαις ὑμῶν.

7. Wohlenberg, *Petrusbrief und Judasbrief*, 202-3. Spitta also mentions the first of Wohlenberg's reasons, but only as an argument against the second construal (*Petrus und Judas*, 112).

8. According to Hofmann the phrase indicates that what is known (γινώσκοντες) is not the object of rational or experiential perception or knowledge; he calls attention to 2 Cor 4:6 as a parallel. Schmidt observes that Deut 8:5 and Josh 23:14 speak of knowing (γινώσκειν) in one's heart using a simple dative rather than a prepositional phrase, and that 1 Kgs 2:44 speaks of the heart knowing. The prepositional phrase is used with the verb "say" (= "think") in Rev 18:7 and Deut 18:21. Schmidt considers the latter passage a particularly close parallel to 2 Pet 1:19-20 (*Mahnung und Erinnerung*, 300).

phrase, below. With respect to the third point, we can observe that the parallel between ὡς λύχνῳ φαίνοντι ἐν αὐχμηρῷ τόπῳ and ἕως οὗ ἡμέρα διαυγάσῃ καὶ φωσφόρος ἀνατείλῃ ἐν ταῖς καρδίαις ὑμῶν is not as close as Wohlenberg suggests. In the former case, a prepositional phrase modifies a participle; in the latter, it would modify one or two verbs.

In what follows, I will argue that the second construal of 1:19-20 is correct, i.e., that the prepositional phrase at the end of 1:19 should be understood as modifying the participle at the beginning of 1:20 (γινώσκοντες).

The main argument for interpreting ἐν ταῖς καρδίαις ὑμῶν as modifying γινώσκοντες in 1:20 is that it makes better sense of 1:19-20 than does the more common construal. As we will see, the common interpretation implies that in v. 19 the author of 2 Peter refers to Jesus's παρουσία as an inner, psychological event, i.e., the author says that Jesus rises "in your hearts." While not impossible, this is not as consonant with the rest of 2 Peter as the interpretation for which I argue; at no other place in 2 Peter does the author refer to the παρουσία as an inner event.[9]

1:19 begins the author's appeal to the prophetic word, a second argument, after the appeal to the transfiguration in 1:16-18, that the author has not followed cleverly devised myths in making the παρουσία of Jesus known to the addressees. By the prophetic word, the author means mainly the prophecies found in the Jewish Bible,[10] but also those contained in Christian writings.[11] The author implies that the prophetic word foretold Jesus's παρουσία and that expectation of it is thus well-founded.

Having referred to the prophetic word, the author urges the addressees to attend to it and supports this invitation by comparing the prophetic word to a lamp shining in a dark place. The latter is the present world,[12] which is

---

There are several biblical passages that speak of knowing in one's heart, using the prepositional phrase with other words whose meaning approximates "know." We find διανοέομαι (thinking) in one's heart in Gen 6:5; Jer 7:31; 19:5; νοέω in Isa 47:7; λογίζομαι in Zech 8:17; διαλογίζομαι in Mark 2:6, 8/Luke 5:22; Luke 3:15; διαλογισμός in Luke 24:38; and ἐνθυμέομαι in Matt 9:4. Cf. Qoh 8:16 which speaks of giving one's heart to know wisdom. The prepositional phrase is used with verbs meaning "say" in many biblical passages in addition to those mentioned by Schmidt; see Deut 8:17; 9:4; 1 Sam 1:13; 27:1; 1 Kgs 12:26; Ps 4:5; 73:8 (LXX); Isa 47:8; 49:21; Jer 5:24; 13:22; Zeph 1:12; Zech 12:5; Jdt 13:4; Tob 4:2; Pss. Sol. 8:3; Matt 24:48/Luke 12:45; Rom 10:6

9. Hofmann and Spitta (*Petrus und Judas*, 111) also see this problem with the common interpretation. Ernst Käsemann avoids this problem by understanding v. 19 as a reference to the inner illumination given by prophecy ("Apologia," 189). As we will see below, it is more likely that the verse refers to Jesus's παρουσία.

10. Kelly, *Peter and Jude*, 321.

11. Contra Bauckham, *Jude, 2 Peter*, 224.

12. Kelly, *Peter and Jude*, 321; cf. Bauckham, *Jude, 2 Peter*, 225.

dark because day has not yet dawned. The clause of 1:19 that immediately precedes the prepositional phrase we are investigating states that the addressees should attend to the prophetic word/lamp shining in a dark place ἕως οὗ ἡμέρα διαυγάσῃ καὶ φωσφόρος ἀνατείλῃ.

Two metaphors—dawn of day and rising of the light-bearer—indicate the end of the period during which the addressees need attend to the prophetic word. The meaning of "day" is relatively unambiguous; it is probably the first instance of an image for the end of the world later used frequently in 2 Peter—the day of judgment (2:9; 3:7), the day of the Lord (3:10), the day of God (3:12), the day of eternity (3:18).[13] The meaning of "light-bearer" is more ambiguous. φωσφόρος is not a common word, and it is often used as an adjective. As a substantive, it most often indicates the planet Venus, i.e., the morning star whose appearance precedes the dawn and heralds it.[14] Therefore, this is usually taken to be its meaning in 2 Peter 1:19; it is often suggested that it alludes to Num 24:17.

One problem with this interpretation is that according to it, dawn and the rising of the morning star would not be mentioned in chronological order, since the appearance of the morning star precedes the dawn. A possible explanation of this is that the two are reversed so that the more vivid expression is mentioned after the less vivid in order to increase its impact, something recommended by Demetrius, *On Style* 50–52 as adding grandeur to style.[15]

However, the best interpretation of φωσφόρος in 2 Peter 1:19 may be to see it as meaning the sun.[16] On this interpretation, the rising of the light-bearer is the appearance of the sun over the horizon shortly after dawn. Hans Windisch and Karl H. Schelkle recognize the attractiveness of this interpretation but do not embrace it because the only otherwise attested use of φωσφόρος as a substantive is to designate the planet Venus.[17] While this

---

13. On the use of this image in Old and New Testaments, see Delling, "ἡμέρα." Wohlenberg argues that ἡμέρα alone without the article or any other specification cannot mean the day of judgment (*Petrusbrief und Judasbrief*, 203).

14. It is used with this meaning in Cicero, *De Natura Deorum* 2.20; Philo, *Her.* 224; Plutarch, *Moralia* 430A; 601A; 925A; 927C; 1028B-D; 1029A-B. On the meaning of the word see Spicq, *Theological Lexicon*, 3:492–93.

15. Another instance of mentioning the less vivid before the more vivid can be seen in 2 Pet 1:9.

16. Cf. Dölger, *Antike und Christentum*, 5, 10–11. T. Levi 18.3–4 portrays the future in terms similar to those used in 2 Pet 1:19. The T. Levi passage speaks of a star that will rise (ἀνατελεῖ), rather clearly referring to Num 24:17. This star is compared to the sun. The star will light up the light of knowledge as the sun the day; it will shine forth like the sun on the earth and remove all darkness.

17. Windisch, *Katholische Briefe*, 90; Schelkle, *Petrusbriefe*, 200n4. Wohlenberg also

is the most common meaning of φωσφόρος as a substantive, φωσφόρος is hardly a technical term for the planet Venus.

The word is used to designate the planet Venus mainly in the context of naming several stars or planets,[18] which is obviously not the context in 2 Peter 1:19. The word is also used as a substantive to mean one or more goddesses, probably Artemis and Hecate.[19] I have found no other example in which φωσφόρος is used as a substantive to mean the sun. However, as an adjective, φωσφόρος most often describes the stars, including the sun, moon, and planets.[20] Likewise, the cognate verb φωσφορέω is most often used to speak of the stars as bearing light.[21] The sun is the pre-eminent light-bearer among the stars.[22] Thus use of φωσφόρος as a substantive to designate the sun would not be at all surprising. Whether φωσφόρος refers to the planet Venus or to the sun, it is probably an image for Christ.[23]

The relationship between these two images—dawn of day and rising of the light-bearer—is not entirely clear. Kelly argues that the dawn of day refers to the end of time in general, while the rising of the morning star refers specifically to Jesus.[24] I think it more likely that the two metaphors constitute hendiadys, a figure of speech in which two terms are used but only one thing or idea is intended, i.e., the second coming of Jesus at the

rejects this interpretation (*Petrusbrief und Judasbrief*, 204).

18. This is the context in the passages listed in note 7 above. For example, in *Her.* 224 Philo says that above the sun are Saturn, Jupiter, and Mars, and below it are Mercury, φωσφόρος (= Venus), and the Moon.

19. It is used with this meaning in Strabo 3.1.9; Plutarch, *Moralia* 1119E; Clement of Alexandria, *Stromata* 1.24.163. For example, the last of these passages refers to Munychia as the location of an altar of φωσφόρος.

20. This is the case in Philo, *Opif.* 29, 53; *Fug.* 184; *Somn.* 1.214; *Mos.* 1.120; 2.102; cf. *Ebr.* 44; Plutarch, *Moralia* 921E; 942D. *Mos.* 1.120; 2.102 make it clear that the stars include the sun, moon, and planets. For example, the latter passage speaks of the candlestick in the south of the sanctuary as an image of the light-bearing stars (φωσφόρων ἀστέρων) and explains this by saying that the sun, the moon, and the others run their courses in the south.

Φωσφόρος is also used as an adjective to designate the eyes as light-bearing (Plato, *Timaeus* 45B; Philo, *Plant.* 169; Plutarch, *Moralia* 98B [quoting Plato]; 928B) and Hecate as light-bearing (Plutarch, *Moralia* 379D [quoting Euripides]).

21. This is the case in Philo, *Opif.* 55, 168; *Her.* 222, 263; *Mos.* 2.103; *Decal.* 49.

22. Three times the sun is the only star Philo mentions by name when he refers to the stars as light-bearing (*Opif.* 29; *Mos.* 1.120; *Her.* 263); twice more only sun and moon are mentioned by name (*Mos.* 2.102; *Opif.* 168); once Philo says that the sun is in the center of the planets that give light (*Her.* 222); and once he says that the sun gives light to the other planets (*Mos.* 2.103).

23. Kelly, *Peter and Jude*, 322; Bauckham, *Jude, 2 Peter*, 226.

24. Kelly, *Peter and Jude*, 321–22.

end of time. The main indication that this should be understood as hendiadys is the line of argument in 3:4-12. In 3:4 the author of 2 Peter quotes the question raised by his opponents—where is the promise of his [Jesus's] παρουσία? The author then responds to this question (in part) by saying that the day of the Lord comes like a thief (v. 10), urging the addressees to await the παρουσία of the day of God. This suggests that the author equates the παρουσία of Jesus and the day that is the beginning of the end of time.

Some commentators understand this verse as referring to the παρουσία both as a physical occurrence and as a psychological event.[25] Although they do not explicitly say so, they seem to think that the dawn of day is the former and the rising of the light-bearer the latter. Other commentators simply see this verse as referring to Jesus's παρουσία as a psychological event, though it is still also understood as a physical occurrence.[26]

Windisch, Ceslas Spicq, and Kelly support their understanding of ἐν ταῖς καρδίαις ὑμῶν as modifying ἀνατείλῃ by referring to passages in which Philo uses language like that found in 2 Peter 1:19 to express the idea of inner enlightenment. Thus in *Ebr.* 44 Philo compares knowledge of God to the sun when it rises (ἀνατείλας) and describes it as the intelligible rays of the light-bearing (φωσφόρου) God that flash on the eye of the soul. Likewise, in *Conf.* 60 Philo speaks of virtue as rising (ἀνατολή) in the soul like the sun. In *Decal.* 49 Philo compares the laws to stars in the soul bringing light (φωσφοροῦντας). Such passages clearly show that the language of 2 Peter 1:19 could be used to describe inner enlightenment. However, they provide no parallel to the use of this language to speak about the spiritual dimension of a physical event such as is supposed to underlie 2 Peter 1:19. Nor, of course, do they provide a parallel to the use of this language to speak of Jesus's παρουσία as an inner event. Thus, these parallels do not diminish the problematic aspect of this interpretation.

Such an interpretation of the verse is not as consonant with the general outlook of 2 Peter as understanding ἐν ταῖς καρδίαις ὑμῶν as modifying the following participle. It is clear from the account of Jesus's transfiguration in 1:16-18, and even more from the account of the end time in 3:10-13, that the author of 2 Peter sees the παρουσία of Jesus and the end of the world as a public, physical event, observable by all. If ἐν ταῖς καρδίαις ὑμῶν is taken as modifying the following participle, the παρουσία is simply a physical event,

---

25. This seems to be the view of Kelly, Hiebert, Mounce, Reicke, Sidebottom, and Windisch.

26. This seems to be the view of Bauckham, Bigg, Schelkle, Spicq, Paulsen, Perkins, Vögtle, and Wohlenberg. Tord Fornberg also takes this view (*Early Church*, 85). Spicq suggests that the dawn of day may refer to Jesus's first coming (*Épitres de Saint Pierre*, 224).

as elsewhere in 2 Peter, and ἐν ταῖς καρδίαις ὑμῶν specifies the locus of the knowing that 1:20 speaks about.

Understanding ἐν ταῖς καρδίαις ὑμῶν as modifying the following participle is not only more consonant with the rest of 2 Peter, it is also more consonant with the understanding of Jesus's παρουσία elsewhere in the New Testament. Nowhere else in the New Testament is the future παρουσία of Jesus something that occurs in the hearts of believers.[27] Of course, it is not at all impossible that the author of 2 Peter might develop an original understanding of Jesus's παρουσία, but in that case we would expect some explanation of the idea, not a rather casual reference to it in a metaphor.

There is no obstacle to understanding ἐν ταῖς καρδίαις ὑμῶν as modifying the following participle. One thing generally overlooked by commentators (and translators) is that the sentence begun in 1:19 is not completed at the end of the verse but continues into 1:20. Thus, whether ἐν ταῖς καρδίαις ὑμῶν is seen as modifying ἀνατείλῃ or γινώσκοντες, the sentence continues after the prepositional phrase. And of course, this makes it possible that the phrase modify the following participle rather than the preceding verb.

Sixty-eight times in the course of 2 Peter a prepositional phrase modifies a verb. Thirty-three times the prepositional phrase precedes the verb,[28] including twelve relative clauses introduced by a prepositional phrase;[29] thirty-five times the prepositional phrase follows the verb.[30] Other things

---

27. On this, see Oepke, "παρουσία κτλ." Such an understanding did develop at a later time. Oepke mentions the later view that the four Sundays of the liturgical season Advent celebrated the coming of Jesus "in carnem, in mentem, in morte, in maiestate" (871).

28. 2 Pet 1:4 διὰ τούτων before γένησθε; 1:18 ἐξ οὐρανοῦ before ἐνεχθεῖσαν and σὺν αὐτῷ before ὄντες; 1:21 ὑπὸ πνεύματος ἁγίου before φερόμενοι; 2:1 ἐν ὑμῖν before ἔσονται; 2:3 ἐν πλεονεξίᾳ before ἐμπορεύσονται; 2:4 εἰς κρίσιν before τηρουμένους; 2:9 ἐκ πειρασμοῦ before ῥύεσθαι and εἰς ἡμέραν κρίσεως before κολαζομένους; 2:10 ὀπίσω σαρκὸς and ἐν ἐπιθυμίᾳ μιασμοῦ before πορευομένους; 2:12 ἐν τῇ φθορᾷ αὐτῶν before φθαρήσονται; 2:13 ἐν ταῖς ἀπάταις αὐτῶν before συνευωχούμενοι; 2:16 ἐν ἀνθρώπου φωνῇ before φθεγξάμενον; 2:17 ὑπὸ λαίλαπος before ἐλαυνόμεναι; 2:18 ἐν πλάνῃ before ἀναστρεφομένους; 3:3 κατὰ τὰς ἰδίας ἐπιθυμίας αὐτῶν before πορευόμενοι; 3:5 ἐξ ὕδατος and δι' ὕδατος before συνεστῶσα; 3:9 εἰς μετάνοιαν before χωρῆσαι; 3:13 κατὰ τὸ ἐπάγγελμα αὐτοῦ before προσδοκῶμεν; 3:15 κατὰ τὴν δοθεῖσαν αὐτῷ σοφίαν before ἔγραψεν; 3:16 ἐν πάσαις ἐπιστολαῖς before λαλῶν.

29. 2 Pet 1:4 δι' ὧν before δεδώρηται; 1:13 ἐφ' ὅσον before εἰμί; 1:17 εἰς ὃν before εὐδόκησα; 2:2 δι' οὓς before βλασφημηθήσεται; 2:12 ἐν οἷς before ἀγνοοῦσιν; 3:1 ἐν αἷς before διεγείρω; 3:4 ἀφ' ἧς before ἐκοιμήθησαν; 3:6 δι' ὧν before ἀπώλετο; 3:10 ἐν ᾗ before παρελεύσονται; 3:12 δι' ἣν before λυθήσονται; 3:13 ἐν οἷς before κατοικεῖ; 3:16 ἐν αἷς before ἐστιν.

30. 2 Pet 1:1 ἐν δικαιοσύνῃ τοῦ θεοῦ ἡμῶν etc. after λαχοῦσιν; 1:2 ἐν ἐπιγνώσει after πληθυνθείη; 1:3 διὰ τῆς ἐπιγνώσεως after δεδωρημένης; 1:5-7 ἐν τῇ πίστει etc. after ἐπιχορηγήσατε; 1:8 εἰς τὴν τοῦ κυρίου ἡμῶν Ἰησοῦ Χριστοῦ ἐπίγνωσιν after

being equal, it is almost as likely that a prepositional phrase precede the verb it modifies as that the phrase follow the verb.

This is also true in cases where prepositional phrases specifically modify participles. This occurs twenty-eight times in 2 Peter. Thirteen times the prepositional phrase precedes the participle;[31] fifteen times the prepositional phrase follows the participle.[32]

There is good reason why ἐν ταῖς καρδίαις ὑμῶν would precede rather than follow γινώσκοντες in 2 Peter 1:19-20. The participle introduces a noun clause that specifies what the addressees are to know. So that this clause can follow immediately after γινώσκοντες, γινώσκοντες is preceded not only by the prepositional phrase but also by a direct object and an adverb. In 3:3 the phrase τοῦτο πρῶτον γινώσκοντες is also used to introduce a noun clause, in this case without being modified by a prepositional phrase. A turn of phrase somewhat parallel to my construal of 1:19-20 is found in 2:3, which begins καὶ ἐν πλεονεξίᾳ πλαστοῖς λόγοις ὑμᾶς ἐμπορεύσονται. Here, a prepositional phrase, an instrumental dative phrase, and a direct object all precede the verb of the clause.

The word καρδία is only used twice in 2 Peter, in 1:19 and 2:14. This makes it hard to determine the precise meaning of the word for 2 Peter. In 2:14 the author of 2 Peter refers to the false teachers as having a καρδίαν γεγυμνασμένην πλεονεξίας. This seems to imply that καρδία here has the meaning it characteristically has elsewhere in biblical literature, i.e., it means the center of the inner life of a human being and thus the seat of all the forces and functions of soul and spirit.[33] In 2:14 καρδία is specifically

---

καθίστησιν; 1:12 περὶ τούτων after ὑπομιμνήσκειν and ἐν τῇ παρούσῃ ἀληθείᾳ after ἐστηριγμένους; 1:13 ἐν τούτῳ τῷ σκηνώματι after εἰμὶ and ἐν ὑπομνήσει after διεγείρειν; 1:15 μετὰ τὴν ἐμὴν ἔξοδον after ἔχειν; 1:17 παρὰ θεοῦ πατρὸς after λαβὼν and ὑπὸ τῆς μεγαλοπρεποῦς δόξης after ἐνεχθείσης; 1:18 ἐν τῷ ἁγίῳ ὄρει after ὄντες; 1:19 ἐν αὐχμηρῷ τόπῳ after φαίνοντι; 1:21 ἀπὸ θεοῦ after ἐλάλησαν; 2:1 ἐν τῷ λαῷ after Ἐγένοντο; 2:7 ὑπὸ τῆς τῶν ἀθέσμων ἐν ἀσελγείᾳ ἀναστροφῆς after καταπονούμενον; 2:8 ἐν αὐτοῖς after ἐγκατοικῶν; 2:11 κατ' αὐτῶν and παρὰ κυρίῳ after φέρουσιν; 2:12 εἰς ἅλωσιν καὶ φθοράν after γεγεννημένα; 2:18 ἐν ἐπιθυμίαις σαρκὸς ἀσελγείαις after δελεάζουσιν; 2:20 ἐν ἐπιγνώσει etc. after ἀποφυγόντες; 2:21 ἐκ τῆς παραδοθείσης αὐτοῖς ἁγίας ἐντολῆς after ὑποστρέψαι; 2:22 ἐπὶ τὸ ἴδιον ἐξέραμα after ἐπιστρέψας; 3:1 ἐν ὑπομνήσει after διεγείρω; 3:2 ὑπὸ τῶν ἁγίων προφητῶν after προειρημένων; 3:3 ἐπ' ἐσχάτων τῶν ἡμερῶν and [ἐν] ἐμπαιγμονῇ after ἐλεύσονται; 3:4 ἀπ' ἀρχῆς after διαμένει; 3:7 εἰς ἡμέραν after τηρούμενοι; 3:9 εἰς ὑμᾶς after μακροθυμεῖ; 3:11 ἐν ἁγίαις ἀναστροφαῖς καὶ εὐσεβείαις after ὑπάρχειν; 3:14 ἐν εἰρήνῃ after εὑρεθῆναι; 3:16 ἐν αὐταῖς and περὶ τούτων after λαλῶν and πρὸς τὴν ἰδίαν αὐτῶν ἀπώλειαν after στρεβλοῦσιν; 3:18 ἐν χάριτι καὶ γνώσει etc. after αὐξάνετε.

31. 2 Pet 1:18 (twice), 21; 2:4, 9, 10, 13, 16, 17, 18; 3:3, 5, 16.

32. 2 Pet 1:1, 3, 12, 17 (twice), 18, 19; 2:7, 8, 12, 20, 22; 3:2, 7, 16.

33. See Baumgärtel and Behm, "καρδία κτλ."

the seat of greed. On my construal καρδία is used in a similar sense in 1:19, i.e., to mean the seat of the knowledge that all prophecy of scripture is not of its own interpretation. Of course, καρδία is also used in a similar sense according to the common construal of 1:19, i.e., the seat of awareness of the παρουσία of Jesus within oneself. Thus the word καρδία is equally compatible with either interpretation.

Conclusion

Considerations of grammar and vocabulary show that it is possible to interpret ἐν ταῖς καρδίαις ὑμῶν as modifying γινώσκοντες, but they do not show that it is impossible to interpret it as modifying ἀνατείλῃ, or even that the former is more likely than the latter. However, if the two interpretations are equally possible on grammatical grounds, the former is preferable because of the meaning it gives the passage. On the latter interpretation, 1:19 speaks of the παρουσία of Jesus either as both a physical occurrence and a psychological event, or only the latter, making use of an idea not found elsewhere in 2 Peter or the rest of the New Testament. On the former interpretation, 1:19–20 simply speaks of the παρουσία of Jesus as a physical event, as elsewhere in 2 Peter, and goes on to speak of the knowledge of prophecy one must have to continue one's expectation of this event.

7

Rhetography and Rhetology of Apocalyptic Discourse in 2 Peter

In this paper I will apply the methodology known as sociorhetorical interpretation (SRI) to the Second Epistle of Peter. The form of SRI that I will use has been developed by Vernon K. Robbins and those associated with him.

I. Description of Sociorhetorical Methodology

SRI is a multi-dimensional approach to texts. The first significant stage of this approach was set out by Robbins in two books—*The Tapestry of Early Christian Discourse: Rhetoric, Society, and Ideology* and *Exploring the Texture of Texts: A Guide to Socio-Rhetorical Interpretation*. At this stage, SRI involved observation and interpretation of five aspects of texts—inner texture, intertexture, social and cultural texture, ideological texture, and sacred texture.

- Inner texture refers to the internal structure of a text, such things as opening-middle-closing, repetitions in the text, progressions, narration, argument, and sensory-aesthetic elements.
- Intertexture is the relationship of the text to things outside itself, the way it incorporates other texts, as well as cultural, social, and historical realities.
- The social and cultural texture of a text consists of its stance toward the culture out of which it arises, its inclusion of cultural values such as honor-shame and purity codes, and its place in its culture.

- Ideological texture "concerns particular alliances and conflicts the language in a text and the language in an interpretation evoke and nurture . . . the way the text itself and interpreters of the text position themselves in relation to other individuals and groups."[1]
- Sacred texture refers to the religious or theological content of a text.

The great value of SRI in this form is the way it unifies various approaches to the New Testament that are often pursued separately. Each of the items that Robbins calls textures of the text is often pursued on its own. And when any of them is pursued individually, there is at least some tendency to see it as an alternative to other ways of interpreting the text. However, SRI provides a framework within which each of these things has a proper place in developing a complete interpretation of the text.

More recently, Robbins has developed SRI in a somewhat different direction. Beginning with an essay titled "The Dialectical Nature of Early Christian Discourse,"[2] Robbins has proposed that there were six basic kinds of early Christian discourse, which he calls "rhetorolects." The six are now known as: wisdom, miracle, prophetic, precreation, priestly, and apocalyptic discourse. Each of these is a "distinctive configuration of themes, topics, reasonings, and argumentations,"[3] and each blends with the others in early Christian texts.

These six rhetorolects are a Christian counterpart of the classical division of rhetoric into judicial, deliberative, and epideictic. These three kinds of rhetoric are associated respectively with the courtrooms, political assemblies, and civil ceremonies of Greek and Roman city-states. Partly because these were not the most important social situations for early Christians, they developed forms of rhetoric associated with other social situations, namely, the intersubjective bodies, households, villages, synagogues, cities, temples, kingdoms, and empires in which they lived and which they imagined.

In order to understand fully a classical speech in written form, one must take into account the setting in which it was intended to be delivered. For example, one must realize that a judicial speech was delivered by an advocate in a courtroom. In the same way, one must situate the six rhetorolects in the context for which each was composed. Robbins has proposed the following description of these contexts.

- Wisdom discourse is spoken in the context of the universe understood as a household over which God presides as a father. Through

1. Robbins, *Exploring the Texture of Texts*, 4.
2. Robbins, "Dialectical Nature," 353–62.
3. Robbins, "Dialectical Nature," 356.

the medium of God's wisdom, people who are God's children produce righteous action and speech.

- Miracle discourse arises in a context in which God is understood as the healer, through a bodily agent, of the malfunctioning bodies of individuals and thus as restoring communities to relationships of well-being.
- Prophetic discourse presumes the context of the universe understood as a kingdom of which God is king. Prophets are individuals to whom God's will has been communicated and who call people to act righteously through prophetic action and speech.
- Precreation discourse presumes the context of the universe seen as an empire of which God is the emperor with an eternal household consisting of his son and others. People can enter into relationship with the emperor through the members of his household.
- Priestly discourse arises in the context of the universe understood as a temple city. Actions in the temple benefit God in a way that activates divine benefits for humans.
- Apocalyptic discourse presumes the context of the universe understood as an empire of which God is the emperor at the head of an army. The divine army will destroy all the evil in the universe and create a state in which the good experience perfect well-being in the presence of God.

These contexts and their elaborations form what Robbins calls the rhetography of the discourse. The argumentation of the discourse forms its rhetology. As Robbins observes, New Testament interpreters have given relatively little attention to its rhetography. Robbins himself has developed the exploration of rhetography by making use of critical spatiality theory and cognitive theory about conceptual blending.[4] The precise meaning of rhetography is still being clarified.

Some instances of the six rhetorolects are primarily pictorial, i.e., rhetography; this is particularly true of narratives. However, such instances also have an argumentative or persuasive dimension, i.e., rhetology. Other instances of these types of discourse are primarily argumentative. However,

---

4. This description of the six rhetorolects and of rhetography and rhetology is based on two essays by Vernon K. Robbins ("Socio-Rhetorical Interpretation"; "Rhetography"). See also the introduction to Robbins, *Invention of Christian Discourse*. For critical spatiality theory Robbins refers to Gunn and McNutt, *'Imagining' Biblical Worlds* among other works. For conceptual blending theory, he refers to Fauconnier and Turner, *Way We Think*.

such instances also have a pictorial dimension. A still unsettled question is the relationship between the six discourses and the five textures discussed by SRI.

II. Application to 2 Peter

In this paper I will discuss rhetography and rhetology in the apocalyptic discourse of 2 Peter. I will restrict myself to 2 Peter 1:16–2:10a; 3:1–13 because these are the most concentrated sections of apocalyptic discourse in the letter. Such discourse is also found elsewhere in 2 Peter, however. For example, Duane F. Watson also regards 2:10b–22 as apocalyptic discourse.[5]

Both passages are part of the picture evoked by the letter as a whole. In this picture the apostle Peter, near the end of his life, writes a testamentary letter so that those he addresses can always remember his teaching (2 Peter 1:1–15; 3:1). Peter and the addressees have many things in common, most basically their faith in Jesus. However, he and the immediate addressees are separated spatially, making a letter rather than oral communication necessary, and he is separated from the ultimate addressees, both spatially and temporally, because they will use the letter to remember Peter's teaching after his death. This framework is basically prophetic discourse. Peter, who identifies himself as a slave and apostle, functions as a prophet in calling those to whom he writes to righteous living because he has been called by God to do so. If Peter is seen as communicating a revelation of the divine plan regarding the history of the universe, this framework could be seen as apocalyptic discourse. Such a view of Peter is not explicit, however, though it comes close to being explicit in 1:16–18. Thus it is probably best to see the basic picture evoked by the letter as prophetic discourse. Within this prophetic framework, the apocalyptic discourse of the letter evokes additional pictures that I will analyze separately.

In the first of the two passages under consideration, apocalyptic discourse sometimes functions as a further framework within which other kinds of discourse are used in support of the apocalyptic discourse. In apocalyptic discourse the universe is seen as analogous to an empire ruled by God, from which God will soon eradicate evil and establish righteousness. The evil of the universe and God's control over it are not obvious, but they are made known by means of a revelation that exposes the character of the universe and the divine plan for it. According to this plan, the history

---

5. Watson, "Oral-Scribal and Cultural Intertexture," in Watson, *Intertexture of Apocalyptic Discourse*. The other essays in this volume discuss apocalyptic discourse in other parts of the New Testament. See also Webb, "Intertexture and Rhetorical Strategy."

of the universe is divided into temporal segments inevitably leading to the culmination of that history. Apocalyptic revelation focuses on the place of those who receive the revelation in the unfolding history of the universe. In Christian apocalyptic discourse the final segment of time begins with the second coming of Christ.[6]

In 2 Peter 1:16–2:10a this picture and variations on it are directly evoked. At times, however, other kinds of discourse, implying different pictures, are used to support the overarching apocalyptic discourse.

a. 1:16–2:10a—Two Arguments That Jesus Will Come Again

1. 1:16–18—First Argument: The Story of Jesus's Transfiguration

Rhetography

In 1:16–18 the author of 2 Peter appeals to the story of Jesus's transfiguration to support his message about the power and coming of Jesus. He does so initially by rejecting the idea that this message derives from cleverly devised myths. This evokes, in order to reject, the picture of someone deliberately concocting the story that Jesus would come again. The author of 2 Peter might be envisioned as the creator of the myth, or he might be envisioned as having adopted the myth from its creator, either knowing that it was a concoction or not.

The message about the power and coming of Jesus evokes the picture of Jesus as the emissary of God who will return at some future time to establish God's reign. "Coming" (παρουσία) was used as a technical term for the coming of a divinity or a person of high rank, especially kings and emperors.[7] Use of this word pictures the return of Jesus as something similar to this; however, this picture is only mentioned, not described. To support the truth of this message, the author of 2 Peter describes a somewhat different picture. He refers to the story told in Mark 9:2–8 and parallels, perhaps especially the version in Matt 17:1–8. Jesus took Peter, James, and John with him up a high mountain. There, Jesus was transfigured, his face and clothing becoming white as light. Moses and Elijah appeared and talked to Jesus. A bright cloud overshadowed them, and a voice from the cloud said, "This is my beloved Son, with whom I am well pleased; listen to him."

---

6. This description of the basic picture underlying apocalyptic discourse is drawn from chapter 8 of Robbins, *Invention of Christian Discourse*.

7. Schelkle, *Petrusbriefe*, 196n2; Spicq, *Épitres de Saint Pierre*, 220.

The author of 2 Peter does not describe this event in detail. What he does say would call this story to the minds of those who knew it. Those unfamiliar with the story of Jesus's transfiguration would only be aware of what the author mentions explicitly. And even those who are familiar with the story would be most aware of the details that are specifically mentioned.

The author of 2 Peter does not specify all who accompanied Jesus, only that he himself was present along with some others. He does mention that they were on a mountain and calls it the holy mountain, a detail not found in the synoptic transfiguration accounts. Likewise, he explicitly mentions God's participation in the event, another detail absent from the synoptic transfiguration accounts. The author says nothing about the witnesses' reaction to what happened or about the presence of Moses and Elijah. More significantly, he mentions the transfiguration of Jesus only rather obliquely by saying that he, the author, and others were eyewitnesses of Jesus's majesty and that Jesus received honor and glory from God. This probably refers to the transformation of Jesus, i.e., something that was seen, but it is expressed in such general terms that it could simply be a reference to the words spoken by the voice. The visual dimension is indicated most directly by the author's references to glory. This glory could be visualized as a kind of radiance that passes from God, the magnificent glory, to Jesus. In Matthew's account of the transfiguration, Jesus's clothing became white as light (φῶς) and a bright (φωτεινός) cloud overshadowed Jesus. The author of 2 Peter might envision something like this and intend that the addressees do so.

In comparison with the Synoptic Gospels' account of Jesus's transfiguration, however, the author of 2 Peter lets the transformation of Jesus recede into the background of the story.[8] The author explicitly reports the words of the voice, "This is my son, my beloved, in whom I am well pleased," and emphasizes that he and others heard it. This is the most important aspect of the story for the author. To underline this, he adds other details not found in the synoptic accounts. He twice mentions that the voice was borne to Jesus, the first time saying that it was borne by the magnificent glory (v. 17) and the second time that it was borne from heaven (v. 18). He also calls God "the father," which is appropriate because the words of the voice say that Jesus is the speaker's son. This presents Jesus and God as members of a family.

---

8. This is also true of the transfiguration account in the Apocalypse of Peter. In this account Moses and Elijah appear in a glorified form, but not Jesus. After the words of the heavenly voice about Jesus, Jesus, Moses, and Elijah are all taken into heaven. This account also refers to the mountain of transfiguration as the holy mountain and speaks of a voice from heaven, details mentioned by 2 Peter but not found in the synoptic transfiguration accounts.

Insofar as this passage calls to mind the story of Jesus's transfiguration as we know it from the Synoptic Gospels, it can be seen as an instance of miracle discourse, in which God is seen as renewing or restoring the bodies of individuals. Insofar as it focuses on the words of the voice directed to Jesus, it is probably an instance of pre-creation discourse, in which Jesus is identified as the eternal son of the heavenly emperor. Insofar as it functions as a revelation of the second coming of Jesus, it is apocalyptic discourse. This is the aspect of the story that is most important for the author.

Rhetology

The argumentative force of this section lies in the blending of miracle and especially pre-creation discourse with apocalyptic discourse. The apocalyptic expectation of the return of Jesus is based on Peter and others' experience of the transfiguration of Jesus. However, it is not clear exactly how Jesus's transfiguration shows that it is right to expect his return. There are several ways one might explicate the force of the argument.

The author implies that what Peter and others experienced when Jesus was transfigured was an experience of Jesus's power and coming.[9] Although the author's description of the transfiguration does not explicitly speak of power, seeing Jesus's majesty, his reception of honor and glory from God, and hearing the words of the voice might reasonably be summarized as an experience of his power. However, in order to be an experience of Jesus's coming, the transfiguration must have been an anticipation of this future event.[10] Richard J. Bauckham argues that the author of 2 Peter understands the transfiguration as Jesus's appointment by God to the role he will exercise at his second coming, in fulfillment of Psalm 2.[11] Otto Knoch argues that the author understands the transfiguration, especially the words of the voice, as God's testimony to the power of Jesus and thus the reliability of Jesus's promise to come again.[12]

Perhaps people have denied that Jesus will come again in glory by arguing that Jesus's earthly life was incompatible with such an expectation. If so,

---

9. Paulsen (*Der Zweite Petrusbrief*, 120) simply sees the transfiguration of Jesus as a general legitimation of the author's message.

10. Neyrey, "Apologetic Use of the Transfiguration," 510–14; Davids, *2 Peter and Jude*, 202.

11. Bauckham, *Jude, 2 Peter*, 219–20; so also Watson, *Invention, Arrangement, and Style*, 102; Davids, *2 Peter and Jude*, 203–6; cf. Vögtle, *Der Judasbrief/Der 2. Petrusbrief*, 164–65.

12. Knoch, *Erste und Zweite Petrusbrief*, 255.

the story of Jesus's transfiguration might be an effective counter-argument.[13] Jesus's temporary transformation and the words of the voice reveal a dimension of Jesus otherwise hidden. But even if the author is not responding to this specific objection, the revelation that Jesus is the eternal son of the Father supports the idea that he will come again because Jesus has not yet acted like the son. If this is the truth about Jesus, it is reasonable to suppose that at some time he will appear in this role and enact it more completely than he has thus far. Attending to the rhetography of this passage shows that the story focuses on God's declaration that Jesus is the beloved son of God with whom God is well pleased. The argumentative power of the passage lies in this.

2. 1:19–2:10a—Second argument: the Prophetic Word

2A. 1:19–21—PART ONE: APPEAL TO THE PROPHETIC WORD

Rhetography

The author of 2 Peter next appeals to the prophetic word in support of his message about the power and coming of Jesus. This reference to the prophetic word evokes a picture of prophecy as it functioned in Israel. As part of God's choice of Israel to be the people of God, from time to time God called certain people to be prophets—that is, people who speak for God—and sent them to the rest of the people to call them back to fidelity to God (e.g., Isa 6; Jer 1). These prophets did not act on their own but were moved by the Holy Spirit. The Holy Spirit fell on the prophets and impelled them to actions they would and could not take by themselves (e.g., 1 Sam 10:5–6, 10–13). In addition, stories about these prophets and their utterances have been written down. The addressees of 2 Peter access the prophetic word through writings rather than by means of direct contact with prophets. This evokes the picture of people studying and pondering the written records of the prophets.

In v. 21 the author develops in some detail a picture of the relationship between prophecy and the Holy Spirit. The author repeats two key terms, "human being(s)" and "borne," in the two halves of the verse and in a chiastic pattern, i.e., first in the just-stated order and then in reverse order. The verse says that prophecy is not a matter of being borne by human will but rather of being borne by the Holy Spirit; the repetition of "borne" (φέρω in

---

13. This may also be the reason for including the story of Jesus's transfiguration in the Synoptic Gospels.

the passive voice) emphasizes the rejection of one source of prophecy and the affirmation of another. "Borne" is used first in the aorist tense, then in the present tense. The former denies that prophecy ever arose from human will; the latter implies that while they were speaking from God, prophets were being borne by the Holy Spirit. In 1:17–18 the author says that the heavenly voice was "borne" to Jesus; use of the same word to speak of the origin of prophecy pictures the latter as comparable to the former. Just as the voice was borne to Jesus, so prophets are borne by the Holy Spirit when they speak from God. By mentioning "human being" at the beginning and the end of v. 21, the author rounds off the sentence, ending where he began. This repetition makes clear the precise participation of human beings in prophecy. Although prophecy does not derive from the will of a human being, it does involve human beings who spoke from God.

The primary picture evoked by this appeal to the prophetic word is that of prophecy in Israel, especially as it is included in the Jewish scriptures. However, prophecy was also an element of the religion of Greece and Rome.[14] These words could also evoke a picture of prophecy as it functioned in this context. For example, one might think of the priestess of Apollo at Delphi, who was known as a prophet, or of the prophets who proclaimed her words. Those for whom the author's words evoked this picture would understand the author's main point, i.e., the divine origin of prophecy. However, the references to prophecy of scripture and, even more, to the Holy Spirit mean that prophecy at Delphi does not match the circumstances presumed in 2 Peter as closely as does prophecy in Israel, and that the latter is probably the picture intended by the author.

The author of 2 Peter does not define or describe the prophetic word at all, except to mention that it is found in written form and derives from the Holy Spirit. He obviously presumes that the prophetic word is well known to those he addresses so that the picture his argument requires is summoned by the term alone. That picture is the picture of prophecy in Israel.

The author supports his appeal to the prophetic word with an explicitly pictorial simile. The addressees should attend to the prophetic word "like a lamp shining in a dark place until day dawns and the light-bearer rises." These words describe a lamp alight in a dark place, perhaps a house. It is dark because it is night. During the night, the lamp is necessary to see, but it will no longer be necessary when day dawns. Like such a lamp, the prophetic word makes things visible that would otherwise not be visible, and so should be used for that purpose.

---

14. Neyrey, *2 Peter, Jude*, 183–84.

The author implies that the prophetic word makes visible the future power and coming of Jesus by predicting it. This is not presently visible because it still lies in the future but also probably because the character of the present world is contrary to the future that will begin with the power and coming of Jesus. The present is like night; the future will be like day. The power and coming of Jesus constitute the dawn of that day.

Rhetology

In this section the force of the argument lies in the blending of prophetic discourse with apocalyptic discourse. The author's second argument for the reliability of the apocalyptic expectation of Jesus's return is the prophetic word. The author summons the picture of prophecy as it functioned in Israel as supporting belief in Jesus's return. The author implies that the prophetic word predicts the return of Jesus; thus expectation of his return is well founded. It is an even more secure argument than the transfiguration because it predicts the power and coming of Jesus more directly.

At this point, the author does not cite any prophecies of Jesus's return; he will be more specific about this in 2:4–10a. He presumes that these prophecies exist and invokes the reliability of the institution of prophecy to support belief in the second coming of Jesus. Insofar as one recognizes that God truly has sent prophets to the people of Israel to guide them, one accepts the reliability of what they said, now written down in the Bible.

It seems probable from 2 Peter 2:4–10a that the prophetic word is partly found in Genesis. Thus, the author seems to view the entire Bible as prophetic, not just those parts that concern people explicitly called prophets.[15] This is confirmed by 2 Peter 3:1–13. Here, the author again implies that Genesis is prophetic, but also implies that prophecy is found in Psalms, the letters of Paul, Isaiah, and quite possibly other parts of the Bible. The author seems to view the entire Bible as having been produced by prophetic activity.

The author encourages the addressees to pay attention to the prophetic word by comparing it to a light shining in darkness. If they accept the validity of the comparison, their spontaneous recognition of the goodness and usefulness of light in the darkness is transferred to the prophetic word and the future it predicts.

Finally, the author speaks of the derivation of prophecy from the Holy Spirit, picturing prophets as speaking under the impetus of the Holy Spirit. Implicitly, this is an argument for its reliability. Explicitly, it is an attempt

---

15. Kelly, *Peter and Jude*, 321; Bauckham, *Jude, 2 Peter*, 224.

to show that prophecy is not of one's own explanation. This is probably intended to reject the idea that the words of prophets can be dismissed as deriving from themselves.[16] Or it might be intended to reject the idea that one can give one's own interpretation to the prophetic word.[17] In either case, the nature of prophecy is used as an argument against a view of prophecy that minimizes its support for the author's apocalyptic expectations. 1:20-21 is an enthymeme in which v. 21 supports the contention that prophecy is not of one's own interpretation (v. 20). The argument can be restated:

> Prophecy that derives from human will is of a prophet's own interpretation.

> Prophecy of scripture was never borne by human will, but being borne by the Holy Spirit, prophets spoke from God.

> Therefore, prophecy of scripture is not of a prophet's own interpretation.

2B. 2:1-3—PART TWO: FALSE PROPHETS AND FALSE TEACHERS

Rhetography

The author of 2 Peter elaborates the picture of prophecy in Israel that he has evoked by saying that there were false prophets among the people as well as true prophets. It was not always clear which of the people who claimed to be prophets—or were thought to be prophets—were in fact prophets. This might remind the addressees of the occasional presentation of conflicting claims to be true prophets in the Jewish scriptures (e.g., 1 Kgs 22:5-28; Jer 28).

The author goes on to predict a similar situation among those he addresses. He says nothing about prophets among them, but says there will be false teachers, which, in turn, also seems to imply the existence of true teachers. Teaching does not evoke as specific a concrete situation as does prophecy. In speaking of prophecy, the author refers mainly to a past activity that is described in some detail in the Jewish scriptures. But in speaking of false teaching, the author refers to a present, or even future, activity that is nowhere described in detail. We do not know exactly when, where, and how these other teachers taught; thus the picture evoked by the reference to false teachers is somewhat ill defined. Peter's main point is that they and their

---

16. Bauckham, *Jude, 2 Peter*, 229-33.
17. According to Bauckham (*Jude, 2 Peter*, 229-33), this is the view of most commentators.

teaching are false and that in the eschatological judgment that is coming they will be destroyed. The images evoked by these descriptions are clear.

There are other references in the New Testament to teachers among the early Christians—Acts 13:1; 1 Cor 12:28–29; Eph 4:11; Jas 3:1. In New Testament usage, the word "teacher" designates one who indicates the way of God from the Torah to a group of students.[18] This includes repetition of the teaching of Jesus, proof from the Torah that Jesus is the Messiah, and deriving directions for Christian living from the Torah.[19] Eph 4:11 suggests that teaching is the responsibility of the pastor or leader of the community. Thus the false teachers mentioned in 2 Peter may be pictured as leaders of the community whose teaching does not correctly indicate the way of God to the members of their community.

Peter's further description of the false teachers, their doctrine, and their destiny evokes a kaleidoscope of pictures, each flashing briefly before the eyes of the addressees before being replaced by another. The teachers secretly introduce their teaching; they hide its true character so that it will be accepted. Its true character is that it leads to destruction, but they conceal this. Either implicitly or explicitly, their teaching is a denial of the master who bought them. This pictures Jesus as someone who has bought the false teachers as slaves from their former owner and is now himself their owner. Jesus is like a householder or perhaps the owner of an enterprise, such as a farm or a mine, who has slaves working for him. Lying behind this picture of Jesus, as the purchaser of the false teachers, is probably another picture of Jesus, as having paid the purchase price by his own death.

The false teachers are characterized by licentiousness, especially sexual misconduct. Many will imitate their licentiousness, bringing the followers of Jesus into disrepute. Following Jesus is described as the way of truth, picturing it as a road that leads human beings to their proper destination. The false teachers are also characterized by greed, i.e., excessive love for money. In this instance, it is used in a transferred sense, referring to the false teachers' zeal to gain control over the addressees. Because of this greed, the false teachers will use counterfeit words to buy the addressees. Speaking of the false teachers as buying the addresses pictures them as shoppers who use their false teaching to acquire the addressees as possessions. The judgment of the false teachers that was handed down long ago and their destruction are personified. Judgment and destruction are pictured as sentient beings who might be idle or asleep, but they are not.

---

18. Rengstorf, "διδάσκω κτλ," 153.
19. Rengstorf, "διδάσκω κτλ," 144–48.

Rhetology

The author develops prophetic discourse somewhat further in order to make a transition back to apocalyptic discourse. He speaks of the existence of false prophets among the people in order to predict the future arrival of false teachers among the addressees. The picture of the false teachers corresponds to that of the false prophets. The argumentative substrate of this may first of all be typological. The false prophets of the past are a type of the false teachers to come.[20] Secondly, this may be seen as a partial explication of the content of the prophetic word, i.e., the future appearance of false teachers and their destruction. And finally, the author implies that the teachers are false because they incorrectly dismiss the prophecies of Jesus's second coming, not recognizing the view of prophecy he has articulated in 1:19–21.

Referring to the teachers as false is an implicit argument that they do not present reliable teaching. The same view is expressed more specifically by saying that they deny the master who purchased them; they deny the second coming of Jesus.[21] The false teachers may also assert that eschatological judgment is idle and the destruction consequent upon it sleeps, two things that the author of 2 Peter denies. The description of the false teachers as licentious and greedy attributes general moral failings to them. Likewise, those who follow them are licentious and bring the way of truth into disrepute. All of these descriptions undermine the ethos of the false teachers and attempt to arouse the pathos of the addressees against them, i.e., emotions of revulsion against the false teachers, leading to rejection of the false teachers. The author of 2 Peter further develops this kind of argument in 2:10b–22.

Finally, the description of the false teachers as being destroyed in the future, which is repeated three times in different ways, provides a basis for rejecting them. Insofar as the addressees accept destruction as the destiny of the false teachers, they have reason not to follow them.

2C. 2:4–10A—PART THREE: PROPHECIES OF THE LAST JUDGMENT

Rhetography

The author of 2 Peter now specifies how the prophetic word predicts the power and coming of Jesus. He does so by describing three occasions when

---

20. Knoch, *Erste und Zweite Petrusbrief*, 259; Paulsen, *Der Zweite Petrusbrief*, 126.
21. Fornberg, *Early Church*, 36.

God judged evildoers and, on two of these occasions, also rescued the upright. This implies that God will do the same thing in the future. Each of these descriptions presents God as judging creation. Although the author of 2 Peter does not explicitly present them this way, the three occasions he describes are often used in apocalyptic discourse to indicate some of the periods into which history has been divided by God.[22] This sequence of historical periods culminates in the end of the world.

The author's descriptions of these three occasions refer to stories told in the Jewish scriptures. What we said above about the author's reference to the story of Jesus's transfiguration also applies to these references. These references would call the biblical stories to the minds of those who knew them. Those unfamiliar with the stories would only be aware of the features of the stories that the author mentions specifically. And even those familiar with the stories would be most aware of the details that are explicitly mentioned. Since the author uses the stories as instances of the prophetic word's prediction of the power and coming of Jesus, he probably presumes at least a general awareness that they are found in the Jewish scriptures.

The author begins by describing God's judgment of the sinful angels. This probably refers to the story in Genesis 6:1–4, in which the sons of God marry human women. This story does not say that the sons of God were angels, that their marriage to human women was sinful, or that God punished them for it, though the second of these may be implied by Genesis 6:5. However, when 1 Enoch retells the story, it includes all three elements (see 1 En. 12.4–6), as does Jude 6, on which the author of 2 Peter depends at this point. Thus the author evokes a picture in which angels left their proper place in heaven and consorted with human women on earth. However, the author of 2 Peter says explicitly only that the angels sinned. If the addressees do not recognize the story to which this alludes, the picture presented is simply that of some unspecified wrongdoing on the part of the angels.

In consequence of their sin, God consigned the angels to Tartarus, where they await final judgment. They are kept in chains of gloom; Tartarus is a dark place. Although the author has not presented a detailed picture of the angels' sin, he is much more specific about their punishment. By referring to the underworld as Tartarus, the author invokes another picture, one in which Zeus consigned the Titans to Tartarus after they rebelled against him. Elements of 2 Peter's presentation, especially use of the word "angels," make it seem very probable that he subordinates this picture to the one derived from the Jewish scriptures and the tradition based on them. Perhaps

22. Sinful angels: 1 En. 86–88; 2 Bar 56:10–14; Jude 6—Noah and the flood: 1 En. 89:1–8; 93:4; 2 Bar 56:15–16; Matt 24:37–39/Luke 17:26–27—Sodom and Gomorrah: Matt 10:15/Luke 10:12; Luke 17:28–30, 32; Jude 7.

because of the parallel between God's punishment of the angels and Zeus's punishment of the Titans, the author of 2 Peter uses the name for the latter's place of punishment. This integration of Tartarus into the picture of divine judgment in Judaism was probably already familiar to the author and addressees.[23]

The author goes on to describe God's judgment of the world in the time of Noah. This evokes the story told in Genesis 6:5–9:29. Because of the wickedness of the human race, God decided to destroy all the people and animals God had created. God told Noah to build an ark for himself, his wife, his three sons and their wives, and two of every kind of animal. When Noah had built the ark and all its passengers were aboard, God sent a flood on the earth that blotted out every other living thing. When the floodwaters receded, God made a covenant with Noah and his descendants.

In referring to the story of Noah, the author of 2 Peter mentions few details. He says only that God brought a deluge on the world of the impious, but guarded Noah, as one of eight, from that deluge. The author does not say that God guarded Noah by means of the ark, nor does he say anything about animals or a covenant. He does, however, include one detail not found in the biblical account. He describes Noah as a "herald of justice," picturing Noah as speaking out against the wickedness of his generation. Although this detail is not part of the biblical account, it is found in other versions of the story of Noah, e.g., Josephus, *Ant.* 1.74.

Finally, the author describes God's destruction of Sodom and Gomorrah after sending the righteous Lot out of Sodom. This evokes the story told in Genesis 18–19. Because of Sodom and Gomorrah's bad reputation, God decided to investigate these cities and destroy them if they were as wicked as their reputation. Their reputation proved to be true, so God rained fire and brimstone on them and destroyed them, after first bringing Lot, his wife, and his daughters out to safety.

Once again, when the author of 2 Peter refers to the picture found in the biblical story (and in Jude 7, on which the author depends here), he mentions few details. He says only that God condemned Sodom and Gomorrah, reducing them to ashes in a catastrophe, and rescued Lot. One of these few details, namely the reduction of Sodom and Gomorrah to ashes, is not found in the biblical account or in Jude 7; however, it is found in Philo, *Migr.* 139. To this the author adds that in treating Sodom and Gomorrah this way, God made them an example of what is about to happen to the impious.

---

23. Bauckham, *Jude, 2 Peter*, 249.

Even more significantly, the author of 2 Peter emphasizes that Lot was oppressed by life among the wicked people of Sodom. The author pictures Lot as a just man who was worn out by his life among the lawless. The author elaborates on this by saying that this just man tortured his just soul day after day by what he saw and heard living among them. In addition to evoking a picture of Lot as suffering from his contact with the wicked, this evokes a picture of the wicked as lawless and, specifically, licentious. The only thing suggestive of this in the biblical account, apart from general references to the people of the cities as wicked, is the story of how the men of Sodom tried to force Lot to hand his guests over to them (Gen 19:4–11). The author of 2 Peter implies that this sort of thing happened repeatedly.

The author concludes from all three descriptions that God knows how to rescue the pious and how to keep the unjust confined for the day of judgment. He further describes the unjust as especially those who go after the flesh in desire for defilement and despise dominion. This implies that the sinful angels, the generation of the flood, the inhabitants of Sodom and Gomorrah, and the false teachers are all guilty of these things. It is clear how this applies to the angels who married human women and the inhabitants of Sodom who wanted sexual relations with Lot's guests; it can easily be supposed to apply to the generation of the flood. In 2:3 the author mentioned the licentiousness of the false teachers. All despise dominion in at least the sense that they do not accept God as their Lord.

Rhetology

This section of the letter supports the denial in 2:3b that the judgment of the false teachers is idle and their destruction is asleep. Thus it continues the apocalyptic discourse of 2:1–3. The argument is an induction from a series of examples.

> God has punished sinners in instance "a"
> God has punished sinners and saved the righteous in instance "b"
> God has punished sinners and saved the righteous in instance "c"
> Therefore, God knows how to save the righteous and punish sinners.

These instances all come from scripture and so serve to explain exactly how the prophetic word supports the author's presentation of the power and coming of Jesus. Grammatically, 2:4–10a is a conditional sentence, of which

vv. 4–8 state a set of circumstances and vv. 9–10a draw a conclusion from the existence of these circumstances.[24]

The argumentative force of the section derives from the succession of three pictures leading to the conclusion expressed in vv. 9–10a. These pictures are presented as parallel to one another and so as establishing a pattern of divine action on which the conclusion is based. Verses 4–7 consist of three parallel conditional clauses, each of them complex in itself; the last is followed by a parenthetical explanatory clause in v. 8. The parallelism of the three clauses (vv. 4, 5, 6–7) is emphasized by various instances of repetition and progression. The phrase "did not spare" is used in v. 4 and repeated in v. 5; the adjective "impious" is used in v. 5 and repeated in v. 6. These three clauses present a chronological progression of events. They also represent a progression in the character of the events. The first clause (v. 4) refers only to God's punishment of the sinful. The second and third clauses (vv. 5, 6–7) refer not only to this but also to salvation of the righteous. The third clause is followed by a parenthetical clause (v. 8) that elaborates the description of the situation from which Lot was saved. Thus there is an increasing emphasis on salvation of the righteous.

There is also a noteworthy parallel between the three conditional clauses and the conclusion in vv. 9–10a; this helps establish that the conclusion truly follows from the conditional clauses. The second and third conditional clauses are the basis for the conclusion that "the Lord knows how to rescue the pious from trial"; the verb "rescue" is used in both v. 7 and v. 9. The first conditional clause is the basis for the conclusion that the Lord also knows "how to keep the unjust confined for the day of judgment," since the sinful angels are explicitly said to be "kept for judgment" in v. 4. There is thus a chiastic relationship between the three conditional clauses and the conclusion; the author first draws a conclusion from the second and third clauses and then from the first clause. This brings the entire period back to its starting point. The author also sees the second part of the conclusion as based on the second and third conditional clauses, however. This is explicit in the comment that what happened to Sodom and Gomorrah was an example of what will happen to the impious. The author's explicit reference to the licentiousness of Sodom and Gomorrah grounds the conclusion that the unjust that God especially knows how to confine for the day of judgment are those who go after the flesh in desire for defilement.

---

24. Contra Gerdmar, *Rethinking the Judaism-Hellenism Dichotomy*, 33.

b. 3:1-13—Further Argument That Jesus Will Come Again

Rhetography

The author of 2 Peter begins this section by referring again to the picture evoked by the letter as a whole, namely the picture of Peter as writing a testamentary letter near the end of his life so that people can remember his teaching in the future. The resumption of this picture, however, does not repeat all of the elements mentioned earlier and introduces some new details. The author does not again explicitly refer to the imminence of his own death or to making it possible to remember his teaching in the future, though he surely presumes the addressees will continue to have these things in mind. On the other hand, he refers to the present letter as the second one he has written, probably thinking of 1 Peter as the first.[25] The purpose of both is to arouse in the memory of the addressees a pure understanding so that they remember the words spoken beforehand by the holy prophets and the commandment given by the apostles of Jesus. His purpose is cognitive; he wants the addressees to have knowledge. The danger he wants to avert is that of forgetting or misunderstanding. At least in part, his teaching is not unique to him, but it is an endorsement of the words of the prophets and the commandment of the addressees' apostles.

This evokes a picture in which this teaching has previously been delivered to the addressees. As in 1:20 the author probably presumes that the words of the prophets have come to them by means of the Bible. In referring to the commandment of the apostles of the addressees ("your apostles"), the author may evoke a picture in which apostles presented this commandment to the addressees either orally or by means of writings like the earlier letter of the author and the letters of Paul. It is clear from 3:15 that the author of 2 Peter regards Paul as having written to the addressees of 2 Peter. Perhaps "your apostles" are, or at least include, Peter and Paul. The teaching of the prophets is presumed to be apocalyptic; it concerns what will happen in the last days and is directed especially to those who will live at that time. The commandment of the apostles is probably the holy commandment mentioned in 2:21,[26] i.e., the commandment to live a holy life in expectation of Jesus's return. Thus the author evokes the basic apocalyptic picture of the world under the rule of God, who is about to bring this world to an end and replace it with another.

---

25. So Bigg, *St. Peter and St. Jude*, 288-89; Kelly, *Peter and Jude*, 352-53; Bauckham, *Jude, 2 Peter*, 286. Davids (*2 Peter and Jude*, 257-59) rejects this view.

26. Kelly, *Peter and Jude*, 354; Watson, *Invention, Arrangement, and Style*, 126.

The author goes on to say that in the last days there will be scoffers who doubt that they are living in the last days because they doubt that there will be any last days. They doubt this because they follow their own desires. This pictures the doubters as ones who reject expectation of the end of the world because it allows them to indulge their appetites. This parallels the prediction that false teachers will arise (2:1) and is probably another expression of the same prediction. The scoffers argue that Jesus will not come again to bring the world to an end because nothing like that has ever happened before. Since the fathers have died, all things continue thus from the beginning of creation. This evokes the anti-apocalyptic picture of world history as an uninterrupted continuum. The author of 2 Peter presents the appearance of those who doubt apocalyptic expectation as an element of that expectation.

In refuting their skepticism, the author invokes various pictures. In refuting their claim that nothing like the return of Jesus to end the world has ever happened before, he refers again to God's destruction of the world in the time of Noah, again evoking the story told in Genesis 6:5–9:29. This time he makes no reference to the salvation of Noah and those with him; he speaks only of God's destruction of the world at that time. However, in 3:5 he puts this destruction in the context of creation, evoking the story told in Genesis 1:2, 6–9. God created the world with a word, first dividing the primeval waters with the dome of the heavens and then gathering the waters below the dome into one place so that dry land appeared.[27] At the time of Noah, God destroyed the world by water and word. At God's word, the waters above and below the dome were released from their boundaries (see Gen 7:11).

The author of 2 Peter describes creation only by saying that long ago there were heavens and an earth constituted from water and through water by the word of God. Someone who did not recognize the allusion to Genesis might have difficulty understanding exactly what that means; however, the author of 2 Peter probably presumes that those he addresses will recognize it. He describes the destruction of the world at the time of Noah as having taken place through water and the word. For those who recognized the author's allusion to Genesis, this would imply that the destruction resulted from God's undoing the work of creation. The author describes the destruction itself as a matter of the world's having been deluged with water. This is the same picture presented earlier in 2:5.

Just as the world was destroyed in the time of Noah, so the present heavens and earth are being kept by the same word for fire on the day of

---

27. See Kelly, *Peter and Jude*, 358–59; Bauckham, *Jude, 2 Peter*, 297; Paulsen, *Der Zweite Petrusbrief*, 160–61; Davids, *2 Peter and Jude*, 268–70.

judgment and destruction of impious human beings. This repeats the picture presented in 2:4 and 9 of sinners and the unjust as being kept for judgment (see also 2:17). Here, the author makes it clear that the judgment involves the entire world and will take place by fire. The statement that the world is being kept for judgment by the word of God probably means that it is predicted in the Bible. The author sees it as predicted by the scriptural accounts of the events he has mentioned in 2:4–8. In 2:5 he presented the reduction of Sodom and Gomorrah to ashes (by fire) as a sign of what will happen to the impious. He may also see the judgment of the world by fire predicted by passages such as Deut 32:22; Mal 3:19; Isa 66:15–16; Zeph 1:18. And he may be thinking that it is predicted by 1 Cor 3:13–15.

In addition to invoking biblical predictions of the judgment of the world by fire, the author's picture might also remind the addressees of the Stoic idea that a conflagration brings the world to an end and is followed by its reconstitution.[28] In the Stoic view this also occurs through the word. If the author intends to evoke this picture, however, it is most likely that he integrates it into the biblical picture of judgment by fire. To mention only one point, the parallel with destruction of the world by water in the time of Noah has no place in Stoic thought.

The author goes on to address the perception that the return of Jesus to end the world has been delayed by saying that time is different for God than for human beings. For God, one human day is like a thousand years and a thousand human years like one day. In this way, he calls attention to a fundamental difference between God and human beings. This pictures God as being outside the human world in a situation where something as basic as time is different than it is in the human world. A short time in the human world may correspond to a long time in God's situation, and a long time in the human world may correspond to a short time in God's situation. The author adds that Jesus has not yet come again because God is giving people a chance to repent before he comes. This portrays God as extremely patient and benevolent toward them.

Finally, the author directly describes God's ending of this world. He first says that the day of the Lord will come unexpectedly like a thief. The author evokes the picture of a thief secretly approaching the person he plans to rob and taking his victim by surprise. The day of the Lord will appear in a similar way. The author has probably taken this picture from 1 Thess 5:2,[29] but it is also found in several other places.[30]

---

28. Bauckham, *Jude, 2 Peter*, 300–301; Neyrey, *2 Peter, Jude*, 240–41.
29. Fornberg, *Early Church*, 25. Bauckham (*Jude, 2 Peter*, 306) disagrees.
30. Matt 24:43–44/Luke 12:39–40; Rev 3:3; 16:15.

The author gives a further description of the end in v. 10 and repeats it in v. 12.

10 And the day of the Lord will come like a thief, on which the heavens will pass away with a rushing noise, and the elements, set on fire, will be dissolved,	12 awaiting and eagerly seeking the coming of the day of God on account of which the heavens, burning, will be dissolved and the elements, set on fire, are melted.

The day of the Lord is also the day of God. On that day, the heavens will pass away with a rushing noise (v. 10) or will be dissolved by fire (v. 12). The picture underlying the first of these may be that of destruction of the heavens by fire, which is explicit in the second; the rushing noise with which the heavens pass away may be the noise of a roaring fire.[31] An eschatological fire will also dissolve or melt the elements of which the world is composed. These elements are probably earth, air, fire, and water.[32] The author may picture the dissolution of the world that consists of various combinations of these elements as resulting from the complete conversion of earth, air, and water into fire. If so, he is adopting the Stoic description of the conflagration that ends the world.

The four clauses that describe the dissolution of the heavens and earth all have the same grammatical structure and all end with the same syllable in Greek, namely *tai*. The words "'heavens," "dissolved," "elements," and "set on fire" are all repeated. The first two are used in different ways, and there are other differences in vocabulary between the two descriptions. This combination of differences and similarities emphasizes the details of the day of the Lord by repeating them in an interestingly varied way.

When the world ends, the earth and the works on it will be discovered. In saying that the earth and the works on it will be discovered, the author may evoke a picture like that presented explicitly in 1 Cor 3:12–15. In this passage Paul says that the nature of the work a person has done in building on the foundation of Christ will be revealed by fire on the last day. Good work will survive the fire; poor work will be burned up. The author of 2 Peter uses this picture to say that the false teachers and their followers will be destroyed on the day of the Lord, and only the upright will remain. Because this is the case, the addressees should live holy and pious lives.

Thus the author of 2 Peter does not envision the destruction of everyone at the end of the world but only the destruction of the impious. In this, the author fundamentally diverges from the Stoic understanding of the

---

31. Bauckham, *Jude, 2 Peter*, 315.

32. According to Bauckham most commentators instead see the elements as the sun, moon, and stars (*Jude, 2 Peter*, 315–16).

conflagration, even though he seems to have adopted the Stoic picture of this conflagration. Just as Noah and his family escaped God's ending of the world by the flood, so the upright will escape God's ending of the world by fire.

And as was the case in the time of Noah, the heavens and earth that have been destroyed will be replaced by new heavens and earth. The author has taken this picture from Isaiah 65:17; 66:22. This will be God's third creation of heaven and earth. God destroyed the first heaven and earth in the time of Noah and then recreated them; on the day of the Lord, God will destroy the second heaven and earth and then recreate them. Justice will dwell in this third heaven and earth. Justice is pictured as a person that lives in the new creation; this picture is adapted from Isaiah 32:16.

Rhetology

By predicting the appearance in the last days of those who will scoff at the expectation of Jesus's return (3:3), the author makes the false teachers he opposes an element of the apocalyptic expectation he advocates. The rise of the false teachers is itself a sign that these are the last days. This implicitly undermines their opposition to expectation of the end of the world. It need not be taken seriously because it is itself part of the chain of events by which God will bring the world to an end. Nevertheless, the author goes on to respond to the arguments of the false teachers.

The false teachers argue that everything remains as it has from the beginning. There is no precedent for the coming of Jesus and the end of the world and thus no reason to think it will happen. The author refutes this argument in vv. 5-6 by describing again (as in 2:5) the flood in the time of Noah. These verses form an enthymeme[33] whose argument can be restated:

> One can only maintain that all things have remained as they are since the beginning of creation if the world has not previously been destroyed.
>
> But the world was destroyed previously by the flood.
>
> Therefore, all things have not remained as they are since the beginning of creation (and one can maintain that the world will be destroyed again).

The picture of the world's destruction in the time of Noah powerfully contradicts the view that all things have remained the same since the beginning

---

33. Watson, *Invention, Arrangement, and Style*, 129.

of creation. The author then concludes that the present heavens and earth are treasured up for destruction by fire by the same word that was operative in the creation and destruction of the first heavens and earth. As we have seen, the author probably presumes that this was predicted by the prophets. Insofar as the author has this in mind, he again invokes the prophetic word as an argument for what he says.

In vv. 8–9 the author responds to an argument that he has not explicitly attributed to the scoffers, namely, the argument that the return of Jesus has been delayed. Apparently the scoffers' skepticism is partly based on the idea that the return of Jesus should have already occurred by their time if it was going to happen at all. Since it has not, they view the expectation as unfounded. The author responds to this in two ways. In v. 8 he makes use of Ps 90:4 to point out that time is different for God than for humans. Although the author does not explicitly say that he is quoting the psalm, he presumably expects the addressees to recognize that he is. And the recognition that he is restating the teaching of an authoritative text is a reason for accepting the teaching. The teaching is that one human day is like a thousand years with God and a thousand human years like one day. Since time has such different meanings for human beings and for God, it is not possible to say that what seems like a long time to human beings is actually a long time for God. Thus human perceptions of time cannot be the basis for saying that God has delayed some action; the divine perception of time is completely different.

The author's second response in v. 9 argues on another basis that God has not delayed to keep the promise of Jesus's return. This argument presumes that "delay" means simple procrastination. If God has a reason for sending Jesus at one time rather than another, this is not delay. The author's picture of God as patient and benevolent makes it impossible to think that God has simply neglected to fulfill the promise of Jesus's return. This enthymeme[34] can be restated:

> One can only say that the Lord is slow to keep his promises if there is no sufficient reason for delay in keeping them.
>
> But the Lord delays out of patience, giving all the opportunity for repentance.
>
> Therefore, the Lord is not slow to keep his promises.

In v. 10 the author offers a final response to the argument that the return of Jesus has been delayed. He says that the day of the Lord will come like a thief, i.e., unexpectedly. Since no one knows when it will come, it is

---

34. Watson, *Invention, Arrangement, and Style*, 130–31.

impossible to say that is has been delayed. The vivid picture of the return of Jesus as analogous to a totally unexpected theft eliminates any possibility that its time could be known. The statement that the day of the Lord will come like a thief is quoted from 1 Thessalonians 5:2, though without indicating this explicitly. Once again, the author may presume that the authority of 1 Thessalonians is a reason to accept this teaching.

In the remainder of v. 10 the author describes the coming of the day of the Lord and ends by saying that the earth and the works on it will be discovered at that time. From this, he draws the conclusion in vv. 11–12 that the addressees need to live holy lives in eager expectation of the day of the Lord. The slavery to corruption of the earth and some of its inhabitants will be clear when they undergo corruption at the end. Likewise, the freedom from corruption of those who do not will be clear. The dissolution of the universe at the end is thus a motive for living virtuously. The same argument is made, in completely different terms, in 1 Thessalonians 5:3–11. In 2 Peter 3:13 the author gives a second reason the addressees should live holy lives. The present heavens and earth will be replaced by new heavens and earth in which justice dwells. One must be just if one hopes to dwell in the new creation along with justice.

III. Contribution of Sociorhetorical Methodology to a New Understanding of 2 Peter

Sociorhetorical methodology makes several contributions to increased understanding of 2 Peter. As I mentioned in the introduction to this paper, SRI in its first stage unifies various approaches that are often pursued separately. It brings together interpretations such as historical-critical exegesis, rhetorical criticism, social scientific criticism, and others. It allows each its proper place in the interpretation of 2 Peter and also calls for the application of each to 2 Peter in cases where that has not been done. In this way, it calls attention to aspects of the text that are often not observed systematically and to the relationship among them.

The form of SRI that I have pursued in this paper makes a similar contribution. As I mentioned in the introduction, what Robbins calls the rhetography of New Testament texts has not received much attention from interpreters. Attending to it brings to light new aspects of the texts. It is also an excellent foundation for discernment of rhetology. As I have tried to show, a more precise awareness of the images conjured up by a text allows us to understand in more detail the arguments of the text and how it makes these arguments. Previous interpreters have attended to the rhetology of texts much more than they have their rhetography. But pursuit of the two in tandem yields new insights into rhetology.

For example, investigating the rhetography of 2 Peter 1:16–18 makes us aware that the author only says explicitly that God the father bestowed honor and glory on Jesus when a voice came from heaven identifying Jesus as his beloved son; Peter and unnamed others witnessed this when they were with Jesus on the holy mountain. Realizing that the author's account of the transfiguration of Jesus focuses on God's declaration that Jesus is his son helps us to understand the argumentative force of the account, its rhetology. The revelation that Jesus is the son of God supports the expectation that Jesus will come again because it is appropriate that someone who did not clearly enact the role of the son of God at his first coming will come a second time to do so.

This form of SRI focuses attention on the mental processes set in motion by reading or hearing the texts. In this respect, it somewhat resembles reader-response criticism and other forms of reader-oriented interpretation. However, SRI focuses on aspects of the experience of reading neglected by other forms of reader-oriented interpretation. Like classical rhetorical analysis, reader-response criticism attends to a wide range of ways a text affects a reader. According to Robert M. Fowler, two central components of reader-response criticism are attention to the temporality of the reading experience and the consequent understanding of meaning as event.[35]

Reader-response criticism focuses on the way reading occurs over time. The reader experiences a text word by word, sentence by sentence, during a period of time extending from the time one begins to read until one finishes reading. As Fowler presents it, this emphasis on the temporality of reading or hearing a text is an alternative to the view that the text is an object, a container for meaning. SRI presumes the temporality of the reading experience and focuses specifically on the ways a text awakens pictures in the imagination of the reader, develops them (or does not), and moves to other pictures. SRI also focuses on the way a text persuades the reader by presenting successive arguments for its contentions.

Reader-response criticism views the reader as construing the meaning of the text as he or she reads or hears the text; the meaning of the text unfolds in the process of reading. Fowler paraphrases M. H. Abrams's way of distinguishing this approach from others:

> Abrams says a literary theory tends to concentrate on either the literary text itself (objective theories), the world reflected in

---

35. On this, see Fowler, *Let the Reader Understand*, 41–58.

the work (mimetic theories), the author of the work (expressive theories), or the audience of the work (pragmatic theories).[36]

Like reader-response criticism, SRI is concerned with the impact of a text on its audience. However, it focuses specifically on the persuasive, argumentative impact of texts. This is not the primary focus of reader-response criticism.

For example, reader-response criticism makes use of speech act theory, which views language as performative.[37] Language does not *say* something as much as *do* something, like the "I do" of a wedding ceremony. This focuses attention on what speech act theorists call *illocution*, what a speaker intends to do by saying something, and its uptake by those who hear it. This is not at all incompatible with SRI, but SRI is concerned with a particular kind of intended effect of a text on its audience, namely its persuasive effect (rhetology), and particular ways of achieving that effect, namely rhetography.

---

36. Fowler, *Let the Reader Understand*, 49, citing Abrams, *Mirror and the Lamp*, 6.
37. Fowler, *Let the Reader Understand*, 47–48.

8

Comparison of Humans to Animals in 2 Peter 2:10b–22

A striking feature of 2 Peter 2:10b–22 is the author's multiple references to similarities and differences between humans and animals. In this passage the author of 2 Peter continues and concludes the criticism of the people he calls "false teachers" that he began in 2:1. In 2:12 the author compares the false teachers to irrational animals. In 2:16 he develops the point that the false teachers are followers of Balaam by observing that a voiceless donkey prevented the madness of Balaam, implicitly contrasting the false teachers with the donkey. And finally in 2:22 the author says that a proverb about the behavior of a dog and a sow applies to those who follow the false teachers and by implication to the false teachers themselves.

In his critique of the false teachers in 2:1–22, the author of 2 Peter is dependent on Jude 4–16.[1] He has taken the comparison of the false teachers to irrational animals from Jude 10. He has also taken the connection of the false teachers to Balaam from Jude 11. Jude, however, mentions Balaam very briefly and makes no reference to Balaam's donkey; the author of 2 Peter has described Balaam more fully and specifically included the behavior of the donkey. The author of 2 Peter has added the proverb to the material he took from Jude. Thus, by comparison with Jude, the author of 2 Peter has greatly increased the use of animal references in his polemic. This use of animals was probably suggested to him by Jude 10, but he has made it much more prominent than it was in Jude.

In what follows, I will illuminate this aspect of 2 Peter 2:10b–22 by investigating comparison of humans to animals by writers older than, and

---

1. On this, see chapter 1, "Use of the Letter of Jude by the Second Letter of Peter."

(roughly) contemporary with, 2 Peter. This will bring 2 Peter's references to animals into sharper focus.

Like Irrational Animals (2 Peter 2:12)

In Jude 10 the author says that those he criticizes are like irrational animals in that they know some things naturally (ὅσα δὲ φυσικῶς ὡς τὰ ἄλογα ζῷα ἐπίστανται). The author also says that his opponents are destroyed by these things they know naturally. It is unclear whether or not this is also true of the irrational animals. If it is, this is another way that the opponents resemble irrational animals. Second Peter's revision of this in 2:12 explicitly says that the false teachers are like irrational animals in being destined by their nature for destruction. The author of 2 Peter eliminated any reference to irrational animals' knowing things naturally; perhaps he did not think it appropriate to speak of irrational animals as having knowledge. Instead he says that they are begotten naturally for capture and corruption (ὡς ἄλογα ζῷα γεγεννημένα φυσικὰ εἰς ἅλωσιν καὶ φθοράν). To this the author adds that the false teachers will be corrupted in the corruption of the irrational animals (ἐν τῇ φθορᾷ αὐτῶν καὶ φθαρήσονται).

In Greek λόγος means both reason and speech; the latter is an outward expression of the former.[2] The idea that humans are distinguished from other animals in that humans reason and speak (i.e., are λογικοί) while other animals do not goes back at least to Aristotle (see, e.g., *De Anima* 433A; *Nicomachean Ethics* 1111B) and was strongly affirmed by the Stoics (see, e.g., Epictetus 1.2.1). Others, especially Platonists, rejected the distinction.[3] For example, in the dialogue *De Animalibus* 10–71 Philo of Alexandria's nephew Alexander presents an extensive argument that animals are rational.[4] Likewise, Plutarch argues that animals are rational in *De sollertia animalium* (*Moralia* 959–985) and *Bruta animalia ratione uti* (*Moralia* 985–992).[5]

---

2. On the relationship between reason and speech, see Sorabji, *Animal Minds and Human Morals*, 80–86. Dierauer says that in its earliest use, the designation of animals as ἄλογα meant that they lacked speech (Dierauer, *Tier und Mensch*, 33).

3. For detailed discussion of the dispute and its ramifications, see Sorabji, *Animal Minds and Human Morals*; cf. also Grant, *Early Christians and Animals*, 9–11.

4. For this treatise, see Terian, *Philonis Alexandrini De Animalibus*. The text and translation of Philo's other writings are taken from the Loeb Classical Library, as are the text and translation of other Greek and Latin writers cited in this essay as far as possible.

5. The view that animals are rational can easily be seen to imply that one should abstain from eating animal flesh. Plutarch makes such an argument in *De esu carnium orationes* I and II (*Moralia* 993A–999B) as does Porphyry in *On Abstinence from Animal*

Some such arguments acknowledge that animals do not speak as humans do, but maintain that animals do reason. Thus the Greek title of Plutarch, *Bruta animalia ratione uti*—Περὶ τοῦ τὰ ἄλογα λόγῳ χρῆσθαι—designates animals as ἄλογα even as it proposes that animals use λόγος (cf. also 992C).[6] Other arguments that animals are rational maintain that at least some animals speak. Thus Alexander in Philo, *De Animalibus* 13–15 argues that birds are capable of rational utterance, and Plutarch, *De sollertia animalium* argues that starlings, crows, and parrots are endowed with rational utterance (προφορικὸς λόγος) (972F–973E).

The idea that animals are irrational is not found in the Hebrew Bible, but it was taken up by Hellenistic Jews. For example, in *De Animalibus* 77–100 Philo rejects his nephew Alexander's argument that animals are rational. Likewise, Wis 11:15–16 says that God punished the Egyptians' worship of irrational serpents and worthless animals by means of irrational animals so they might learn that one is punished by the very things by which one sins. There are many other references to irrational animals in Hellenistic Jewish literature.[7] It is presumably from here that Jude has derived the idea that animals are irrational, and 2 Peter has derived it from Jude.

The author of 2 Peter describes irrational animals as begotten naturally for capture and corruption. This is not a common idea about animals, though it is not unparalleled. Aristotle argued that animals exist for the sake of humans (see Aristotle, *Politics* 1256B), meaning that they exist to be eaten as well as to provide service, clothes, and tools. The Stoics held a similar view. According to Plutarch, the Stoics (he specifically mentions Chrysippus) maintain that the pig by nature (φύσει) has come to be in order to be killed and eaten (Fragment 193). Richard Bauckham says the idea that certain animals were born to be slaughtered and eaten was common in the ancient world and cites three examples: Juvenal 1.141; Pliny, *Nat.* 8.81; b. B. Metz. 85a.[8] The first of these speaks of boars as an animal born for the sake of banquets (*apros, animal propter convivia natum*). The second says concerning rabbits that nature has generated fertile animals that are harmless and good to eat (*natura innocua et esculenta animalia fecunda generavit*). The third presents Rabbi Judah the Prince as telling a calf that was being taken to be slaughtered that the calf had been created for this.

Food.

6. Animals are also called ἄλογα in the Greek title of Philo, *De Animalibus*. They are also said to have λόγος in Plutarch, *Bruta animalia ratione uti* 991F, 992D–E.

7. See 4 Macc 14:14, 18; Philo, *Post.* 161; *Abr.* 266–7; *Mos.* 1.272; *Spec.* 1.148; 2.69; 4.121; *Virt.* 81, 117, 125, 133, 140, 148, 160; Josephus *Ag. Ap.* 2.213; *Ant.* 10.262.

8. Bauckham, *Jude, 2 Peter*, 263.

These passages certainly speak of animals as born to be slaughtered and eaten, and this is generally similar to what 2 Peter says. However, 2 Peter says specifically that animals are born for capture and corruption. "Capture" seems to imply that animals are born to be hunted, either by humans or by other animals. "Corruption" refers to disintegration that results either from being eaten or simply from decay.[9] The author of 2 Peter seems most concerned to portray animals as mortal, destined for death and decay. This is similar in thought, but not language, to what is said in Ps 49:12, 20—"Mortals cannot abide in their pomp; they are like the animals that perish." In the Greek translation of this psalm, though not in the Hebrew text, the animals are explicitly described as irrational (τοῖς κτήνεσιν τοῖς ἀνοήτοις—Ps 48:13, 21). In Targum Neofiti 1 on Numbers, Balaam's donkey refers to itself as an unclean beast that dies in this world and does not enter the world to come, contrasting itself to the children of Abraham, Isaac, and Jacob.[10] This is quite similar to the thought of 2 Peter, though the targums do not explicitly refer to the donkey as irrational.

Comparison of humans to irrational animals is fairly common and serves various purposes.[11] Sometimes the point is simply that humans are unlike irrational animals because they are rational. Epictetus argues that rational and irrational animals have in common such things as eating, drinking, resting, and sexual intercourse, but only rational animals have understanding (1.6.12–22; cf. 4.7.7). At other times, the point is that humans are enough like irrational animals that behavior toward the latter should be a pattern for the way one treats humans. In *Spec.* 4.121 Philo says that one should learn from dealing with irrational animals how to deal with humans (cf. Josephus, *Ag. Ap.* 2.213). Philo argues that the Mosaic laws concerning proper treatment of irrational animals and plants are intended to train people in proper treatment of one another (*Virt.* 131–34, 140, 160). At still other times, the point is that some humans are like animals in lacking rationality. In *Praecepta gerendae reipublicae* Plutarch says that enticing a mob by currying favor with it rather than by persuasion is like catching and herding irrational animals (*Moralia* 802E). Galen says that children, who do not yet have reason, fight with one another like animals (*De Placitis Hippocrates*

---

9. On this, see chapter 3, "The Soteriology of the Second Letter of Peter," especially 40–42.

10. Targum Neofiti 1, 127. Cf. the similar statement in Targum Pseudo-Jonathan, 254.

11. Of course, those who maintain that animals are rational frequently compare humans and animals, but they are not comparing humans to what they regard as irrational animals. Plutarch's comparison of humans to pigs in *Bruta animalia ratione uti* is discussed below.

et Platonis 5.5.1–5). *Corpus Hermeticum* 4.5 describes those who are not Gnostics as having perceptions like those of irrational animals.

Most often, humans are compared with irrational animals to make some more specific point. Sometimes humans are compared with irrational animals to say that they possess some good quality of animals or even that they are inferior to animals in possessing some good quality. Fourth Maccabees 14:14, 18 says that irrational animals and humans are alike in having sympathy and love for their offspring. In *Ant.* 10.262 Josephus says that even the irrational lions who consumed the enemies of Daniel considered the wickedness of those enemies a reason for punishing them. In this way, he suggests that these irrational creatures regard wickedness the same way humans should. In *Post.* 161 Philo says that irrational creatures are greatly superior to humans with regard to the senses of hearing and smell (cf. also *Abr.* 266–67). Similarly, Plutarch says that nature is a stepmother to humans, but a mother to irrational animals because of the animals' size, speed, and vision (Fragment 121). In *De amore prolis*, Plutarch argues that irrational animals follow nature more closely than do rational ones (*Moralia* 493B–E). Elsewhere, Plutarch says that humans should imitate irrational animals (Fragment 118), and in *De Stoicorum repugnantiis* he criticizes the Stoics because they do not consistently use the behavior of irrational animals as a model for human behavior (*Moralia* 1045B). Second Peter 2:16 invokes this kind of positive comparison of humans and irrational animals; Balaam's donkey, which is sometimes called an irrational animal (Philo, *Mos.* 1.272; *Virt.* 117), is presented as superior to Balaam in this verse.

At other times, humans are compared to irrational animals to say that they possess some bad quality of animals, especially their excessive appetite. For example, in *Spec.* 1.148 Philo compares desire to a licentious and unseemly irrational animal (ἀλόγου θρέμματος) and says that the belly is its manger. Musonius Rufus says that we liken gluttons to unreasoning animals (ζῴοις ἄφροσι—18B).[12] Clement of Alexandria says that humans who live in order to eat are like irrational animals whose life is their belly and nothing else (*Paidagogus* 2.1.4).

Second Peter's comparison of the false teachers to irrational animals falls into this general category. However, the specific way in which they resemble irrational animals is very different. As we have seen above, the main point of comparison is that both irrational animals and the false teachers are destined for death and decay. In other words, they are alike in having this inherent character. I have found no close parallel to a comparison of

---

12. The text and translation of Musionius Rufus are taken from Lutz, *Musonius Rufus*.

this kind; the closest is Psalm 49, which is quoted and discussed above. The reason may be that many would simply take it for granted that humans and animals are alike in this way. Those who thought they differed in this respect would not make such a comparison. It would mainly arise where humans could either be like or unlike animals in this way. Second Peter thinks that Christians are destined to escape death and decay, to be sharers in divine nature (see 2 Peter 1:5). But the false teachers will not share this destiny; they will be like irrational animals instead.

Unlike Balaam's Donkey (2 Peter 2:16)

Jude 11 says about those it criticizes that "they go the way of Cain, and abandon themselves to Balaam's error for the sake of gain, and perish in Korah's rebellion." Second Peter's revision of this in 2:16 eliminates the references to Cain and Korah and expands the reference to Balaam. Presumably comparison of the false teachers to Balaam served the author's purpose better than the triple comparison made by Jude.[13] Expanding the reference to Balaam also allowed the author of 2 Peter to mention Balaam's donkey explicitly. This enabled him to develop the theme of comparing the false teachers to animals. As I have noted above, this comparison emphasizes a positive feature of an animal.

In describing Balaam's donkey, the author of 2 Peter says that Balaam received a rebuke of his lawbreaking when a voiceless donkey, having spoken with a human's voice, prevented the madness of the prophet (ὑποζύγιον ἄφωνον ἐν ἀνθρώπου φωνῇ φθεγξάμενον ἐκώλυσεν τὴν τοῦ προφήτου παραφρονίαν). The author of 2 Peter has taken this from Numbers 22:28–30. These verses tell how the Lord opened the mouth of Balaam's donkey to reproach Balaam for beating the donkey. It is possible that this beating is what the author of 2 Peter means by Balaam's lawbreaking and his madness. However, it seems more likely that the author understands lawbreaking and madness more broadly. If so, he probably presumes the elaboration of the story of Balaam in non-biblical sources in which the donkey rebukes Balaam for his general failings, not simply for beating the donkey. According to Bauckham the targums to Numbers 22:30 attribute to the donkey a speech in which she rebukes Balaam for his foolishness.[14] In Targum Neofiti the donkey rebukes Balaam for lacking understanding and argues that if

---

13. On this, see Caulley, "'They Promise Them Freedom.'"
14. Bauckham, *Jude, 2 Peter*, 268. Bauckham mentions specifically Frg. Tg., Tg. Ps.-J., Tg. Neof.

Balaam is unable to curse the donkey, he will surely be unable to curse the Israelites. The donkey's speech in Targum Pseudo-Jonathan is quite similar.[15]

One indication that the author of 2 Peter is not directly dependent on the biblical text at this point is that he uses the word ὑποζύγιον for Balaam's donkey; the LXX uses ὄνος as does Josephus (see *Ant.* 4.109–10). However, Josephus speaks of the donkey as having a φωνὴν ἀνθρωπίνην; these are very close to the words used by 2 Peter and are not found in the biblical text. Philo uses ὑποζύγιον in reference to Balaam's donkey (*Mos.* 1.269). When Philo treats the words of the donkey as a rebuke spoken by various life pursuits in *Cher.* 35, they rebuke the person as proud-necked.

Second Peter's point is that the donkey acted more righteously than did Balaam; Balaam was inferior to the donkey in this respect, as are the false teachers who follow Balaam. We have noted above that Philo refers to Balaam's donkey as an irrational animal. The story of Balaam is an instance of an irrational animal's being superior to the false teachers. They are not like this particular irrational animal, but are inferior to it.

The author of 2 Peter describes the donkey as voiceless. This probably does not mean that the donkey is incapable of making a sound but rather that it is incapable of speech. As we have noted above, speech and rationality were closely related in Greek thought. Thus, in *On Abstinence from Animal Food* 3.3, Porphyry says that voice (φωνή) is external reason (προφορικὸς λόγος). The description of the donkey as voiceless may be intended to indicate that it was irrational.[16]

Like a Dog and a Sow (2 Peter 2:22)

Second Peter 2:22 is one of the author's additions to the material he adapted from Jude. It is the culmination of his critique of the false teachers and of his comparison of them to animals. The author says concerning the followers of the false teachers and the false teachers themselves that the meaning of the true proverb has applied to them: a dog having turned back to his own vomit, and a sow, having been washed, to wallowing in the mud (συμβέβηκεν αὐτοῖς τὸ τῆς ἀληθοῦς παροιμίας· Κύων ἐπιστρέψας ἐπὶ τὸ ἴδιον ἐξέραμα, καί· Ὗς λουσαμένη εἰς κυλισμὸν βορβόρου).

---

15. Targum Neofiti 1, 127, 254.

16. In the passage cited Porphyry is arguing that since animals have voices, they are therefore rational. He specifically mentions canine and bovine speech alongside barbarian and Greek. As was noted above, a similar argument is found in Philo, *De Animalibus* and Plutarch, *De sollertia animalium*. In *Politics* 1253A Aristotle separates voice and reason. He says that animals have voice (φωνή) but not speech (λόγος) that manifests reason.

The first part of the proverb comes from the Bible, specifically from Proverbs 26:11; the second part apparently comes from *The Story of Ahikar* 8.15/18. Neither source is cited verbatim; Bauckham thinks the two may have been combined by Hellenistic Jews before 2 Peter used the combination.[17] One thing suggesting this is that the author refers to this as a single proverb although it has two distinct parts.

Dogs and pigs are among the specific animals described as irrational with which humans are compared in the passages discussed above in connection with 2 Peter 2:12. Dogs are the irrational animals with which humans are compared with respect to good qualities in Philo, *Post.* 161; *Abr.* 266–67; *Spec.* 4.121; Plutarch, *De amore prolis* 493C. Pigs are the irrational animals with which humans are compared with respect to bad qualities in Philo, *Spec.* 1.148. Both dogs and pigs are mentioned negatively in Musonius Rufus 18B.

In addition to these passages, humans are often compared to dogs and pigs when the latter are not specifically called irrational animals. And these comparisons follow a pattern similar to that of the passages mentioned above: humans are compared to dogs with respect to both positive and negative qualities; humans are almost always compared to pigs with respect to negative qualities.[18]

One specific context in which humans are compared to dogs and pigs (as well as other animals) is that of physiognomy, the assessment of a person's character from their outer appearance. One of the methods of doing this is to infer the relationship between appearance and character in humans from the relationship between the two in animals, on the assumption that the two are similar. In pursuing this approach to physiognomy, the inferences based on dogs and pigs are sometimes positive, sometimes negative. In the case of the dog, the two are approximately equal; in the case of the pig, the latter preponderate.

---

17. Bauckham, *Jude, 2 Peter*, 273.

18. In contemporary English usage as in first-century Greek and Latin, comparing someone to a pig is almost always negative—e.g., making a pig of oneself, pigging out, sweating like a pig, male chauvinist pig—but comparing someone to a dog is more positive than in the first century—e.g., dogged determination. This is based on the more favorable estimate of dogs in our culture—the dog is man's best friend. However, the negative comparison is still found—e.g., son of a bitch.

a) Comparison of Humans to Dogs

Otto Keller divides dogs in the ancient world into five large groups: Spitz-type dogs, shepherd's dogs, street dogs, greyhounds, and mastiffs.[19] Humans are usually compared negatively to street dogs; they are compared positively to other kinds of dogs.

Humans are also compared to dogs in a neutral way. Judges 7:5 speaks about humans lapping water like a dog. In *Somn.* 1.108 Philo says that just as barking is peculiar to a dog, so is reasoning to a human. Seneca makes a similar point somewhat more elaborately in *Epistles* 76. In *Somn.* 2.267 Philo interprets the statement about a dog in Exodus 11:7 as referring to the tongue that is dog-like in barking so loud. Musonius Rufus argues that just as the trainers of dogs make no distinction in the training of male and female, so women should study philosophy (4, Lutz 44–45). And Musonius argues that just as a dog was not created for pleasure, neither were humans (17, Lutz, 106–109). Epictetus frequently draws conclusions about human beings from the characteristics and behavior of dogs. For example, in 1.2.34 he argues that humans differ in their abilities by asking if all dogs are skilled in tracking. In 2.23.24 he argues that human faculties are all useful though differing in value by saying that a dog is useful though less so than a slave. In 3.1.1–6, 23, 45 he argues that human beauty consists in possessing the excellence proper to a human by saying that this is true of dogs. Similar arguments are found in 3.26.26; 4.1.85, 124; 4.8.42.

Odyssey 20.9–13 compares the heart of Odysseus, filled with wrath against evil deeds, to a dog defending her puppies. According to Keller, Plautus and Horace use "little dog" (*catellus*) as a term of endearment for humans. And Pindar refers to Pan as the unexcelled dog of the great gods.[20] Another example of a positive comparison of humans to dogs is found in Philo, *Decal.* 114–15; here, Philo says that humans should imitate the example of dogs who guard their masters and die for them.

In Pseudo-Aristotle, *Physiognomica* the following physical characteristics are said to indicate positive traits on the basis that this is true of dogs:

> a deep voice goes with courage (807A)
>
> a narrow waist marks the hunter (810B)
>
> lips thin and pendulous such that part of the upper lip overhangs the lower signify pride of soul (811A)
>
> a somewhat long, flat forehead means quickness of sense (811B)
>
> a large head means quickness (812A)

19. Keller, *Antike Tierwelt*, 1:91.
20. Keller, *Antike Tierwelt*, 1:128.

hair on the point of the chin indicates a bold spirit (812B).

Negative comparisons of humans to dogs focus on several aspects of canine behavior. In *Gig.* 35 Philo says that undisciplined pleasures are like dogs in that they fawn on us then turn against us and their bite is fatal. Bad rulers are compared to dogs in the same respect in *Prob.* 90. In 2.22.9 Epictetus compares the changeable dispositions of humans to dogs that first play with one another and then begin to fight over a piece of meat thrown among them. Humans are also compared to mad dogs. In *Contempl.* 40 Philo says that under the influence of drink, some humans behave like mad dogs, bellowing and attacking and biting each other. Other comparisons of humans with mad dogs are found in Horace, *Epistles* 2.2.75; Josephus, *J.W.* 6.196; *Ant.* 7.209; Ignatius, *Eph* 7.1; Augustine, *City of God* 22.21.[21]

Humans are also described as like dogs in being shameless. In *Ag. Ap.* 2.85 Josephus says that Apion displays the shamelessness of a dog (see also Horace, *Epistles* 1.2.26). Humans are particularly like dogs with respect to their shameless eating and sexual activity. In *J.W.* 5.526 Josephus says that those besieged in Jerusalem continued like dogs to maul the carcass of the people.[22] In *Ant.* 12.213 Josephus says that Hyrcanus accused his fellow diners of eating bones along with meat like dogs, while he discarded the bones like a human. In *Epistles* 72 Seneca says that foolish humans behave like dogs in waiting eagerly for whatever Fortune may throw them, bolting it, and then waiting for more; the wise man, however, is indifferent to what may come his way. Musonius Rufus says that gluttons imitate the shameless greediness of dogs (18B, Lutz, 116–17).[23] In *City of God* 14.20 Augustine says that Cynics hold the shameless view, worthy of dogs, that no one should be ashamed to engage in sexual intercourse in a public place. The dog that is mentioned in Deuteronomy 23:18 (Hebrew v. 19) may be a reference to a male prostitute who is called a dog because his behavior is similar to that of a dog.[24]

---

21. In *De sollertia animalium* 963C–F Plutarch argues that one would not speak of a dog as having become mad if the dog were not rational to begin with.

22. Dogs are very often described as eaters of carrion; this may be one of the main reasons referring to someone as a dog is usually pejorative. For instances of this in the Bible, see Exod 22:31; 1 Kgs 16:4; 20:19, 23, 24, 38; 2 Kgs 9:10, 36; Ps 68:23; Jer 15:3. This presentation of dogs is also frequent in Josephus, sometimes in direct dependence on the Bible. For examples of this, see *J.W.* 4.324; 6.637; *Ant.* 6.187; 8.270, 289, 361, 407 (= 1 Kgs 20:19), 417; 9.124 (= 1 Kgs 20:23); 15.289. See also Luke 16:21 where dogs are said to lick the sores of Lazarus.

23. Dogs are described as greedy in Isa 56:11; see also Philo, *Mos.* 1.130.

24. Burns, "Devotee or Deviate."

In addition to negative comparison of humans with dogs focusing on the aggressiveness and shamelessness of dogs, there are other comparisons that do not make explicit the behavior that makes them alike. It is likely, however, that aggressiveness and shamelessness form at least part of the basis for these unspecific comparisons. One example of this can be seen in the use of the name Cynic (= dog-like) for a philosophical school.[25] In 1 Sam 17:43 Goliath asks David if Goliath is a dog that David comes to fight him with sticks. In the LXX David replies that Goliath is worse than a dog. This is reproduced by Josephus in *Ant.* 6.186. Such general derogatory comparison of humans with dogs can also be seen in a number of other biblical passages that denigrate humans as lowly.[26] In other passages the comparison implies that humans have an evil character.[27] In all of these passages people are presented as comparable to dogs in some unspecified but negative way.[28]

In Pseudo-Aristotle, *Physiognomica* the following physical characteristics are said to indicate negative traits on the basis that this is true of dogs:

> a projecting upper lip and gums mark the abusive (811A)
>
> if the tip of the nose is pointed, it means irascibility (811A)
>
> a smooth brow marks the flatterer (811B)
>
> fiery eyes mean impudence (808B)

Note that except for Proverbs 26:11, people are not said to be like dogs specifically in that they return to their own vomit. One of the main ways in which humans are compared to dogs is with respect to their repulsive eating habits; however, returning to their own vomit is mentioned only in Proverbs and 2 Peter.[29]

b) Comparison of Humans to Pigs

A rather elaborate instance of positive comparison of humans and pigs is found in Plutarch, *Bruta animalia ratione uti* (*Moralia* 985–992), in which

---

25. On this, see Dierauer, *Tier und Mensch*, 181.

26. 1 Sam 24:14; 2 Sam 3:8; 9:8; 16:9; 2 Kgs 8:13; Mark 7:27/Matt 15:26. The lowliness of dogs is implied in Qoh 9:4—"a living dog is better than a dead lion."

27. Ps 22:16, 20; 59:6, 14; Phil 3:3; Rev 22:15.

28. Keller (*Antike Tierwelt*, 1:98) lists some additional instances in which humans and others are called dogs either to denigrate them or to indicate their evil character; see also Dierauer, *Tier und Mensch*, 11n27.

29. The Gospel of Truth (NHC I 33:15–16) says, "Do not return to what you have vomited to eat it." This converts the description of behavior found in Proverbs and 2 Peter into a warning against that behavior, but without mentioning that this is the behavior of a dog.

Plutarch argues that pigs and other animals are rational, not irrational. In this dialogue Odysseus tries to persuade Circe to transform the humans she has turned into animals back into humans. According to the Odyssey, Circe had turned half of Odysseus's men into pigs and had earlier turned other humans into other animals. Circe tells Odysseus that she will turn them back into men if he can persuade the animals that this is best. So that Odysseus can make his argument, Circe enables one of the animals to talk.[30] This is apparently a pig called Gryllus (= grunter or pig).

Gryllus responds to Odysseus's first effort to persuade by saying that Odysseus is trying to worsen, not improve, their situation by turning them back into humans, who are the most unfortunate of all animals. Odysseus answers by suggesting that it may have been a pre-existing inclination to swinishness that caused him to become a pig (986D–E). Later, Odysseus expresses admiration of Gryllus's argumentative ability despite his present swinishness (988E–F). These are instances of the negative comparison of humans to pigs. Gryllus rejects this slur and goes on to argue that beasts surpass humans in courage. In support of this Gryllus says that courage is found among both male and female beasts and so is natural to them; he cites as an example the sow of Crommyon (987F). Gryllus also points out that poets say a man is like a boar in valor, but never that a boar is like a man in valor (988D).[31] Later, Gryllus argues that animals surpass humans in temperance. One example is that sows attract boars without the use of artificial fragrances. The two are attracted to the nuptial union by mutual affection. Both celebrate at the proper time a love without deceit or hire. After conception, they cease sexual intercourse. Nor is homosexual mating found among beasts (990C–D).[32]

Humans are compared with pigs negatively, as they are with dogs, with respect to their aggressiveness, their eating habits, and their sexual behavior. The LXX of 2 Sam 17:8 compares David's soldiers to a savage pig on the plain. In *Somn.* 2.87–89 Philo says that some humans are more fierce and malicious than wild boars. In Leviticus Rabbah 13 (114c) the pig of Leviticus 11:7 is interpreted as referring to Rome because Rome is a thief, a housebreaker, and a robber. Likewise, in Avot of Rabbi Nathan 34 the wild boar of

---

30. This ability to talk is referred to as producing and understanding speech (λόγον), something animals are ordinarily not able to do (986B).

31. Idomeneus is compared to a boar in this way in *Iliad* 13.470–75. In Pseudo-Aristotle, *Physiognomica* coarse hair is said to indicate courage as can be seen from the coarse hair of the wild boar (806B).

32. Similar positive presentations of the sexual temperance of animals, but without explicit reference to pigs, are found in Plato, *Laws* 840D–E; Philo, *De Animalibus* 48–49; Plutarch, *De amore prolis* 493E–F.

Psalm 80:13 (Hebrew v. 14) is interpreted as referring to Rome because the boar injures and kills people.[33] According to the Epistle of Barnabas 10.1–3, Moses prohibited eating pig (χοῖρον)[34] (Lev 11:7; Deut 14:8) to prohibit association with humans who are like pigs in ignoring their owner when they have food and squealing when they are hungry. In 18B (Lutz, 116–17) Musonius Rufus says that gluttons behave like pigs. In *Spec.* 3.36, 113 Philo says that those who have sexual intercourse for pleasure rather than for procreation behave like pigs.[35]

In addition to these ways of comparing humans with pigs that are similar to the ways they are compared with dogs, humans are also compared with pigs in preferring to live in dirt. In *Republic* 535E Plato says of someone who does not mind being found ignorant that he rolls in the mud of ignorance like a pig (θηρίον ὕειον) (cf. *Laws* 819D). In *Agr.* 144–45 Philo says that Moses compares sophists to swine because they are at home in a mode of life that is thick and muddy and in all that is most ugly. In *Spec.* 1.148 he says that desire like a pig rejoices to make its home in the mire. And Musonius Rufus in 12 (Lutz, 86–87) speaks of humans as being like swine and rejoicing in their own vileness. See also Horace, *Epistles* 1.2.26; 2.2.75; Epictetus 4.11.11, 29, 31. This is close to the comparison implied in 2 Peter, but it lacks the specific idea of returning to the mud after having been washed.

As is the case with comparison of humans to dogs, humans are sometimes compared with pigs without specifying the negative behavior of the pigs that the comparison presumes. Very likely the aggressiveness, shamelessness, and liking for dirt are at least part of the basis for this. Thus Proverbs 11:22 says that a beautiful woman without good sense is like a gold ring in a pig's snout.[36]

In Pseudo-Aristotle, *Physiognomica* the following physical characteristics are said to indicate negative traits on the basis that this is true of pigs:

> lips thin and hard are a sign of base breeding (811A)

---

33. Philo refers to the aggressive behavior of boars in *Prov.* 2.57; *De Animalibus* 51, 70 but without comparing it to human behavior. On the aggressive behavior of wild pigs in the ancient world, see Keller, *Antike Tierwelt*, 1:389–93.

34. That this word is synonymous with the more common ὗς/σῦς is indicated by the use of the two with the same meaning in the same context in Josephus, *Ag. Ap.* 2.137 and 141.

35. Pseudo-Aristotle, *Physiognomica* 808B says that violent sexual excitability is found in pigs.

36. Keller (*Antike Tierwelt*, 1:404) mentions a couple of instances in which humans are called pigs to denigrate them. A generally negative assessment of pigs is implied by the proverb cited by Plato (*Laches* 196D) "any pig would know."

a nose thick from the tip means dullness of sense (811A)

a small forehead means stupidity (811B)

eyebrows that droop on the nasal and rise on the temporal side indicate silliness (812B)

c) Comparison of Humans to Both Dogs and Pigs

In view of the similar ways humans are compared with dogs and pigs, it is not surprising that the two are sometimes mentioned together as they are in 2 Peter.[37] The seventh-century BCE poet Semonides speaks of ten different types of women or wives as deriving from eight different animals along with the earth and sea (Fragment 7). Two of the animals are the pig and the dog. The wife derived from the pig is dirty and eats too much. She lies in mud (βορβόρωι) throughout her house and wallows (κυλίνδεται) in it. She sits on a dunghill and grows fat. The wife derived from the dog wants to stick her nose in everything and barks incessantly. Later, the wife derived from the sea is said at times to be as ferocious as a dog with puppies.

In Matt 7:6 Jesus says, "Do not give what is holy to dogs; and do not throw your pearls before swine (χοίρων), or they will trample them under foot and turn and maul you."[38] Here the people referred to as dogs and swine are seen as like those animals in their aggressive behavior.[39] In *Epistles* 1.2.26 Horace says that Ulysses, if he had drunk from Circe's cup, would have lived like a filthy dog or a hog delighting in mire. In *Epistles* 2.2.75 he describes the busy streets of Rome by saying that here runs a mad dog, there rushes a sow begrimed with mire. Musonius Rufus in 18B (Lutz, 116–17) says that gluttons are greedy like swine or dogs. Epictetus contrasts the behavior of dog and pig, saying that the former does not roll in the mud (κυλίεται ἐν βορβόρῳ) while the latter does; humans should imitate the former (4.11.31). b. Shabb. 155b says that no one is poorer than a dog or richer than a pig; this is because no one gives food to a dog, but pigs are fattened for slaughter.

37. They are sometimes mentioned together without comparing them to human beings. In the LXX of 1 Kgs 20:19; 22:38 it says that sows and dogs eat blood; only dogs are mentioned in the Hebrew text, and the former passage is 21:19. In *De Animalibus* Philo speaks of the wild boar and dog as well as other animals. P. Oxy. 840, lines 33–34 mentions waters into which dogs and pigs are thrown day and night. On dogs and pigs, see Grant, *Early Christians and Animals*, 6–7.

38. On this verse, see Lips, "Schweine füttert man, Hunde nicht."

39. The first element of this exhortation is quoted in Didache 9:5 and applied explicitly to the Eucharist. A parallel to this first element is found in b. Bek. 15a; b. Tem. 130b. Commenting on Deut 12:15 it says that one should not release holy (food) in order to let the dogs eat it.

All of this shows that criticism of people by comparing them to dogs and pigs is rather common in the context of 2 Peter. However, the specific ways they are criticized in 2 Peter are not common. The author of 2 Peter did not originate his comparison but rather derived it from a proverb. Nevertheless, it is an unusual use of the comparison that suited the purposes of 2 Peter very well.

In 2:18–22 the author of 2 Peter warns the addressees against following the false teachers by returning to the defilements of the world after having been saved from them (v. 20). The behavior of the dog and pig mentioned in v. 22 is a very good analog to such backsliding. Having expelled something harmful from his body, the dog returns to it; having been washed clean, the sow makes herself dirty again. The washing may refer to baptism (cf. also 1:9).[40]

Conclusion

As we have seen, comparison of humans to animals is very common in the ancient world. This comparison can be neutral, simple observations of ways that humans and animals are alike. It can also be positive, a way of praising humans as superior to or for possessing the good qualities of animals. Comparison of humans with animals can also be negative, a way of criticizing humans for possessing the bad qualities or for lacking the good qualities that animals have. Second Peter's comparison of humans with animals is of this last kind. In 2 Peter 2:12, 22 the author criticizes humans for possessing bad qualities of animals; in 2 Peter 2:16 the author implicitly criticizes humans for lacking the good qualities of Balaam's donkey.

Although 2 Peter's comparison of humans to animals is generally similar to comparisons made by others, we have also seen that the specific way 2 Peter compares them is unique. No other author compares humans to irrational animals in that both are destined for capture and corruption, as 2 Peter does in 2:12. No other author has used the story of Balaam or the proverb about the dog from Proverbs 26:11 to characterize humans negatively as 2 Peter does in 2:16, 22. And finally, no other author has used the proverb from *The Story of Ahikar* 8.15/18 to describe humans' return to circumstances from which they have been rescued as 2 Peter does in 2:22.

Such negative comparison of humans to animals can be rather dangerous. Richard Sorabji has shown in detail how the idea that animals are irrational supported the conclusion that humans could make any use of

---

40. Grundmann, *Judas und Petrus*, 101.

animals they chose.[41] Comparing humans to animals might support a similar conclusion about those humans. The author of 2 Peter is certainly not drawing such conclusions himself, and his comparison of humans to animals is nuanced and complex. However, his comparison of his opponents to animals could provide the foundation for such a conclusion by others. Such a reading of 2 Peter can be seen in Robert Paul Seesengood's paper, "'Irrational Animals, Creatures of Instinct, Bred to Be Caught and Killed': Hybridity, Alterity, and Name-Calling in 2 Peter 2," presented at the 2007 annual meeting of the Society of Biblical Literature.

41. Sorabji, *Animal Minds and Human Morals*, 107–219.

9

The Gospels of Matthew and John in the Second Letter of Peter

A. The Gospel of Matthew in 2 Peter

The single most prominent way Jesus tradition appears in 2 Peter is its account of what is usually called the transfiguration of Jesus in 1:16-18. Although it is generally recognized that this is the same story as is told in Mark 9:2-8/Matt 17:1-8/Luke 9:28-36,[1] few commentators think the author of 2 Peter derives the story from one or more of these Gospels. Instead, they see 2 Peter as making independent use of the tradition that underlies the Gospels. By contrast, I will argue that 2 Peter derived its account of the transfiguration from the Gospel of Matthew.

In part, the common view may reflect the commentators' presuppositions. Those who think 2 Peter was written by Peter obviously would not think he depends on the Gospels; Peter knew the transfiguration of Jesus from his own experience.[2] Those who do not think 2 Peter was written by

---

1. There is another extensive but rather different account of the transfiguration in the Apocalypse of Peter as well as briefer accounts in Acts of Peter 20; Acts of Thomas 143; Acts of John 90; and Gospel of Philip NHC II 58:5-10; on these. see Bauckham, *Jude, 2 Peter*, 212. As in 2 Peter, the accounts of the transfiguration in the Apocalypse of Peter and the Acts of Peter are given by Peter himself. These accounts are probably dependent on that of 2 Peter.

2. I have found eight commentaries published in the twentieth and twenty-first centuries that regard 2 Peter as having been written by Peter. They are Bigg, *St. Peter and St. Jude*, 242; Wohlenberg, *Petrusbrief und Judasbrief*, xxvii; Mounce, *Living Hope*, 99; M. Green, *Peter and Jude*, 13-39; Moo, *2 Peter and Jude*, 23-24; G. Green, *Jude and 2 Peter*, 150; Harvey and Towner, *2 Peter and Jude*, 9-16; Giese, *2 Peter and Jude*, 6-11. Of course, the authorship of 2 Peter is discussed not only in commentaries but also in

Peter, but do think it was written fairly early, e.g., 60–100, might not think it depends on the Gospels because the Gospels, written at approximately the same time, would not have been available to the author of 2 Peter.

The main basis, however, on which commentators explicitly argue that 2 Peter does not derive its account of the transfiguration from the Gospels is that the account in 2 Peter differs from the accounts in the Gospels. There are many differences. The Gospel accounts, which also differ somewhat among themselves, all agree that Jesus took Peter, James, and John with him up a mountain. There, Jesus was transfigured, his clothing becoming intensely white. Moses and Elijah appeared and talked to Jesus. A cloud overshadowed them, and a voice from the cloud said, "This is my Son; listen to him."[3]

The author of 2 Peter does not specify all who accompanied Jesus, only that he himself was present along with some others. Like the accounts in the Synoptic Gospels, the author mentions that he and the other witnesses of Jesus's transfiguration were on a mountain. However, he calls it the holy mountain, a detail not found in the synoptic transfiguration accounts. The author of 2 Peter also explicitly mentions God's participation in the transfiguration, another detail absent from the synoptic accounts. The author of 2 Peter says nothing about the presence of Moses and Elijah or about the witnesses' reaction to what happened. More significantly, he mentions the transfiguration of Jesus only rather obliquely, saying that he, the author, and others were eyewitnesses of Jesus's majesty and that Jesus received honor and glory from God. This probably refers to the transformation of Jesus, i.e., something that was seen, but it is expressed in such general terms that it could simply be a reference to the words spoken by the voice. The visual dimension is indicated most directly by the author's references to glory. In comparison with the Synoptic Gospels' account of Jesus's transfiguration, however, the author of 2 Peter lets the transformation of Jesus recede into the background of the story. The visual element is apparently less important than the auditory element.

New Testament introductions and other writings, and some of these argue that Peter was the author. One example of this is Robinson, *Redating the New Testament*, 173–99. Robinson argues that Jude composed 2 Peter acting as the agent of Peter.

3. In the Apocalypse of Peter's account, Moses and Elijah appear in a glorified form, but not Jesus. After the words of the heavenly voice, Jesus, Moses, and Elijah are all taken into heaven. This account refers to the mountain of transfiguration as the holy mountain and speaks of a voice from heaven, details mentioned by 2 Peter but not found in the synoptic transfiguration accounts.

Richard J. Bauckham has argued at greatest length that 2 Peter 1:16-18 is independent of the gospel transfiguration accounts.[4] Bauckham discusses a number of differences between them like those listed above. He does not regard such differences as implying that 2 Peter's account is independent of the synoptic accounts because they could result from the author's redaction of the synoptic accounts. There are two differences, however, that he thinks show its independence. (1) While in all three synoptic accounts the voice is said to come from the cloud, in 2 Peter it is described as borne from heaven. (2) More importantly, the words of the voice in 2 Peter differ from those in the synoptic accounts. Here again Bauckham notes differences that in his estimation do not imply the independence of 2 Peter, but argues that two differences do imply independence. (a) μου (my) is repeated after ἀγαπητός (beloved) and (b) ἐν ᾧ, found in Matt 17:5, though not in Mark or Luke, has been replaced by εἰς ὃν (in whom).

Robert J. Miller has responded to Bauckham in detail, arguing that these three differences are more likely to derive from redaction of Matt 17:1-8 by the author of 2 Peter than from an independent tradition. Miller contends that these differences on which Bauckham focuses are too slight to make it more probable that 2 Peter represents an independent tradition than that it depends on the Gospel of Matthew.[5] I agree.

Neither Bauckham nor Miller discusses whether or not the Gospel of Matthew was available to the author of 2 Peter, though Miller obviously presumes that it was. I also think this probable. Their respective dates of composition do not seem to present an obstacle to use of Matthew by 2 Peter. The Gospel of Matthew was probably written 80-90. It seems to have been used by Ignatius of Antioch (e. g., *Smyrn.* 1.1 refers to Matt 3:15), who probably died c. 108. And according to the Two-Source Theory, Matthew used the Gospel of Mark which was probably written c. 70.[6]

Second Peter was probably written about 125. This is implied by the reference to Paul in 3:15-16. In 3:15 the author of 2 Peter first refers to what Paul wrote to the recipients of 2 Peter, then states that Paul says the same thing in all his letters. This implies the existence of a collection of letters of

---

4. Bauckham, *Jude, 2 Peter*, 205-10. Davids (*2 Peter and Jude*, 198-99) and G. Green (*Jude and 2 Peter*, 223-24) agree with Bauckham. Others who take a similar position include Schelkle, *Petrusbriefe*, 199n1; Kelly, *Peter and Jude*, 319; Paulsen, *Der Zweite Petrusbrief*, 118-19.

5. Miller, "Independent Attestation." Gilmour agrees with Miller (*Significance of Parallels*, 95-97, 120) as does Lee (*Jesus' Transfiguration*, 138-39). Denis Farkasfalvy has also argued that 2 Peter's account of the transfiguration is dependent on Matthew's ("Ecclesial Setting," 5-7), but he thinks 2 Peter has elements of Luke's account as well as Matthew's. Helmut Koester speaks of "written gospels" as the source of 2 Pet 1:14, 16-18 (*History and Literature*, 296); so also Trobisch, *First Edition*, 88.

6. For this dating, see Kümmel, *Introduction to the New Testament*, 119-20.

Paul. Exactly when such a collection was made is unknown. Some argue that Paul himself began such a collection.[7] Most see the collection as likely to have been made c. 100.[8] It is again Ignatius of Antioch who first refers to multiple letters of Paul (*Eph.* 12:2; *Rom.* 4:3).

In 3:16 the author of 2 Peter says that the ignorant and unstable twist difficult elements of Paul's letters as they do the other scriptures. This implies that the author of 2 Peter puts the letters of Paul into the same category as the Jewish scriptures, which were also accepted as authoritative by Christians. This presumably happened some time after the collection of Paul's letters. By c. 140 Marcion used a collection of ten letters of Paul that he regarded as authoritative. If 2 Peter was written c. 125 and the Gospel of Matthew was written 80–90, it is entirely possible that the author of 2 Peter knew the Gospel of Matthew.

It is widely acknowledged that 2 Peter 1:16–18 resembles Matt 17:1–8 more than it does the other transfiguration accounts.[9] The two accounts are most similar in reporting the words of the voice quoted in 2 Peter 1:17 and Matt 17:5.

> 2 Peter 1:17 ὁ υἱός μου ὁ ἀγαπητός μου οὗτός ἐστιν, εἰς ὃν ἐγὼ εὐδόκησα
>
> Matt 17:5 οὗτός ἐστιν ὁ υἱός μου ὁ ἀγαπητός, ἐν ᾧ εὐδόκησα

There are four differences between the two (including the two differences already mentioned above): (1) in 2 Peter οὗτός ἐστιν (this is) follows rather than precedes ὁ υἱός μου ὁ ἀγαπητός (my beloved son); (2) μου (my) is repeated after ἀγαπητός (beloved); (3) ἐν ᾧ has been replaced by εἰς ὃν (in whom); and (4) ἐγὼ (I) has been added after εἰς ὃν (in whom).[10] These differences seem more likely to reflect 2 Peter's rather free use of Matthew than its derivation from an independent tradition.[11]

---

7. Trobisch, *Paul's Letter Collection*; Murphy-O'Connor, *Paul the Letter-Writer*, 114–30.

8. E.g., Kümmel, *Introduction to the New Testament*, 480–81.

9. See, for example, Bauckham, *Jude, 2 Peter*, 148; Davids, *2 Peter and Jude*, 199; G. Green, *Jude and 2 Peter*, 223.

10. Second Peter also omits the last two words of Matt 17:5, namely ἀκούετε αὐτοῦ (hear him). As Bauckham observes (*Jude, 2 Peter*, 206–7), the words of the voice in 2 Pet 1:17 are equally close to those found in Clementine *Homilies* 3:53 (οὗτός ἐστιν μου ὁ υἱός ὁ ἀγαπητός, εἰς ὃν εὐδόκησα), which also mentions that the voice came from heaven. The fourth-century date of the Clementine *Homilies* makes it impossible for 2 Peter to be dependent on them; however, the Clementine *Homilies* could depend on 2 Peter.

11. In terms of the categories described by Vernon K. Robbins in *Exploring the Texture of Texts* and *Tapestry of Early Christian Discourse*, 2 Peter's use of Matt 17:1–8 can

It is possible to surmise why the author of 2 Peter might have made these changes. (1) The author might have put οὗτός ἐστιν after ὁ υἱός μου ὁ ἀγαπητός so that the words of the voice disclose the identity of God's son rather than the identity of Jesus as in Matthew. Since both versions identify Jesus as God's son, the difference is not great. But the words in 2 Peter can be seen as the answer to the question "Who is God's son?" while the words in Matthew answer the question "Who is Jesus?" (2) The repetition of μου after ἀγαπητός changes the latter from a simple adjective to a substantive in apposition to υἱός. This makes ἀγαπητός more emphatic. (3) Use of εἰς ὃν with εὐδοκέω rather than ἐν ᾧ is uncommon. One other place it is found is Matt 12:18. Second Peter 1:17 might have been influenced by this passage in Matthew. (4) The addition of ἐγώ puts more emphasis on the speaker, making it emphatic that God is well pleased with Jesus.

Such a free use of Matthew is consonant with other instances in which 2 Peter is thought to make use of a source. Examples of this can be seen in 2 Peter's use of use of Jude 4–18 in 2 Peter 2:1–3:3 and 2 Peter's use of Genesis 6:1–19:29 in 2 Peter 2:4–8.[12] Consider the way the author of 2 Peter used Jude 4(–5) in 2 Peter 2:1–3.

Jude 4(–5)/2 Peter 2:1–3

	2:1 Ἐγένοντο δὲ καὶ ψευδοπροφῆται ἐν τῷ λαῷ, ὡς καὶ ἐν ὑμῖν ἔσονται ψευδοδιδάσκαλοι, οἵτινες
4 παρεισέδυσαν γάρ τινες ἄνθρωποι, οἱ πάλαι προγεγραμμένοι εἰς τοῦτο τὸ κρίμα, ἀσεβεῖς, τὴν τοῦ θεοῦ ἡμῶν χάριτα μετατιθέντες εἰς ἀσέλγειαν	παρεισάξουσιν αἱρέσεις ἀπωλείας,
καὶ τὸν μόνον δεσπότην καὶ κύριον ἡμῶν Ἰησοῦν Χριστὸν ἀρνούμενοι.	καὶ τὸν ἀγοράσαντα αὐτοὺς δεσπότην ἀρνούμενοι, ἐπάγοντες ἑαυτοῖς ταχινὴν ἀπώλειαν·

---

be seen as an example of one kind of oral-scribal intertexture, specifically a recitation that uses some of the narrative words in the biblical text plus a saying from the text (*Exploring the Texture of Texts*, 42–43; *Tapestry of Early Christian Discourse*, 104–5).

12. On the former, see chapter 1, "Use of the Letter of Jude by the Second Letter of Peter."

	2:2 καὶ πολλοὶ ἐξακολουθήσουσιν αὐτῶν ταῖς ἀσελγείαις, δι' οὓς ἡ ὁδὸς τῆς ἀληθείας βλασφημηθήσεται· 2:3 καὶ ἐν πλεονεξίᾳ πλαστοῖς λόγοις ὑμᾶς ἐμπορεύσονται· οἷς τὸ κρίμα ἔκπαλαι οὐκ ἀργεῖ, καὶ ἡ ἀπώλεια αὐτῶν οὐ νυστάζει.
5 Ὑπομνῆσαι δὲ ὑμᾶς βούλομαι, εἰδότας ὑμᾶς πάντα, ὅτι [ὁ] κύριος ἅπαξ λαὸν ἐκ γῆς Αἰγύπτου σώσας τὸ δεύτερον τοὺς μὴ πιστεύσαντας ἀπώλεσεν	

The author of 2 Peter changed the aorist of Jude 4 (παρεισέδυσαν) into future tense (ἔσονται, παρεισάξουσιν) in order to transform Jude's critique of a group presently confronting its addressees into prediction of a group that will confront the addressees of 2 Peter in the future. The author of 2 Peter prefaced his condemnation of these future opponents, the false teachers, with the statement that false prophets arose among the people, i.e., the people of Israel. The author of 2 Peter also combined rewritten versions of the main clause (παρεισέδυσαν γάρ τινες ἄνθρωποι) and final participial phrase (τὸν μόνον δεσπότην καὶ κύριον ἡμῶν Ἰησοῦν Χριστὸν ἀρνούμενοι) of Jude 4 in 2 Peter 2:1; he rewrote the second participial phrase from Jude 4 (τὴν τοῦ θεοῦ ἡμῶν χάριτα μετατιθέντες εἰς ἀσέλγειαν) in 2 Peter 2:2; and he rewrote the first participial phrase from Jude 4 (οἱ πάλαι προγεγραμμένοι εἰς τοῦτο τὸ κρίμα) in 2 Peter 2:3. Second Peter's reference to the people of Israel in 2:1 and its three references to destruction of the false teachers in 2:1, 3 may have been suggested by Jude 5. This is at least as thorough a revision of Jude 4(-5) as was involved in the adaptation of Matt 17:1-8 in 2 Peter 1:16-18.[13]

Another place where Jesus tradition appears in 2 Peter is 2:20b. Here the author of 2 Peter says τὰ ἔσχατα χείρονα τῶν πρώτων (the last things [have become] worse than the first). This is a verbatim quotation (with one difference) of the words of Jesus in Matt 12:45/Luke 11:26 τὰ ἔσχατα τοῦ ἀνθρώπου ἐκείνου χείρονα τῶν πρώτων (the last things of that person [are] worse than the first). The author of 2 Peter might have derived these words from Matthew, from Luke, from the Q source on which Matthew and Luke relied, or from oral tradition. However, if 2 Peter derived its account of the

---

13. In terms of Robbins's categories, 2 Peter's use of Jude is a different kind of oral-scribal intertexture than is its use of Matt 17:1-8; 2 Peter's use of Jude can be seen as recontextualization (*Exploring the Texture of Texts*, 48–50; *Tapestry of Early Christian Discourse*, 107). In terms of the categories described by William L. Schutter in *Hermeneutic and Composition* and elaborated somewhat by John H. Elliott in *1 Peter*, 2 Peter's use of Jude can be seen as an example of citation involving a sufficient quantity of text and degree of correspondence, but without an introductory formula (*1 Peter*, 13).

transfiguration from Matthew, there is no reason to suppose that it derived these words from any other source.[14]

B. The Gospel of John in 2 Peter

The second most prominent use of Jesus tradition in 2 Peter (after the transfiguration account) is the statement in 1:14 that Jesus has revealed to Peter the imminence of his death. It seems likely that this refers to the saying of Jesus in John 21:18. In this verse Jesus says to Peter, ἀμὴν ἀμὴν λέγω σοι, ὅτε ἦς νεώτερος, ἐζώννυες σεαυτὸν καὶ περιεπάτεις ὅπου ἤθελες· ὅταν δὲ γηράσῃς, ἐκτενεῖς τὰς χεῖράς σου, καὶ ἄλλος σε ζώσει καὶ οἴσει ὅπου οὐ θέλεις. (Amen, Amen I say to you, when you were younger, you girded yourself and walked around where you wished; but when you become old, you will stretch out your hands, and another will gird you and bring you where you do not wish.) In the following verse the evangelist comments that Jesus said this to show by what kind of death Peter would glorify God.

The saying does not describe Peter's death in much detail; it mainly indicates that someone will bring Peter's life to an end against his will. Nor does it say much about the time of Peter's death, only that it will happen when Peter has grown old. Nevertheless, this saying is likely to underlie 2 Peter 1:14. It is once again Bauckham who has argued this most fully.[15] He contends that 2 Peter 1:14 presupposes there was a well-known prediction of Peter's death by Jesus and argues that John 21:18 is most likely to be that well-known prediction. Bauckham does not, however, think that the author of 2 Peter derived the prediction from the Gospel of John. Instead, he thinks the author knew the tradition underlying John.

Bauckham mentions two reasons for not thinking 2 Peter depends on John: (1) 2 Peter may be earlier in date than John, and (2) 2 Peter is far removed from John in theological character. With regard to (1), the Gospel of John was probably written no later than 110. This is implied by the existence of Papyrus 52 containing John 18:31-33, 37-38, and dated 135-50 CE, as well as a number of other somewhat later papyri containing John (Papyri 66, 75; Egerton 2). These texts make it clear that the Gospel had to have been

---

14. This falls into the same categories as 2 Peter's use of Jude; see preceding note.

15. Bauckham, *Jude, 2 Peter*, 199-201. Paulsen (*Der Zweite Petrusbrief*, 115), Davids (*2 Peter and Jude*, 195-96), and G. Green (*Jude and 2 Peter*, 212) agree with Bauckham. Bigg (*St. Peter and St. Jude*, 264) also takes this position. Hans Windisch thinks it more likely that the reference is to some other, perhaps lost, word of Jesus (*Katholische Briefe*, 88). Karl H. Schelkle suggests that there is no reference to a specific saying but only to general knowledge of nearness of death (*Petrusbriefe*, 195); Kelly (*Peter and Jude*, 313-14) takes a similar view.

written by 110 to allow time for it to reach Egypt and be circulated in several copies there.[16] As discussed above, I think 2 Peter was written about 125. Thus their dates of composition do not make it impossible for the author of 2 Peter to have known the Gospel of John. With regard to (2), the two writings are different in theological character, but they also resemble each other, at least in their Christology. Both of them assert the identity of Jesus with God (John 1:1, 18; 20:28; 2 Peter 1:1) and at the same time present Jesus as distinct from God (John 1:1-2; 2 Peter 1:2).[17]

The saying of Jesus in John 21:18 is not otherwise attested. Since there is no obstacle to use of John by the author of 2 Peter, it is simplest to suppose that the author refers to this saying as it is found in the Gospel of John.[18]

C. An Echo of the Gospel of John in 2 Peter

In light of 2 Peter's probable use of the Gospels of Matthew and John, it is reasonable to think there might be less obvious ways 2 Peter echoes one or the other. I use the word "echo" as Richard B. Hays uses it in his book *Echoes of Scripture in the Letters of Paul*. Following John Hollander, Hays uses "echo" to refer to a type of allusion in which there is a broad interplay between one text and the text it echoes.[19] I suggest that 2 Peter 1:3–11 echoes John 15:1–17.

The subject of 2 Peter 1:3–4 is τῆς θείας δυνάμεως αὐτοῦ (his divine power) in v. 3. The antecedent of αὐτοῦ (his) is probably Ἰησοῦ τοῦ κυρίου ἡμῶν (Jesus our Lord), the last substantive mentioned.[20] When it says in v. 4

---

16. This is argued by Brown, *Gospel According to John I–XII*, lxxxii–lxxxiii. Brown thinks the earliest possible date is 75 CE (*Gospel According to John I–XII*, lxxxv–lxxxvi).

17. On the Christology of 2 Peter see chapter 2, "The Christology of the Second Letter of Peter."

18. Trobisch also understands 2 Pet 1:14 as a reference to the Gospel of John (*First Edition*, 87). As noted above, Koester speaks of "written gospels" as the source of 2 Pet 1:14, 16–18 (*History and Literature*, 296). In terms of Robbins's categories, this use of John can be seen as yet another kind of oral-scribal intertexture, namely recitation of a saying using words different from the authoritative source (*Exploring the Texture of Texts*, 42; *Tapestry of Early Christian Discourse*, 104).

19. Hays, *Echoes of Scripture*, 20. Hays makes use of Hollander, *Figure of Echo*. Robbins categorizes echo as a kind of cultural intertexture (*Exploring the Texture of Texts*, 60–62; *Tapestry of Early Christian Discourse*, 110). In terms of Schutter and Elliott's categories, the ways I suggest 2 Peter echoes John can be seen as incipient allusions, dependent on an exegetical tradition for their recognition (*Hermeneutic and Composition*, 36; *1 Peter*, 14).

20. So Grundmann, *Judas und Petrus*, 69; Fornberg, *Early Church*, 144; Bauckham, *Jude, 2 Peter*, 177; Starr, *Sharers in Divine Nature*, 31–34; Davids, *2 Peter and Jude*,

that "he" has given precious and very great promises, the antecedent of "he" is again probably Jesus. The remainder of v. 4 says that he has given these promises in order that through them the addressees might become θείας κοινωνοὶ φύσεως (sharers of divine nature). Thus the ultimate content of the promises is that their recipients become sharers of divine nature.

There is no other text known to me in which Jesus is said to promise or promises that people will become sharers of divine nature. It is seldom said in early Christian literature that Jesus makes promises (one instance is 2 Clem. 5.5) and nowhere that he promises sharing in divine nature. This raises the question on what basis 2 Peter presents Jesus as making such promises. I suggest that 2 Peter is paraphrasing the statements of Jesus in the Gospel of John that Jesus's disciples are in him (ἐν ἐμοί), especially as they are found in John 15:1–17. Second Peter uses entirely different language than is found in John. If 2 Peter is dependent on John, it is not primarily a linguistic dependence. The main argument for seeing dependence here is that it offers the best explanation of where and when the author of 2 Peter understood Jesus as making the promises to which he refers. However, there are also some more explicit connections between John 15:1–17 and 2 Peter 1:3–11 that lend support to this hypothesis.

In John 6:56 Jesus says, "The one who eats my flesh and drinks my blood remains in me and I in him (ἐν ἐμοὶ μένει κἀγὼ ἐν αὐτῷ)." In John 14:20 Jesus says, "On that day you will know that I am in my Father and you in me and I in you (ὑμεῖς ἐν ἐμοὶ κἀγὼ ἐν ὑμῖν)." This language is most concentrated in John 15:1–17, Jesus's extended presentation of himself as the true vine and his followers as branches of the vine. He refers to the branches as being "in me" in v. 2; urges them to remain "in me" twice in v. 4; and discusses the implications of remaining "in me" in vv. 5–7. He then urges his disciples to remain "in my love" in vv. 9–10.

These sayings of Jesus in the Gospel of John do not take the form of promises, i. e., statements about what will happen in the future. Rather, they are descriptions of an existing state—being in Jesus—often coupled with an exhortation to remain in that state. However, they can be understood as implicit promises of what results from association with Jesus, from faith in him. In speaking to those who have already believed, Jesus speaks of this promise as already having been fulfilled for them.

---

168. Kelly disagrees (*Peter and Jude*, 300); likewise G. Green understands the antecedent as θεοῦ (*Jude and 2 Peter*, 181). Ceslas Spicq understands the passage as speaking about Jesus's divine power and his call of the author and addressees, but argues that this should not be seen as asserting anything other than that God was working through Jesus (*Épitres de Saint Pierre*, 210).

It is reasonable to suppose that the author of 2 Peter would understand Jesus's speech in John about being and remaining in him as a matter of sharing in divine nature because the author of 2 Peter regards Jesus as God (1:1) and sees Jesus as having divine power (1:3). Thus being in Jesus is sharing in the divine nature of Jesus. It seems that the author of John might agree with this because John regards Jesus as the incarnation of the Word (John 1:14) who is God (1:1, 18; 20:28).

The language in which 2 Peter expresses this idea might have come from combining Paul with John. As we have seen, 2 Peter knows the letters of Paul (3:15-16). Second Peter might reasonably see Paul's language about being in Christ (ἐν Χριστῷ) or in the Lord (ἐν κυρίῳ)[21] as equivalent to Jesus's talk in John about his disciples' being in him. And Paul sometimes expresses the idea of being in Christ as a matter of sharing (κοινωνίαν) in Christ (1 Cor 1:9; 10:16; Phil 3:10).[22]

As we have noted, Jesus's speech in John about his disciples' being in him presumes that the promise of union with Jesus has already been kept for them. Somewhat similarly, 2 Peter 1:4 does not clearly indicate when the promise of sharing in divine nature will be kept. Perhaps the author thinks it has already been kept for those he addresses. In light of 2 Peter as a whole, however, we might suppose that this promise will be kept when the promise (ἐπαγγελία) of Jesus's parousia is kept (3:4; cf. 1:16), when Jesus's followers will enter Jesus's eternal kingdom (1:11). If the author of 2 Peter understands Jesus's promise of sharing in divine nature as having been made in John 15:1-17, he may see the eschatological dimension of this promise in the statement that branches not remaining in Jesus and bearing fruit will be cast into fire (John 15:6).[23] The author of 2 Peter may see this as happening when the world is destroyed by fire (2 Peter 3:7, 10-12).

Support for the idea that 2 Peter 1:3-11 echoes John 15:1-17 is provided by more explicit connections between the two. Taking them in the order in which they appear in 2 Peter, the first of these is that both passages put great emphasis on ἀγάπη (love). In 2 Peter 1:5-7 love is the final rung on the ladder of virtues that the addressees are urged to ascend because of what Jesus has done for them (φιλαδελφία [brotherly love] is the penultimate

---

21. On these phrases, see Best, *One Body in Christ*, 1-33; Fitzmyer, *Paul and His Theology*, 89-90; Dunn, *Theology of Paul the Apostle*, 396-401. Fitzmyer counts 165 instances of these phrases in the letters of Paul, including the phrase "in him," where the antecedent of "him" is Christ. Dunn counts 83 instances of "in Christ" and 47 of "in the Lord."

22. On the similarity between 2 Peter and Paul in this respect, see Starr, *Sharers in Divine Nature*, 189-203.

23. Cf. the similar picture in Matt 3:10/Luke 3:9 and Matt 7:19.

rung). In John 15:9-17 Jesus's exhortation to remain in him is followed by the exhortation to remain in his love (vv. 9-10) by keeping his commandment (v. 10) that his disciples love one another as Jesus has loved them (vv. 12-17).[24]

The second more explicit connection between the two passages is that both speak of the need to bear καρπός (fruit). Second Peter 1:8 says that those who ascend the ladder of virtue will not be ἀκάρπους (fruitless). John 15:1-17 discusses extensively the need for the branches remaining in Jesus, the true vine, to bear fruit. If a branch does not bear fruit, it is removed (v. 2). A branch cannot bear fruit if it does not remain in the vine (vv. 4-5). Bearing fruit is equivalent to being a disciple and glorifies Jesus's father (v. 8). Jesus has chosen his disciples to bear lasting fruit (v. 16).[25]

The third more explicit connection between the two passages is that both speak of cleansing/pruning. Second Peter 1:9 says that those who do not ascend the ladder of virtue have forgotten the καθαρισμοῦ (cleansing) of past sins. John 15:2-3 says that Jesus's father καθαίρει (prunes) the branches in the true vine, Jesus, so that they will bear more fruit (v. 2). Jesus says that his disciples are already καθαροί (pruned/cleansed) because of the word Jesus has spoken to them (v. 3).

A fourth explicit connection between the two passages is that both speak of Jesus's election of his followers. Second Peter 1:10 says that ascending the ladder of virtue makes one's ἐκλογήν (election) secure. In John 15:16 Jesus says that he has ἐξελεξάμην (chosen) his disciples.[26]

---

24. Love is also prominent elsewhere in 2 Peter and John. Second Peter uses ἀγάπη only in 1:7, but uses the cognate adjective ἀγαπητός (beloved) six times, describing God's attitude toward Jesus (1:17) and the author's attitude toward those he addresses (3:1, 8, 14, 17) and toward Paul (3:15). In John the Father's love for Jesus, mentioned in 15:9, also appears in 3:35; 10:17; 17:23, 24, 26. Jesus's love for his disciples, also mentioned in 15:9, also appears in 11:5; 13:1, 23; 14:21; 19:26; 21:7, 20. Jesus's command that his disciples love one another as he has loved them, found in John 15:12, 17, is also reported in 13:34-35. In addition, John speaks of God's love for the world in 3:16; Jesus's love for the Father in 14:31; the need to love Jesus in 8:42; 14:15, 21, 23, 24, 28; and the Father's love for those who do in 14:21, 23; 17:23.

Love is also prominent in the letters of Paul, above all in 1 Corinthians 13. Cf. also Paul's statement that love fulfills the whole law in Rom 13:8-10; Gal 5:14.

25. Use of "bearing fruit" as a metaphor for virtuous living is very common in the New Testament. It is found in Matt 3:8-10/Luke 3:8-9; Matt 7:16-20/Luke 6:43-45; Matt 12:33; in the parable of the sower and its interpretation in Mark 4:1-9, 13-20/Matt 13:1-9, 18-23/Luke 8:4-8, 11-15; in the parable of the weeds in Matt 13:24-30; Luke 13:6-10; John 12:24; 1 Cor 14:14; Gal 5:22-23; Eph 5:9-11; Phil 1:11, 22; Titus 3:14; Heb 12:11; 13:15; Jas 3:17-18; Jude 12.

26. Does 2 Pet 1:9 (τυφλός, ἁμαρτιῶν) also echo John 9:40-41 (τυφλοί, ἁμαρτίαν)? Does 2 Pet 1:9-10 (τυφλός, πταίσητε) also echo Matt 15:14 (τυφλοί, πεσοῦνται)?

Indirect support for the idea that 2 Peter 1:3–11 echoes John 15:1–17 is provided by other ways 2 Peter 1:3–11 may echo the Gospel of John. Second Peter 1:3 says that Jesus's divine power has given author and addressees all things for life through full knowledge of the one who called them, i. e., Jesus. On the assumption that "full knowledge" is closely related to faith, this statement may echo statements in John about the relationship between faith and life. Faith is said to lead to life in John 20:31, and to eternal life in John 3:15, 16, 36; 5:24; 6:40, 47. This connection between faith and life probably also underlies the statements that the water Jesus gives will become a spring of water gushing up to eternal life (John 4:14), that the Son of Man will give food that endures for eternal life (John 6:27), etc.

Second Peter 1:3 also says that Jesus called the author and addressees through his glory. This may echo the emphasis on Jesus's glory in the Gospel of John. In John the glory of Jesus is first mentioned in 1:14, and is subsequently mentioned another sixteen times.[27]

Second Peter 1:4 speaks of escaping the corruption in the world (cf. also the defilements of the world mentioned in 2:20). This may echo the presentation of the world as hostile to Jesus and his followers in the Gospel of John. This theme is first announced in John 1:10, which says that the world did not know the Word; it appears most strongly in statements that the world hates Jesus and his followers (John 7:7; 15:18–19; 17:14). It is expressed in other ways another fourteen times.[28]

Hays lists seven tests for the presence of an echo:[29]

1. Availability of the proposed source of the echo
2. Volume—degree of explicit repetition of words or syntactical patterns as well as prominence of source text and rhetorical stress on echo
3. Recurrence—how often is source text cited
4. Thematic coherence—how well does echo fit into line of argument
5. Historical plausibility
6. History of interpretation

---

27. See John 2:11; 5:44; 7:39; 8:54; 11:4; 12:16, 23, 41; 13:31, 32; 16:14; 17:1, 5, 10, 22, 24.

28. See John 1:29; 8:23; 12:31; 14:17, 27, 30; 16:8, 11, 20, 33; 17:9, 16, 25; 18:36.

29. Hays, *Echoes of Scripture*, 29–32. A more recent discussion of these same criteria can be found in Huizenga, *New Isaac*, 58–65. A somewhat different list of criteria is found in MacDonald, *Mimesis and Intertextuality*, 2–3.

7. Satisfaction

I have argued that 2 Peter was written long enough after the Gospel of John that the latter could have been available to the author of 2 Peter (1). I have shown above that there is a significant volume of verbal connection between John 15:1–17 and 2 Peter 1:3–11. Both passages are prominent in the respective writings of which they are part (2). I do not perceive echoes of John 15:1–17 in any other part of 2 Peter, but I have identified another citation of John in 2 Peter and will mention a possible third citation below; I have also noted possible echoes of other parts of John in 2 Peter 1:3–11 (3). I have tried to show that this echo fits very well into the argument of 2 Peter 1:3–11 (4) and contributes to a satisfactory understanding of the passage (7). To me it seems plausible that second-century readers/hearers of 2 Peter who were familiar with the Gospel of John would have heard the echo of John 15:1–17 in 2 Peter 1:3–11 for which I have argued (5). However, I am not aware that anyone has previously suggested the presence of this echo (6).

D. Another Echo of the Gospel(s) of John and/or Matthew in 2 Peter

I suggest that 2 Peter 2:1 echoes the accounts of Peter's denial of Jesus found in the Gospels of Matthew and John. Second Peter 2:1 describes the false teachers as τὸν ἀγοράσαντα αὐτοὺς δεσπότην ἀρνούμενοι (denying the master who purchased them). The master is Jesus; he purchased the false teachers by his death. This may echo the story that Peter denied (ἠρνήσατο) Jesus as Jesus was being condemned to death (Matt 26:70, 72; John 18:25, 27; see also Mark 14:68, 70; Luke 22:57). Since this story is found in all four Gospels, 2 Peter could echo any of them. But since there is reason to think 2 Peter knew and used the Gospels of Matthew and John, it is most parsimonious to presume that the author echoes one or both of them in 2:1.

This echo provides a nice irony in which Peter accuses the false teachers of the very sin of which he himself was guilty. Having made the same mistake himself, Peter is well able to understand how the false teachers have gone wrong.

The author of 2 Peter has taken this reference to denying Jesus from Jude 4, but has modified it in ways that make it conform more fully to Peter's denial of Jesus. Jude 4 speaks of τὸν μόνον δεσπότην καὶ κύριον ἡμῶν Ἰησοῦν Χριστὸν ἀρνούμενοι (denying our only master and lord Jesus Christ). This contains the basic idea of denying Jesus. But 2 Peter 2:1

changes this into τὸν ἀγοράσαντα αὐτοὺς δεσπότην ἀρνούμενοι (denying the master who purchased them). Adding the description of the master as the one who purchased them heightens the treachery of their denial. But it also makes their denial more like that of Peter, who denied Jesus as he was being condemned to death.

E. Concluding Comments

The idea that 2 Peter used Matt 17:1–8 in 2 Peter 1:16–18, Matt 12:45 in 2 Peter 2:20b, and John 21:18 in 2 Peter 1:14 adds to our picture of the early church. It entails that the Gospels of Matthew and John were known to the author of 2 Peter. It is explicit in 2 Peter 3:15–16 that the author knows a collection of Paul's letters and regards them as scripture. We can also say that he knows of at least two of the Gospels that later were regarded as scripture.

The perception of an echo of John 15:1–17 in 2 Peter 1:3–11 answers a central question raised by the latter passage, namely, when did Jesus promise that his followers would be sharers in divine nature? However, the perception of the echo also illuminates the passage in various other ways. Most importantly, it helps to explain what is meant by sharing in divine nature. Understood as an echo of John 15:1–17, sharing in divine nature can be understood as meaning union with Jesus, whose nature is divine.

The perception of an echo of Matthew and/or John in 2 Peter 2:1 adds an ironic dimension to our understanding of the latter passage.

10

Faith and Faithfulness in 2 Peter

The Second Letter of Peter has little to say explicitly about either faith or faithfulness. It does, however, speak of what is meant by "faith" and "faithfulness" in what it says about knowledge and virtue.

Faith as Knowledge

Faith is mentioned rather seldom in 2 Peter—πίστις (faith) is used twice, in 1:1, 5; πιστεύω (to believe) and πιστός (faithful) are not used at all.[1] The two references to faith are rather prominent, however. The first is in the first verse of the letter; the second reference makes faith the first rung on the ladder of virtue in 1:5-7.

By contrast, with its infrequent references to faith, 2 Peter very frequently speaks of knowledge—ἐπίγνωσις (full knowledge) is used four times (1:2, 3, 8; 2:20); ἐπιγινώσκω (to know fully) is used twice (both in 2:21); γνῶσις (knowledge) is used three times (1:5, 6; 3:18); γνωρίζω (to make known) is used once (1:16); γινώσκω (to know) is used twice (1:20; 3:3); the synonym οἶδα (to know) is used three times (1:12, 14; 2:9); the

---

1. These words constitute .18 percent of the words found in 2 Peter (2/1098). This is less than any other non-narrative writing of the NT except 2 John, which does not use the words at all. Among narrative writings of the NT, Revelation, Matthew, Luke and Mark use these words less frequently than 2 Peter; these words constitute .12 percent of Revelation (12/9834); .13 percent of Matthew (24/18,305); .13 percent of Luke (26/19,428); and .17 percent of Mark (19/11,242). On the other hand, these words are used more frequently by Acts (.3 percent [56/18,382]) and John (.64 percent [99/15,416]). Among non-narrative writings, the lowest incidence of these words after 2 Peter is found in 2 Corinthians (.25 percent [11/4469]); the highest is found in 1 Timothy (2.08 percent [33/1588]). Statistics are based on Morgenthaler, *Statistik*.

antonym ἀγνοέω (to be ignorant) is used once (2:12); the antonym ἀμαθής (ignorant) is used once (3:16). To these can be added the reference to forgetting (λήθην λαβών), another antonym of knowing, in 1:9, and uses of words referring to remembrance, another synonym of knowledge—ὑπομιμνῄσκω (to remind) in 1:12, its cognates ὑπόμνησις (remembrance) in 1:13; 3:1 and μνήμη (remembrance) in 1:15; and a verb cognate to the last of these, μιμνῄσκομαι (to remember), in 3:2. Yet another antonym of knowing, λανθάνω (to escape the notice of), is used in 3:5, 8.[2]

There is reason to think that 2 Peter sees a close relationship between faith and knowledge and speaks of the former mainly by speaking about the latter. The most direct indication of this is found in 1:1-7. In v. 1 the letter is addressed to those who have received πίστις (faith) equal in honor to ours (= Simeon Peter, the sender of the letter, along with unspecified others).[3] In v. 2 the sender wishes that favor and peace may be multiplied for the addressees by ἐπίγνωσις (full knowledge) of God and Jesus. In v. 3 the sender refers to Jesus's having given him and the addressees all things for life and piety through ἐπίγνωσις (full knowledge) of the one who called them, i.e., Jesus. In vv. 5-7 the sender of the letter says that since Jesus has done this, the addressees should ascend a ladder of virtues whose first rung is πίστις (faith).

This alternation of the terms "faith" and "full knowledge" does not explicitly equate the two. However, faith at least has a cognitive element; one must know what one believes.[4] And going immediately from speaking about the reception of faith in 1:1 (presupposed in v. 5) to speaking about full knowledge as the means by which favor and peace are multiplied and Jesus has given all things for life and piety suggests that full knowledge is nearly synonymous with faith for 2 Peter. If this is so, 2 Peter seems to see the cognitive element of faith as its most important aspect. This can be seen as a reconfiguration of the characteristically Jewish term "faith" into the more Hellenistic term "knowledge."[5]

---

2. These words constitute 2.28 percent of the words found in 2 Peter (25/1098); they are used twelve times more often than the words for faith.

3. I do not think that 2 Peter was actually written by Peter; I regard it as having been written by an unknown author who composed the letter as a testament of Peter, probably in about 125 CE.

4. Faith is virtually identified with knowledge in Jas 2:19, where it is understood as meaning only such affirmation of the existence of God as that made by demons.

5. For general discussion of 2 Peter's relationship to its environment see Fornberg, *Early Church*. Cf. also Gerdmar, *Rethinking the Judaism-Hellenism Dichotomy*. On the meaning of faith, see Bultmann, "πιστεύω κτλ"; Bultmann discusses Philo on 201-2. Note also Bultmann's comments on the relationship between faith and knowledge in the Gospel of John (226-27).

This reconfiguration may have been necessary because in a Hellenistic context "faith" could be taken to mean "opinion" as opposed to "knowledge," i.e., an inferior way of knowing. Thus in *Resp.* 7.533E–534A Plato speaks of faith as one of two kinds of opinion (δόξα), contrasting them with two kinds of intellection (νόησις); cf. also *Resp.* 6.511D-E; *Tim.* 29C. A different view of faith can be seen in the writings of the Hellenistic Jew Philo of Alexandria. Despite Philo's dependence on Plato, under the influence of the Jewish Scriptures, Philo regards faith as the highest kind of knowledge.[6] For example, in *Ebr.* 40 Philo equates faith with knowledge (ἐπιστήμη), and unbelief (ἀπιστία) with having false opinion (ψευδοδοκέω). And in *Abr.* 271 Philo parallels faith in God with sound sense (φρόνησις) and wisdom (σοφία). In *Virt.* 216 Philo describes Abraham's faith as a matter of knowing the truth that there is one cause above all and that this cause provides for the world and all that is in it (cf. also *Prov.* 2.72). The author of 2 Peter expresses an understanding similar to this by speaking of knowledge rather than faith.

On the other hand, faith and knowledge are not completely synonymous for the author of 2 Peter; both terms are included in the ladder of virtues in 1:5–7. At least in this context there is a distinction between them. We will consider the nature of the distinction below. In general, however, it seems that the author of 2 Peter speaks of knowledge where someone writing in a Jewish context would have spoken of faith.

The two references to faith in 2 Peter give no indication as to what might be the object or content of faith. Likewise, some references to knowledge do not specify its content (e.g., 1:5–6). Many of the references to knowledge, however, do indicate its content. Taken together, these provide a rather full picture of the way 2 Peter conceives this knowledge. It is first described as knowledge of "God and Jesus our Lord" (1:2). It is next described as knowledge of "the one who called us by his glory and virtue" (1:3), i.e., Jesus. In 1:8 it is described as knowledge of "our Lord Jesus Christ," and in 2:20 and 3:18 as knowledge of "our Lord and savior Jesus Christ."

Thus the knowledge with which 2 Peter is concerned is primarily knowledge of Jesus. It is knowledge that Jesus is Lord,[7] that he possesses glory and virtue,[8] that he is Christ,[9] that he is savior,[10] and that he has

---

6. On this, see Wolfson, *Philo*, 1:143–54, esp. 151–54.

7. In addition to the passages already mentioned, Jesus is called Lord in 1:11, 14, 16, and probably 3:2.

8. The glory of Jesus is also mentioned in 1:17; 3:18.

9. In addition to the passages already mentioned, Jesus is called Christ in 1:1 (twice), 11, 14, 16.

10. In addition to the passages already mentioned, Jesus is called Savior in 1:11 and probably 3:2.

called the author and addressees. All of these attributes of Jesus describe him as savior. Jesus is Lord because he is the master who purchased his followers (2:1). "Christ" (= messiah) identifies Jesus as the fulfillment of Israel's hopes for salvation. Jesus's glory and virtue are the means by which he has called his followers; 1:10-11 implies that this is a call to enter "the eternal kingdom of our Lord and savior Jesus Christ." Referring to the danger of forgetting the cleansing of past sins (1:9) suggests that knowledge of this cleansing of sins is another way to describe knowledge of the salvation accomplished by Jesus.

Most of this knowledge of Jesus as savior is knowledge of what Jesus has done in the past or is now doing. However, the idea that knowledge of Jesus as savior is knowledge that he has called people to enter his eternal kingdom indicates that this knowledge includes things that will happen in the future. This is explicit in 1:16, where the author speaks of having made known the power and coming of Jesus; knowledge of Jesus includes knowledge that he will come again. The knowledge of Jesus's second coming entails knowledge of the nature of scriptural prophecy that foretells it (1:20). Therefore the author writes to arouse the addressees to remember the words spoken by the prophets (3:1-2), and he says that those who twist the meaning of Scripture are ignorant (3:16). Knowledge of Jesus's second coming includes knowledge that in the last days scoffers will question it (3:3). The destruction of the world in the time of Noah escapes the notice of these scoffers (3:5-6); it should not escape the addressees' notice that time is different for God than for humans (3:8).[11]

Knowledge of Jesus also includes knowledge of how to live virtuously; thus in 2:20-21 knowledge of "our Lord and savior Jesus Christ" is parallel to knowing the way of justice. In 2:20 the author speaks of escaping the defilements of the world by full knowledge of Jesus and again being implicated in them; in 2:21 he speaks of fully knowing the way of justice and turning away. Full knowledge of Jesus seems to be equivalent to full knowledge of the way of justice, at least in some measure. The phrase "way of justice" makes use of the common metaphor in which a pattern of behavior is visualized as a road one travels. And in 2:21 the way of justice is parallel to the holy commandment. The verse speaks first of fully knowing the way of justice and then of turning away from the holy commandment, apparently equating the two. The holy commandment is the commandment to follow the way of justice. Therefore the author writes to arouse in the addressees' memory to remember the commandment of their apostles (3:1-2). In the references to

---

11. According to 1:14, Peter knows that his death is imminent because Jesus has revealed it to him. This is a more personal knowledge of the future that is part of Peter's knowledge of Jesus.

knowledge and remembrance of "these things" in 1:12–15, the antecedent of "these things" is probably the need for virtue argued in 1:3–11.

Another way in which knowledge of Jesus includes knowledge of how to live virtuously is that Jesus himself has acted virtuously. It is partly because Jesus is characterized by justice (1:1) that knowledge of him is knowing the way of justice. Because Jesus has called his followers by means of his virtue (1:3), they know what virtue is.

Faithfulness as Virtue

Although 2 Peter does not speak of faithfulness, it has much to say about virtue and vice. It seems that in 2 Peter faithfulness is spoken of as virtuous living.

Second Peter uses δικαιοσύνη (justice) as a general name for virtue.[12] As we have just noted, δικαιοσύνη characterizes "our God and savior Jesus Christ" (1:1). Jesus's δικαιοσύνη is manifested in giving everyone faith equal in honor, i.e., treating them fairly and without favoritism.[13] Noah, who was saved from the flood, was a herald of δικαιοσύνη (2:5).[14] As we have seen, Christian life can be called the way of δικαιοσύνη (2:21). The new heavens and earth that the followers of Jesus await will be a world in which δικαιοσύνη dwells (3:13). In 1:13 the author describes his own behavior as δίκαιος (just), and in 2:7–8 he refers to Lot as δίκαιος. The author seems to see Lot as a type of those he addresses. Just as Lot was saved from Sodom and Gomorrah when the cities were destroyed by fire, the addressees will be saved when the present heavens and earth are destroyed by fire. Like them, Lot was a just man living among those engaged in licentiousness and lawless deeds. The author of 2 Peter describes those he criticizes as ἄδικος (unjust) in 2:9 and speaks of their ἀδικία (injustice) in 2:13, 15.

Δικαιοσύνη is the opposite of the lawlessness that characterizes the residents of Sodom and Gomorrah (ἄθεσμος, 2:7; ἄνομος, 2:8), Balaam (παρανομία, 2:16) and those who threaten the addressees (ἄθεσμος, 3:17).[15]

Despite using δικαιοσύνη as a general name for the virtue that should characterize Christians, in 1:3–11, the author's most extensive description

---

12. On δικαιοσύνη, see Schrenk, "δίκη κτλ," 192–210.

13. Bigg, *St. Peter and St. Jude*, 250; Kelly, *Peter and Jude*, 297; Bauckham, *Jude, 2 Peter*, 168.

14. Philo says that Noah was saved from the destruction of the deluge because of his justice (*Abr.* 56; *Praem.* 22).

15. On the relationship between justice and observance of the law, see Schrenk, "δίκη κτλ," 192–93.

of this virtue, he uses different terms. In 1:1 the author had said that the addressees received faith by the δικαιοσύνη of Jesus. In v. 3 the author says that Jesus has called him and the addressees through his glory and ἀρετή (virtue), using ἀρετή as a synonym for δικαιοσύνη. This can be seen as the author's reconfiguration of δικαιοσύνη, a term characteristic of Jewish writers, into ἀρετή, a characteristically Hellenistic term for excellence connoting excellence that is recognized and honored.[16]

Of course, δικαιοσύνη is also a very prominent term in the ethical reflections of Greek writers. It is sometimes used as a term for virtue in general, but it is most frequently seen as a specific virtue, i.e., that virtue by which a person receives what is due to him or her.[17] In the Greek translation of the Hebrew Bible, and in works dependent on it, δικαιοσύνη is a general term for virtue, but virtue understood as God's saving fidelity to his covenant with Israel and Israel's corresponding fidelity to the will of God.[18] This understanding of δικαιοσύνη would probably not be immediately apparent in a Hellenistic context, and this may make ἀρετή a better term than δικαιοσύνη for 2 Peter's purposes. Ἀρετή does not connote God's fidelity or humans' doing of God's will, but it does indicate virtue in general without the specific connotation of acting equitably that is often carried by δικαιοσύνη.

The reconfiguration of δικαιοσύνη into ἀρετή is peculiar to 1:3-11; ἀρετή appears only here in 2 Peter (in vv. 3, 5). In the remainder of the letter, as we have seen, the author reverts to the language of δικαιοσύνη. In other parts of the letter, however, the author also uses εὐσέβεια (piety) as a synonym for δικαιοσύνη. This may already be intimated in 1:3, where the author says that Jesus has given the author and addressees all things for life and εὐσέβεια, suggesting that εὐσέβεια is a general name for virtue. The author's use of justice and piety as synonyms is most explicit in 2:5-9. In v. 9 the author contrasts the εὐσεβής (pious) with the ἄδικος (unjust), clearly implying that piety and justice are the same thing. This contrast sums up the earlier contrast between, on the one hand, Noah as the herald of justice (v. 5) and the just Lot (three times in vv. 7-8), and, on the other hand, the world of the ἀσεβής (impious) destroyed by the flood (v. 5) and the fate of the impious of which Sodom and Gomorrah are an example (v.

---

16. On the meaning of ἀρετή, see Danker, *Benefactor*, 318; Neyrey, *2 Peter, Jude*, 156. In the NT apart from 2 Peter, ἀρετή is used only in Phil 4:8; 1 Pet 2:9. This and other such reconfigurations had earlier occurred among Hellenistic Jews such as Philo.

17. Schrenk, "δίκη κτλ," 193. This meaning of δικαιοσύνη seems to inform 2 Pet 1:1 to some degree. Aristotle discusses justice at some length in *Eth. nic.* 5.1-7.

18. Schrenk, "δίκη κτλ," 195-96. It is used in this sense in NT literature, especially the Gospel of Matthew and the letters of Paul.

6). Somewhat similarly, in 3:7–13 the author says that the end of this world will be the destruction of the impious (v. 7); it is necessary to have pieties (v. 11) because we await a new world in which justice dwells (v. 13).[19]

According to Werner Foerster, εὐσέβεια means reverence for divinities, cultic worship of them, and respect for the order sustained by them.[20] In 2 Peter εὐσέβεια is especially the opposite of the slander that characterizes the false teachers. In 2:10 the false teachers are said to slander the glorious ones. In 2:12 the false teachers are said to slander what they do not understand, probably expressing in different words the same idea as 2:10. By contrast, in 2:11 the angels are said to refrain from slanderous judgment of the false teachers. According to 2:2, because many will follow the false teachers, the way of truth will be slandered.[21]

Like ἀρετή, εὐσέβεια and ἐγκράτεια (self-control), two of the other terms used for virtues in 1:5–7, correspond to the terminology of Hellenistic popular philosophy and are rare in the NT, though they are also found in early Christian literature outside the NT.[22] Use of εὐσέβεια and ἐγκράτεια can be seen as a development and particularization of the reconfiguration of δικαιοσύνη into Hellenistic terms. Ἐγκράτεια is not used elsewhere in 2 Peter, but as we have seen, εὐσέβεια is used elsewhere, as are antonyms of both. In this way, the reconfiguration of δικαιοσύνη into Hellenistic terms is found throughout 2 Peter.

As we have already seen, 2 Peter not only reconfigures δικαιοσύνη into Hellenistic terms but continues to speak of δικαιοσύνη. Similarly, 2 Peter uses other terms for virtue that are not derived from Hellenistic popular philosophy. These include ὑπομονή (endurance), φιλαδελφία (brotherly love), and ἀγάπη (love). The first of these, ὑπομονή, was a recognized virtue in Hellenistic culture, but was also important in Judaism and

---

19. Danker (*Benefactor*, 343) suggests that εὐσέβεια generally refers to attitudes or performance relative to gods or other authority figures, while δικαιοσύνη refers to conduct relative to people in general. In view of 2 Peter's use of the terms as synonyms, this distinction does not seem to be operative in 2 Peter.

20. Foerster, "σέβομαι κτλ," 178.

21. Throughout 2 Peter, the author uses conventional vituperation to characterize the false teachers; on this, see G. Green, *Jude and 2 Peter*, 20–22. This makes it somewhat uncertain to what extent he represents their behavior accurately. However, there is no uncertainty about the values of the author.

22. Bauckham, *Jude, 2 Peter*, 174–75; on ἐγκράτεια, see Grundmann, "ἐγκράτεια κτλ." Aristotle discusses ἐγκράτεια at some length in *Eth. nic.* 7.1–11. In the NT apart from 2 Peter, εὐσέβεια is found only in Acts 3:12 and the Pastoral Epistles (1 Tim 2:2; 3:16; 4:7, 8; 6:3, 5, 6, 11; 2 Tim 3:5; Titus 1:1), and ἐγκράτεια is found only in Acts 24:25; Gal 5:23. However, the cognate verb (ἐγκρατεύομαι) is also found in 1 Cor 7:9; 9:25, and the cognate adjective (ἐγκρατής) is found in Titus 1:8.

early Christianity and not as a borrowing from Hellenism.[23] The last two, φιλαδελφία and ἀγάπη, are distinctively Christian. In Hellenistic literature φιλαδελφία is used to refer to love among family members; Christian use of it to refer to love among Christians is something new.[24] Likewise, Christian emphasis on ἀγάπη is peculiar to Christianity.[25]

The ladder of virtue presented in 1:5-7 includes eight virtues. Four of them have already been discussed at some length: πίστις (faith), ἀρετή (virtue), and γνῶσις (knowledge), the first three listed, and εὐσέβεια (piety), which is the sixth. The remaining four are: ἐγκράτεια (self-control), ὑπομονή (endurance), φιλαδελφία (brotherly love), and ἀγάπη (love). None of these is mentioned elsewhere in 2 Peter, but all are illuminated by use of related words, synonyms, and/or antonyms in other places.

Ἐγκράτεια (self-control) can be understood in relation to the topic of ἐπιθυμία (desire) in 2 Peter.[26] Ἐπιθυμία is the source of the corruption in the world (1:4; cf. 2:10; 3:3), and ἐπιθυμία can tempt those who have escaped corruption to embrace it again (2:18). Ἐγκράτεια is self-control in the face of ἐπιθυμία.

The main kind of ἐπιθυμία the author of 2 Peter has in view seems to be inordinate sexual desire, i.e., ἀσέλγεια (licentiousness).[27] Ἀσέλγεια is equated with ἐπιθυμία in 2:18. The false teachers are also said to be licentious in 2:2. In 2:7 licentiousness is said to characterize Sodom and Gomorrah. In 2:14 the false teachers are described as having eyes full of an adulteress. However, the author may also be thinking of other kinds of ἐπιθυμία, namely πλεονεξία (greed) and τρυφή (luxuriousness).[28] According to the author of 2 Peter, the false teachers are characterized by greed (2:3, 14) and they regard luxuriousness during the day a pleasure (2:13).

Ὑπομονή (endurance) is synonymous with being established in the truth (1:12) and having stability (3:17). The opposite is the instability that

23. Bauckham, *Jude, 2 Peter*, 186; Davids, *2 Peter and Jude*, 181. Apart from 2 Peter, ὑπομονή is used thirty times in the NT; the cognate verb ὑπομένω is used seventeen times.

24. According to Hans Freiherr von Soden, there are no examples of this usage outside Christian writings ("ἀδελφός κτλ," 146; cf. also Davids, *2 Peter and Jude*, 182-83). In the NT apart from 2 Peter, φιλαδελφία is used in Rom 12:10; 1 Thess 4:9; Heb 13:1; 1 Pet 1:22; the cognate adjective φιλάδελφος is used in 1 Pet 3:8.

25. Stauffer, "ἀγαπάω κτλ," 37. Apart from 2 Peter, ἀγάπη is used 115 times in the NT.

26. Several manuscripts have the title ἐγκράτεια ψυχῆς before Sir 18:30. Sir 18:30, 31 warn against following ἐπιθυμία.

27. In 1 Cor 7:9 ἐγκρατεύομαι is used with reference to control of sexual desire.

28. Aristotle identifies τρυφή as the opposite of ἐγκράτεια in *Eth. nic.* 7.1. Sir 18:32 warns against τρυφή after having warned against ἐπιθυμία in the preceding two verses.

characterizes the author's opponents (3:16) and those who follow them (2:14).

Φιλαδελφία (brotherly love) literally means love among members of a family. The author of 2 Peter probably uses it metaphorically to mean love for other followers of Jesus who are seen as equivalent to family members; the author of 2 Peter calls the addressees brothers (ἀδελφός) in 1:10 and Paul a brother in 3:15.

The final virtue mentioned in 1:5–7 is ἀγάπη (love). In 1:17 God the Father calls Jesus his ἀγαπητός (beloved) son. The author of 2 Peter addresses those to whom he writes as beloved in 3:1, 8, 14, 17. He calls Paul beloved in 3:15.

Thus in 2 Peter, faithfulness is seen as justice. But just as 2 Peter reconfigures the characteristically Jewish term "faith" into the more Hellenistic term "knowledge," so it reconfigures "justice," a term used by Jewish writers to mean God's faithfulness and humans' right conduct before God, into "virtue" and a number of other Hellenistic terms (while continuing to use "justice" and other Jewish and Christian terms for virtue). I will refer to all of these as virtue, using this as a general term for the many good qualities the addressees of 2 Peter are urged to pursue, and the avoidance of the many bad qualities against which they are warned. In 2 Peter, the theme of faith and faithfulness is the theme of knowledge and virtue. Much of the talk about virtue in 2 Peter can be seen as a general exhortation to do good and avoid evil. The specific qualities that seem to be emphasized the most include self control over desire (especially sexual desire), avoidance of slander, and love.

Knowledge and Virtue

In 2 Peter the relationship between knowledge and virtue is somewhat complex. We must first of all note that for the author of 2 Peter, knowledge is a virtue. Both faith and knowledge are rungs on the ladder of virtue in 1:5–7. Thus the question of the relationship between knowledge and virtue is more precisely the question of the relationship between the virtue of knowledge and other virtues. Aristotle (*Eth. nic.* 1.13; 2.1) divided virtues into two categories: the intellectual (διανοητικός) and the moral (ἠθικός). The former include wisdom, understanding, and prudence; the latter include liberality and temperance. For the author of 2 Peter, faith/knowledge is an intellectual virtue. The question of the relationship between knowledge and virtue can be understood as the question of the relationship between intellectual and moral virtue.

1. Knowledge Should Lead to Virtue

If the author of 2 Peter equates faith and knowledge, then the ladder of virtue in 1:5-7 indicates that knowledge should lead to virtue, i.e., intellectual virtue should lead to moral virtue. The first rung on the ladder is faith (= knowledge) and the second is virtue.[29] This is also indicated by 1:3, which says that Jesus's divine power has given the author and addressees all things for life and piety through full knowledge of him; full knowledge of Jesus is the source of the virtue of piety. And it is indicated by 1:9, which says that lack of virtue derives from blindness and forgetfulness. It may also be indicated by 2:12, which says that the false teachers slander things of which they are ignorant. This can be seen as the principal argument of 2 Peter as a whole: knowledge must lead to virtue; if it does not, it is not proper knowledge.

One reason 2 Peter thinks knowledge should lead to virtue is that, as we have seen, knowledge includes knowing how to live virtuously and that it is necessary to do so. In order to understand the latter more fully, it is helpful to consider the soteriology of 2 Peter.[30] Second Peter 2:1 speaks of Jesus as "the master who bought" the false teachers and, presumably, all Christians. This indicates that 2 Peter understands humans as needing salvation because they are enslaved. Jesus saves them by purchasing them from their previous owner and making them his own slaves. Knowledge of Jesus is salvific because Jesus's purchase of humans from their former owner does not take full effect until it is known to have occurred. Until they know they have been purchased by Jesus, humans continue to act like the slaves of their former owner. Once they know Jesus has purchased them, they can act on the freedom Jesus has given them. Prior to their purchase by Jesus, humans could not act virtuously because they were enslaved. Knowing that Jesus has purchased them is knowledge that Jesus has given them the freedom to act virtuously.

As this description makes clear, Jesus's purchase of his followers gives them the opportunity for freedom from their former master, but they must actualize this opportunity. This is why knowledge should lead to virtue. Virtuous living is the enactment of the freedom that results from Jesus's purchase of humans. Failing to live virtuously is remaining in, or returning to, one's former enslavement, negating one's salvation. This parallels the Pauline understanding of the relationship between the indicative and the imperative. E. P. Sanders expresses this relationship by distinguishing

---

29. In *Virt.* 216 Philo says that Abraham, having gained faith, the most secure of the virtues (τὴν τῶν ἀρετῶν βεβαιοτάτην), also gained with it all the others.

30. On this, see chapter 3, "The Soteriology of the Second Letter of Peter."

between "getting in" and "staying in." "Getting in" to the community of the redeemed is not based on one's behavior; it is the free gift of God. "Staying in" that community is based on one's behavior.[31]

2. Virtue Should Lead to Knowledge

Not only does 2 Peter argue that knowledge should lead to virtue, it also says that virtue should lead to more knowledge, i.e., that moral virtue should lead to additional intellectual virtue. Thus, on the ladder of virtue (1:5–7), the first rung is faith; the second is virtue; and the third is knowledge. The first step in ascending the ladder is faith (= knowledge); that leads to virtue; and that virtue, in turn, leads to further knowledge. This relationship between virtue and knowledge is also presented in 1:8, which says that possessing and exceeding in the virtues of vv. 5–7 makes one neither idle nor fruitless for full knowledge of Jesus. The final exhortation of the letter to grow in knowledge of Jesus (3:18) should be understood in light of this. One grows in knowledge by behaving virtuously. Thus 2 Peter seems to see knowledge as something that should issue in virtue and virtue as something that should issue in further knowledge. In this, 2 Peter may go beyond Paul.

In the phrase found in 1:8, εἰς τὴν τοῦ κυρίου ἡμῶν Ἰησοῦ Χριστοῦ ἐπίγνωσιν (for/in full knowledge of our Lord Jesus Christ), εἰς can be taken as indicating the condition to which the qualities in vv. 5–7 bring one, or in a more general sense, as indicating the source from which the qualities named in vv. 5–7 proceed. Most commentators argue for the former view, understanding the preposition εἰς as having its ordinary meaning.[32] Others argue the latter view on the grounds that 1:2 and 3 show that the believer begins with knowledge of God; such interpreters understand εἰς as having the less specific meaning it acquired in Koine Greek.[33] The author of 2 Peter clearly does think the believer begins with knowledge of God and thinks the virtues listed in 1:5–7 should grow out of this. But to me it seems most likely that in v. 8 he presents knowledge of God as also growing out of the virtues (cf. Col 1:10). One both begins with knowledge of God and then grows in knowledge of God as a result of living virtuously.

---

31. Sanders, *Paul and Palestinian Judaism*, 513. On the ethical implications of freedom from sin and death in Pauline thought, see Conzelmann, *Outline*, 275–82.

32. These include Windisch, *Katholische Briefe*, 86–87; Schelkle, *Petrusbriefe*, 191; Spicq, *Épitres de Saint Pierre*, 214; Grundmann, *Judas und Petrus*, 74; Paulsen, *Der Zweite Petrusbrief*, 111; Knoch, *Erste und Zweite Petrusbrief*, 242–43; G. Green, *Jude and 2 Peter*, 197.

33. See Bigg, *St. Peter and St. Jude*, 258–59; Kelly, *Peter and Jude*, 307–8; Bauckham, *Jude, 2 Peter*, 188–89; Davids, *2 Peter and Jude*, 185.

As is the case with the idea that knowledge should lead to virtue, it is easier to see that 2 Peter thinks virtue should lead to knowledge than it is to understand why. Part of the explanation may be found in the idea that knowledge of one's salvation must be put into practice in order to be effective. Virtuous living is necessary to complete and maintain the knowledge of salvation. If one returns to one's former enslavement, the knowledge of salvation has been negated as a practical matter. But 2 Peter does not seem to be thinking only that virtue is necessary to avoid negating knowledge; somehow virtuous living increases knowledge. Perhaps the explanation is that by putting knowledge of virtue into practice, one increases knowledge of this virtue and thus of the knowledge from which it flows.

3. A Dialectical Relationship between Knowledge and Virtue

If knowledge leads to virtue, which, in turn, leads to additional knowledge, and that, in turn, leads to additional virtue, etc., 2 Peter may presume an ongoing progression of growth in knowledge and virtue.[34] Perhaps this progression underlies the ladder of virtue in 1:5-7.[35] The virtues that are the rungs of this ladder may alternate between those that emphasize cognition and those that emphasize behavior, between intellectual virtues and moral virtues. The ascent of the ladder then involves progression through succeeding levels of knowledge and virtue. We might visualize this as a staircase in which each flight of stairs changes direction 180 degrees. Each virtue corresponds to a flight of stairs; the side of the staircase on which half of the flights begin corresponds to cognitive virtue, and the other side corresponds to active virtue. As one ascends the stairs, one moves back and forth between virtues that emphasize cognition and virtues that emphasize behavior (see diagram on page 162).

The first four parts of the staircase can easily be understood this way. By faith (= knowledge that Jesus is the savior who will come again), one can

34. This is somewhat similar to Aristotle's idea that intellectual and moral virtues must work together. Intellectual virtue, especially prudence, must guide moral virtue, and prudence must be completed by moral virtue; see *Eth. Nic.* 6.13.

35. Windisch (*Katholische Briefe*, 86), Bauckham (*Jude, 2 Peter*, 185), Paulsen (*Der Zweite Petrusbrief*, 110), and Davids (*2 Peter and Jude*, 178) do not think there is any internal logic to vv. 5-7. This is also asserted by Vögtle (*Tugend-und Lasterkataloge*, 189), but he nevertheless suggests an internal logic (189-91); so also Schelkle, *Petrusbriefe*, 190-91. J. Daryl Charles (*Virtue*, 145-46n91) rejects the view that the list of virtues is largely random and proposes an understanding of their logical progression (140-45, 156-57). Venerable Bede also proposes an explanation of the logic of vv. 5-7 in his commentary on 2 Peter ("*In epistulas VII catholicas*," 263-64); Grundmann offers an interpretation of the logic of v. 6 (*Judas und Petrus*, 73).

supply virtue because faith includes knowledge of how to live virtuously and the need to do so. By virtue, one can supply further knowledge because acting on one's knowledge of virtue expands that knowledge, adding practical knowledge to the theoretical knowledge with which one began.[36] By one's theoretical and practical knowledge, one can supply the specific virtue of self-control with respect to one's desires.[37] In light of 2 Peter as a whole, we can surmise that it is especially theoretical knowledge of the second coming of Jesus and the practical experience of attempting to live a generally virtuous life that can help one specifically to resist the contrary temptations of desire.

The remaining parts of the staircase do not as clearly display such an ongoing progression from knowledge to virtue, to more knowledge, to more virtue, etc. The fifth and seventh parts of the staircase, namely endurance and brotherly love, are not as obviously intellectual virtues as are the first and third parts, namely faith and knowledge. However, we may also see this same dialectic in the last four parts of the staircase. By self-control, one can supply endurance. In 2 Peter endurance may mean specifically persisting in knowledge of Jesus's second coming.[38] In Hellenistic thought endurance is related to courage, but in Jewish thought and in the NT it connotes reliance on God, particularly God's action in the future.[39] Insofar as one controls desire by means of knowledge of the second coming, this self-control may reinforce the knowledge on which it is based and thus increase it, helping to make it habitual.

By endurance, one can supply piety. This is another general name for virtue, as we have seen, but perhaps especially refers to avoiding slander of God and Jesus by expressing doubt that Jesus will come again. Persistence in knowledge of the second coming obviously leads very directly to piety in this sense. But it also leads to piety in a more general sense. Knowing that

---

36. This suggests that γνῶσις connotes specifically the knowledge that comes from the experience of trying to live virtuously, which would be one element of the knowledge that is generally synonymous with faith in 2 Peter. Bauckham (*Jude, 2 Peter*, 186) suggests something similar to this. Spicq (*Épitres de Saint Pierre*, 213), Grundmann (*Judas und Petrus*, 73), and Knoch (*Erste und zweite Petrusbrief*, 242) understand "knowledge" as the ability to distinguish good from evil.

37. Aristotle discusses the relationship between knowledge (ἐπιστήμη) and the virtue of self-control in *Eth. Nic.* 7.2–3.

38. Commenting on 2 Pet 1:6, Danker says, "In the face of skepticism about an early termination of the world's existence, Auctor invites his addressees to await it patiently; see especially 3:8–9" (*Benefactor*, 461).

39. See Hauck, "μένω κτλ," 581–86; G. Green, *Jude and 2 Peter*, 194. Thus in 1 Thess 1:3 Paul speaks of the Thessalonians' "endurance of hope in our Lord Jesus Christ"; cf. also Rom 8:25; 15:4; Heb 10:36.

the final judgment will occur provides a motivation for virtuous living of all kinds.

By piety, one can supply brotherly love. As we have seen, brotherly love probably refers to love for other Christians, who are regarded as brothers and sisters. Thus it depends on the knowledge that they are brothers and sisters. Perhaps piety is the means by which one can supply brotherly love because it allows one to see other Christians as brothers and sisters. Insofar as piety means respect for the order created by Jesus, it entails recognition of the fraternal relationship among his followers that Jesus has established.[40] In addition, piety sums up the growth in knowledge and virtue that precedes it, including increasing control of one's desires. Desire, especially sexual desire and greed, can cause one to see other people as merely a means to the satisfaction of these desires. Control of desire can allow one to see other people as brothers and sisters, family members, not objects of desire.

By brotherly love, one can supply love. Seeing others as brothers and sisters helps one to have the attitude of love that is proper to other members of one's family and to act on it. And this can lead to more general love, love for everyone and everything.

In this way, 1:5–7 can be seen as proposing that one progresses from knowledge to virtue, to more knowledge, to more virtue, etc., until one arrives at love, the pinnacle of this development. This evaluation of love is reminiscent of Paul's praise of love in 1 Cor 13 and is consonant with other virtue lists that end with love, e.g., those found in 2 Cor 8:7 and Herm. Vis. 3.8.7. In 1:8, however, the author of 2 Peter says that possessing all these virtues keeps one from being idle or fruitless for full knowledge of Jesus. This suggests that even love is not the end of the staircase of virtue, but that it leads to further knowledge and the continuation of the dialectic (cf. also 3:18).

Summary

In 2 Peter faith and faithfulness are reconfigured into knowledge and virtue. Knowledge is mainly knowledge of Jesus as savior, who will come again, and knowledge of how to live virtuously. Justice is a general name for virtue in 2 Peter, but it is reconfigured into other more Hellenistic virtues. The specific virtues receiving the most emphasis are self control over desire, especially inordinate sexual desire, pious avoidance of slander, and love.

---

40. The cognitive foundation of brotherly love is visible in 1 Thess 4:9 and 1 Pet 1:22. The former speaks of brotherly love as based on having been taught by God; the latter speaks of brotherly love as deriving from obedience to the truth.

162 A VOYAGE AROUND THE SECOND LETTER OF PETER

The author of 2 Peter sees knowledge as leading to virtue, both because knowledge includes knowledge of how to live virtuously and because virtuous living is necessary to avoid undoing the salvation that results from knowledge. The author of 2 Peter also sees virtue as leading to more knowledge. In 1:5–7 the author presents a vision of Christian life as a progressive ascent from knowledge to virtue, to more knowledge, to more virtue, etc., as one grows in Christian perfection.

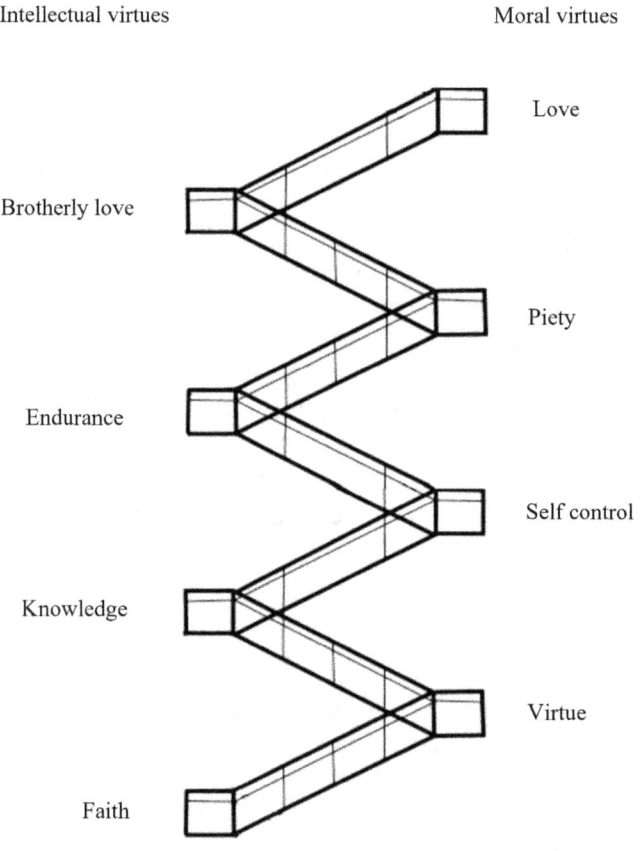

2 Peter 1:5-7 - The Staircase of Virtue

11

Reading the Earliest Copies of 2 Peter

The three earliest extant copies of the second letter of Peter are found in the following manuscripts: Papyrus 72—third century; Codex Sinaiticus—fourth century; and Codex Vaticanus—fourth century.[1]

These and other early copies of 2 Peter have been studied intensively in the effort to determine the earliest recoverable text of 2 Peter, and many of the differences among them have been identified in critical texts of the New Testament. The results of such text criticism are now taken as the beginning point for interpretation of 2 Peter. Text criticism, however, divides manuscripts into variation units and to a great extent considers them piecemeal, not as a whole. Thus much less attention has been given to reading these manuscripts in their entirety and to the meaning of a particular manuscript's various readings taken together.

There have been efforts to see how the perspective of their scribes is reflected in manuscripts. Such efforts might be expected to yield interpretation of the manuscripts as a whole, but generally this has not been the result. Attempting to identify the outlook of the scribes has required distinguishing any changes introduced by the scribes from what they found in the texts they copied. This is the procedure followed by Bart Ehrman in *The*

---

1. A facsimile of the P72 text of 1 and 2 Peter accompanies Martini, *Beati Petri Apostoli Epistulae*; a facsimile of Codex Sinaiticus has been published as *Codex Sinaiticus: A Facsimile* and is available online at http://www.codex-sinaiticus.net/en; a facsimile of the Codex Vaticanus New Testament has been published as *Τα Ιερα Βιβλια*; and a facsimile of the complete Codex Vaticanus has been published as *Bibliorum Sacrorum Graecorum Codex Vaticanus B*.

Orthodox Corruption of Scripture.² This procedure yields an interpretation of certain features of the manuscripts, but not the manuscripts as a whole.

The title of Eldon Jay Epp's *The Theological Tendency of Codex Bezae Cantabrigiensis in Acts* suggests that it is an analysis of Acts as found in Codex Bezae Cantabrigiensis. However, that is not exactly the case. Rather, Epp's actual goal was to identify theological tendencies of the "Western" tradition insofar as it is accessible from Codex Bezae. This involved discounting elements of the text that arose later than the second century.³

Although little attention has been given to understanding early manuscripts as a whole, this is worth investigating. During the first 1400 years of Christian history, before there were printed copies of the New Testament, it was available only in manuscripts. During this period, most of the people in any given place probably did not have access to more than one copy of any biblical writing. As far as they were concerned, their copy simply was the writing.⁴ Since no two manuscripts of any writing agree with one another in every respect, readers' understanding of these writings would have varied as their copies of them varied. This makes it interesting to ask how readers would have understood the earliest copies of 2 Peter. How would their understanding of it have varied because of the differences among these copies?

In what follows, I will discuss each of the three earliest copies of 2 Peter in turn and consider what 2 Peter would have meant to the readers of each one. My concern will be the meaning of the manuscripts as they stand. For this purpose, it does not matter whether the distinctive features of the manuscripts were produced by the scribes who wrote them or were found already in their exemplars. I will identify the most significant textual features of these copies of 2 Peter by comparing them with the text of 2 Peter in *The Greek New Testament*.⁵ This is what I mean when I refer to the probable or likely original text.⁶ In discussing the earliest copies of 2 Peter, I will discuss the meaning of 2 Peter as found in the corrected texts. The one exception is that where possible, I will interpret the text marked with dots. I

---

2. Ehrman, *Orthodox Corruption of Scripture*, 31. This is also the approach taken by Royse in *Scribal Habits* when he discusses the theological changes introduced by the scribes of papyrus manuscript.

3. Epp, *Theological Tendency*, 27–28. Epp provides a review of subsequent investigations on the same lines in "Anti-Judaic Tendencies in the D-Text of Acts: Forty Years of Conversation" in Epp, *Perspectives of New Testament Textual Criticism*, 699–739.

4. Cf. Epp's statement that "these variant texts were for some Christians at some time and place *the* 'original' text" (*Theological Tendency*, 13).

5. Aland et al., *Greek New Testament*.

6. On the complexity of the term "original text" see Epp, "Multivalence of the Term 'Original Text' in New Testament Textual Criticism" in Epp, *Perspectives of New Testament Textual Criticism*, 551–93.

do so because marking the text with dots does not eliminate it as completely as other methods of correction; the dotted text is still there to be read.

Reading the corrected text is quite straightforward in the case of Papyrus 72 and Codex Vaticanus. As we will see below, almost all of the corrections of 2 Peter in Papyrus 72 seem to have been made by the original hand, and there are very few corrections of 2 Peter in Codex Vaticanus. The case of Codex Sinaiticus is different. In this manuscript, there are many corrections of the text of 2 Peter. While some of them seem to have been made before the text left the scriptorium, a number of them seem to have been made much later. Even so, the corrected text of Codex Sinaiticus is one of the earliest copies of 2 Peter.

I. Papyrus 72

Like the other early copies of 2 Peter we are considering, the one found in P72 was part of a codex; Tommy Wasserman calls it the Bodmer Miscellaneous Codex.[7] Unlike the other codices containing early copies of 2 Peter, the Bodmer Miscellaneous Codex was a papyrus codex. The pages of this codex are also smaller than those of the other codices that contain early copies of 2 Peter; they measure 6 inches by 5.5 inches, about half the size of the other codices' pages (though the latter also differ considerably in size). Each page has a single column of text. In 2 Peter the pages mostly have 17–19 lines of text. The size of the codex suggests that it was produced for private use rather than for public reading in the church.

The most important difference between the Bodmer Miscellaneous Codex and the other codices we are considering is that the former is not a biblical codex. As the name suggests, the Bodmer Miscellaneous Codex contains a miscellany of eleven writings, probably written by four different scribes, bound together in the following order:

    Nativity of Mary
    3 Corinthians
    11th Ode of Solomon
    Jude
    Melito, Homily on the Passover
    Fragment of a liturgical hymn
    Apology of Phileas
    LXX Psalms 33:2–34:16

7. Wasserman, "Papyrus 72."

1–2 Peter

Readers of this early copy of 2 Peter would not have been informed by the codex in which they found it that they were reading part of the Bible. They may have known in other ways that this text was an authoritative writing for the Christian church, but they read it in an anthology of various writings. Some of them are biblical writings (Jude; Ps 33:2–34:16, 1–2 Peter), but others are not.

P72 is the name given to the texts of Jude, 1 and 2 Peter that are part of this codex. All were written by the same scribe. This scribe was much less skilled than the scribes who wrote the other early copies of 2 Peter we are considering. Someone who recognized the scribe's many errors would have received the impression that the writer of 2 Peter was not highly literate in Greek. I count 131 itacisms and other errors based on replacing a letter or letters with similar sounding letters.[8]

There are also cases of simple misspellings, where a single letter is used in place of a double letter (Γομορας 2:6; ἐρυσατο 2:7; φυλασεσθαι 3:17) or a double letter used in place of a single letter (μαλλιστα 2:10; βαλλααμ 2:15; ἀσσελγια 2:8,18). Three times, a ς is added to the end of a word (επειθυμειας 2:10; συνεστωσης 3:5; πλανης 3:17). A final ν is omitted from ηδονη in 2:13; a final ς is omitted from αληθου in 2:22; and a final ς is substituted for ν in τρυφης in 2:13.

There are a number of instances where a syllable is repeated by mistake:

1. και before καιπερ (1:12)
2. ει before ειδοτας (1:12)
3. του repeated (1:14)
4. σα repeated in εβασασανιζειν (2:8)
5. και repeated (2:12)

In 3:3 a syllable may have been omitted by mistake, i.e., εν omitted before ενπεγμονη.

Finally, a number of other errors have been corrected in the manuscript.[9] There is a dot to mark the error above the κ of κγνωσιν in 1:5 and

---

8. See Appendix A. These and other scribal errors have been cataloged by Testuz, *Papyrus Bodmer VII–IX*, 29–34; Kubo, *P72 and the Codex Vaticanus*, 8–30; Royse, *Scribal Habits*, 545–614.

9. Royse counts twenty-two corrections by the original hand in 2 Peter (*Scribal Habits*, 559), but I cannot find the correction he mentions in 2:4b. Perhaps this is the correction he mentions elsewhere in 2:5. Royse identifies two corrections by a second hand, namely in 1:8 and 3:16 (*Scribal Habits*, 569).

the κ of διεχγειριν in 1:13; in the former case, the κ has also been erased but is still visible. Likewise, there are dots to mark the errors over the θ of αποφθευγοντας in 2:18 and the second κ of κοσκμος in 3:6. In a number of cases, a letter has been erased and another letter written in its place. Thus, in 1:7 there is an erasure under the second λ in φιλαδελφια; under the α of τοιασδε in 1:17; under the ως of επειλυσεως in 1:20; in 2:5 a letter has been erased between αλλ and ογδοον; there is an erasure under the ης of εντολης in 3:2; and one after the γ of στηριγμου in 3:17. In a number of cases a missing letter or word has been written above or at the end of the line. Thus in 1:8 του seems to have been added at the end of the line after τη; the υ missing from ουκ has been added above it in 2:4; what looks like εις has been added above something scratched out before το διγμα in 2:6; the η missing from τηρειν has been added above it in 2:9; what looks like the second ε missing from ελευσονται has been added above it in 3:3; the λο missing from βουλομενος and the τι missing from τινας have been added above them in 3:9; υμας has been added after υπαρχειν in 3:11; and ω has been added above a scratched out letter in αμωμητοι in 3:14. There are also some other kinds of corrections. In 2:16 ξ appears to have been written over some other letter in ελεγξιν. Likewise, in 2:19 δ has been written over a ζ in δουλοι. In 2:17 the ο of υπο has been crossed out. Finally, in 3:16 ταις has been written after the last line, completing the word αυταις left incomplete at the end of the last line.

Another thing contributing to the impression that the scribe was not highly literate in Greek is the presence of a marginal note in Coptic. This is found in 2:22, where the Greek word αληθου has the Coptic gloss ΠΜΕΙ.

All of this shows that the scribe of P72 was not adept. James Royse quotes Carlo Martini as saying:

> gli *errori* veri e propri dello scriba sono assai numerosi, e dimostrano una diligenza assai mediocre e una conoscenza piuttosto incerta della lingua greca
>
> (the true and proper *errors* of the scribe are rather numerous and demonstrate a rather mediocre diligence and a quite uncertain knowledge of the Greek language).[10]

Readers of P72 might not only have concluded that its scribe was not expert but also have seen 2 Peter itself as a document manifesting a low level of literacy.

---

10. Royse, *Scribal Habits*, 580, quoting Martini, *Beati Petri Apostoli Epistulae*, xviii.

The Bodmer Miscellaneous Codex was found, along with other manuscripts, in a jar near Dishna in Egypt, not far from a Pachomian monastery.[11] The manuscripts may also have been written in that area.

The Meaning of 2 Peter in Papyrus 72

I will discuss five ways in which the distinctive features of 2 Peter in P72 have the effect of giving the letter a meaning significantly different from that of the probable original text.

1. Jesus as Divine

The most important distinctive feature of 2 Peter in P72 is its presentation of Jesus as divine to a greater degree than is done by the probable original text of 2 Peter. This occurs most clearly in 1:2; the version of this verse in P72 does not include και. The verse speaks of του θυ Ιηυ του κυριου ημων (God, Jesus our Lord), rather than του θεου και Ιησου του κυριου ημων (God and Jesus our Lord) as in the likely original text. While the latter apparently distinguishes Jesus from God, the text in P72 identifies Jesus as God.

This peculiarity of P72 has often been noted. Because it coheres with peculiarities of two other documents copied by the same scribe, namely Jude and 1 Peter, it may be an intentional change, or at least seems to be one that reflects the views of the scribe. In Jude 5 P72 speaks of θεος χριστος as having saved Israel from Egypt, while the probable original text speaks of κυριος. And in 1 Peter 5:1 P72 speaks of the sufferings of θεου, while the likely original text speaks of the sufferings of Χριστου.[12] All three of these peculiarities have the effect of presenting Jesus as God.[13]

What is not always noted is that this omission of και from 2 Peter 1:2 in P72 extends a presentation of Jesus as divine that is already prominent in the likely original text of 2 Peter. This is clearest in 1:1, which speaks of του θεου ημων και σωτηρος Ιησου Χριστου (our God and savior Jesus Christ),

---

11. Wasserman, "Papyrus 72," 32.

12. On this passage, see Beare, "Text of 1 Peter in Papyrus 72," 255; Martini, *Beati Petri Apostoli Epistulae*, xxiv.

13. See King, "Notes on the Bodmer Manuscript," 54–57; Ehrman, *Orthodox Corruption*, 85–86; Niklas and Wasserman, "Theologische Linien?," 161–88, esp. 184–85; Royse, *Scribal Habits*, 609–14. Ehrman suggests that the P72 version of 2 Pet 1:2 is anti-Adoptionistic.

probably identifying Jesus Christ as God. However, there are many other elements of 2 Peter that support this same identification.[14]

The likely original text of 2 Peter 1:2 probably distinguishes Jesus from God. This moderates the identification of Jesus as God in 1:1, indicating that the identification of Jesus as God is not a simple, straightforward matter.[15] The version of 1:2 found in P72 eliminates this moderation of the identification of Jesus as God and so makes it a more simple, straightforward matter.

Another peculiarity of 2 Peter in P72 that may express the identification of Jesus as God is the use of δι ου (through whom) at the beginning of 1:12 rather than διο (therefore) as in the likely original text. In the latter 1:12 states the conclusion from the preceding argument—because of its importance, the author will always remind the addressees about what he has just said. The text in P72 says instead that the author will remind the addressees through "our Lord and savior Jesus Christ." The phrase "through Jesus Christ" and its equivalents is rather common in the letters of Paul. For example, in Rom 1:8; 7:25 Paul gives thanks to God through Jesus Christ (cf. also Rom 16:27). A closer parallel is provided by Paul's statement in Rom 15:30 that he exhorts the addressees through our Lord Jesus Christ. In itself, this language does not necessarily imply the divinity of Christ; in the letters of Paul it is one aspect of Paul's central idea that to be a Christian is to exist in union with Christ. However, apart from such a context, as in 2 Peter, the idea that the author of 2 Peter acts through Christ can easily be seen as expressing an understanding of Christ as divine.

2. Salvation From Desire

Other peculiarities of 2 Peter in P72 suggest that humans need to be saved from desire while the likely original text sees them as needing salvation from corruption. In 1:4 P72 speaks of having escaped την εν τω κοσμω επειθυμιαν φθοραν (the desire in the world that is corruption) rather than της εν τω κοσμω εν επιθυμια φθορας (the corruption in the world by desire) as in the likely original text. The text in P72 says that one needs salvation from desire, which is corruption, while the likely original text says that one needs salvation from corruption, which results from desire. In the probable original text of 2 Peter, corruption is understood both literally as

---

14. On this, see chapter 2, "The Christology of the Second Letter of Peter."

15. However, if the και in the likely original text is understood as epexegetical, this text too can be seen as restating the identification of Jesus with God—"God, even Jesus our Lord." It is not ordinarily understood this way, probably because simple identification of Jesus as God is not common in the New Testament.

meaning physical destruction/disintegration and metaphorically as meaning spiritual destruction/disintegration. Metaphorical corruption leads to literal corruption.[16] By speaking of desire as corruption in 2 Peter 1:4, the text of P72 conceives corruption in purely metaphorical terms and as consisting of desire. Perhaps that same understanding of corruption should be seen throughout 2 Peter in P72.

In 2:10 P72 speaks of επειθυμειας σαρκος (desire for flesh [presuming that the final ς of επειθυμειας is a spelling error]) while the likely original text has επιθυμια μιασμου (desire for defilement). Since this verse also speaks of going after the flesh, the different expressions in P72 and the probable original text have the same general meaning. However, the text of P72 puts more emphasis on desire specifically for the flesh. Desire for the flesh is also more satisfactory than desire for defilement as a description of the mental state of the unjust.

Finally, P72 omits μεστους (full) from 2:14. Without this adjective, the verse speaks of "having the eyes of an adulteress" rather than "having eyes full of an adulteress" as does the likely original text. The former presents the false teachers as using their eyes in the same way as an adulteress, i.e., to seek out adultery; the latter presents them as using their eyes only to gaze on an adulteress, intending to engage in adultery with her. These two expressions are very close in meaning, but the former emphasizes slightly more than the latter that desire is the thing from which one needs salvation.

3. Testamentary Letter From Peter

Two other peculiarities of 2 Peter in P72 improve its presentation as a testamentary letter from Peter. In 1:15 P72 has σπουδαζω (I am eager) rather than σπουδασω (I will be eager) as in the likely original text.[17] P72 describes Peter's present state of mind as he writes the letter, where the likely original text speaks of Peter's future state of mind. The text of P72 better suits 2 Peter's presentation of Peter as composing 2 Peter as a testamentary letter.

Somewhat similarly, in 3:16 the text of P72 has στρεβλωσουσιν (they will twist) while the probable original text has στρεβλουσιν (they twist). In this way, P72 presents misinterpretation of the letters of Paul as something that will happen in the future, instead of speaking of it as something happening now, as the likely original text does. This brings the passage into

---

16. On this, see chapter 3, "The Soteriology of the Second Letter of Peter."

17. Sinaiticus has the same thing as P72 at this point. The reading has the same significance in both, but in Sinaiticus this does not seem to be part of a general theme of its version of 2 Peter even to the rather limited extent that it does in P72.

greater conformity with 2 Peter's general presentation of the false teachers as arriving in the future.

4. Prophecy and Scripture

In 1:20 P72 speaks of προφητια και γραφη (prophecy and scripture) rather than προφητεια γραφης (prophecy of scripture), as in the probable original text. While the latter identifies prophecy as part of scripture, the former speaks of prophecy as something that exists alongside scripture. Perhaps 2 Peter in P72 envisions prophecy as a living institution among Christians, somewhat as in the letters of Paul (see, e.g., 1 Cor 14). Prophecy and scripture are alike in not being of one's own explanation, but it is prophecy, not scripture, to which 2 Peter appeals here. The author may imply that early Christian prophets predict the second coming of Jesus and that this is a foundation for the validity of this expectation that is more secure than the transfiguration mentioned in 1:16–18. In the likely original text of 2 Peter, in which prophecy is part of scripture, the argument in 2:4–10a can be understood as a specification of how the prophetic word in scripture predicts the second coming of Jesus. In P72 2:4–10a may be understood as a separate, scriptural argument alongside the argument from prophecy. The prophets mentioned in 3:2 could be these early Christian prophets.

5. Simplified Eschatology

A final important aspect of 2 Peter in P72 is its simplification of the eschatology found in the likely original text of 2 Peter. In 3:8 P72 says that μια ημερα παρα κω ως χιλια ετη ως ημερα μια (one day with the Lord is like a thousand years like one day) rather than μια ημερα παρα κυριω ως χιλια ετη και χιλια ετη ως ημερα μια (one day with the Lord is like a thousand years and a thousand years like one day), as in the probable original text.[18] At this point, the author of 2 Peter is apparently responding to the idea that

18. Codex Sinaiticus again says something very similar to P72 at this point, namely μια ημερα παρα κυ ως χιλια ετη ως ημερα μια (one day from the Lord is like a thousand years like one day). This differs from P72 only in having the genitive rather than the dative case after παρα. This does not seem to be part of a general theme of Sinaiticus's version of 2 Peter even to the limited extent that it does in P72. Both P72 and Codex Sinaiticus's versions might have arisen by parablepsis as the scribe's eye jumped from the first χιλια ετη to the second. This, however, would only have been apparent to someone who compared either of them with a text that included the probable original version. The ordinary reader of either P72 or Codex Sinaiticus would presumably have understood its meaning as I explicate it here.

the parousia of Jesus has been delayed by arguing that time is different for God than for humans. The text of P72 simply says that one day for God is like a thousand years for humans. Because what seems like a long time to humans is a very short time to God, what seems like a delay to humans is not a delay for God.

This is also the main point of the likely original text of the verse. However, it not only says that one day with God is like a thousand years but also that a thousand years (with God) is like one day. The text of P72 might suggest that by using the formula one day = one thousand years it is possible to calculate divine time. The likely original text suggests rather that divine and human time are completely incommensurable. One cannot maintain that the parousia of Jesus has been delayed not merely because a long time for humans is a short time for God but rather because divine and human time are completely different and no conclusion about the former can be based on the latter.

Another aspect of 2 Peter's eschatology is presented distinctively by P72 in 3:10. Here the text of P72 says that γη και τα εν αυτη εργα ευρεθησεται λυομενα (the earth and the works on it will be discovered dissolved) while the likely original text does not include the last word—λυομενα (dissolved). The meaning of the likely original text is unclear; I suggest that the author is thinking that eschatological fire will destroy all injustice and only the just will remain, having thus been revealed. By adding the word λυομενα, the text of P72 clarifies this statement as meaning that the earth and the works on it will be dissolved along with the elements that, it has just been said, will be dissolved.

II. Codex Sinaiticus

Codex Sinaiticus, like Codex Vaticanus to be discussed below, is a parchment codex. Its pages are 15 inches by 13.5 inches, with four columns on each page and 47 lines per column. Presumably, this large book was intended for public reading in the church. Also like Codex Vaticanus, Codex Sinaiticus is a biblical codex. It is assumed that it contained the entire Old Testament even though the first part of the Old Testament, namely Genesis to 1 Chronicles, is now missing. The codex contains the entire New Testament along with two writings not now considered part of the New Testament, namely the Epistle of Barnabas and the Shepherd of Hermas. Readers of this copy of 2 Peter would have been informed by the codex that they were reading part of the Bible.

The scribe who wrote 2 Peter in Codex Sinaiticus was much more adept than the scribe of P72. Nevertheless, Codex Sinaiticus has more scribal errors than Codex Vaticanus. I count fifty-five itacisms and other errors based on replacing a letter or letters with similar sounding letters in 2 Peter.[19]

There is one case of misspelling where part of a word is omitted, namely ηραν instead of ημεραν in 2:9. A ν is mistakenly added to τη in 1:7. In 2:18 the letters θη have been mistakenly added to the word ματαιοτητος; there are dots over these letters, presumably to mark the error.

In 2:12 γεγενημενα may be a misspelling of γεγεννημενα, replacing a double ν with a single ν. In 2:14 μοιχαλιας may be a misspelling of μοιχαλιδος, perhaps based on misunderstanding the word as it was read. Although μοιχαλιας is found at this same point in two other manuscripts, namely A and 33, it does not seem to be part of the vocabulary of the Greek language.

Twice, a word is repeated by mistake: ουδ is repeated after ακαρπους in 1:8 and ελευθεριαν is repeated in 2:19. In both cases, there are dots over the repeated word.

A number of other errors have been corrected in the manuscript:

1. The most extensive such correction is found in 1:12–13. The words καιπερ ιδοτας και εστηριγμενους εν τη παρουση αληθια. δικαιον δε ηγουμαι, εφ οσον ειμι εν τουτω τω σκηνωματι, διεγιριν υμας were omitted from the original text and have been added at the bottom of the page with an arrow to indicate where they should be inserted.

2. A similar but less extensive correction is found in 3:12, where the words και σπευδοντας were omitted and have been added in the margin with a tilde to indicate where they should be inserted.

3. In a rather large number of cases a missing letter or word has been written above the line. Thus the επι missing from χορηγησατε has been added above it in 1:5; in 2:5 there are lines through the last two letters of an original κοσμον, and ω has been written above them; in 2:9 ο and υ have been written above the last two letters of an original πιρασμων; in 2:12–13 an original και φθαρησονται αδικουμενοι has been corrected to καταφθαρησονται αδι κομιουμενοι by adding a stroke to the top of the ι in και to convert it into a τ, writing an α above the line after it, and writing ομι above the line after the κ in αδικουμενοι (dots have been put above αδι to mark them as an error); in 2:16 an original βεωορσορ has been corrected to βεωοσορος by putting a line through the first ρ and writing ος above the line after the second ρ (dots have been put above εω to mark them as an error);

---

19. See Appendix B.

in 2:16 εν has been written above the line before ανθρωπου; in 2:18 an original του οντως has been corrected to τους ολιγως by writing a σ above the line after του, erasing ν and writing λ over it, adding ι at the end of the line, and converting τ into γ by erasing part of the letter; in 2:19 an abbreviation for και has been written above the line before δεδουλωται; in 3:5 an original συνεστωτα has been corrected to συνεστωσα by putting a line through the second τ and writing a σ above it; in 3:11 an original ημας has been corrected to υμας by putting a line through the η and writing υ above it; in 3:15 an original αγεισθαι has been corrected to ηγεισθαι by putting a line through the α and writing η above it; and in the same verse an original δοθειαν has been corrected to δοθεισαν by writing a σ above the line.

4. In other cases, in addition to the ones already mentioned, dots have been written above words or letters, presumably to mark them as errors. In 1:3 there are dots over the phrase τον θν και, which immediately follows the preposition προς; in 2:1 there are dots over the phrase εν τω λαω; in 2:9 there are dots over the word πεφυλακισμενους, which immediately follows αδικους δε.

5. In still other cases, in addition to the ones already mentioned, a letter has been erased and another letter written over it. In 1:18 an original ουν seems to have been converted to συν in this way; in 2:2 η οδος has been converted to η δοξα by putting a line through the first ο, erasing the ς and writing ξ over it, and adding an α at the end of the line; in 2:3 what looks like an original εκπορευσονται was converted into ενπορευσονται by erasing the κ and writing ν over it; in 2:4 what looks like an original η was converted into ει by writing it over the η; in that same verse an original ζοφοις has been converted into ζοφου by putting a line through the final ς and changing the ι into υ; in 3:4 a letter has been erased and replaced by a κ with an extra stroke serving as an abbreviation for και.

6. In 2:10 επιθυμιας has been corrected to επιθυμια by putting a line through the ς; in 2:21 the letters σι and a line indicating a final ν have been added at the end of a line after επιγνου to complete the word. Likewise in 2:22 δε has been added at the end of a line after συμβεβηκεν.

The scribe of 2 Peter in Sinaiticus is the one identified by Constantin Tischendorf as scribe A, an identification confirmed by subsequent investigations.[20] Two other scribes also contributed to Sinaiticus (though not 2

---

20. See Milne and Skeat, *Scribes and Correctors*, 18-29; Jongkind, *Scribal Habits*,

Peter), namely Tischendorf's scribes B and D. A is less adept than D, but more adept than B. Milne and Skeat say that scribe D is "the most correct, who alone reaches the standard of good literary papyri," and that "Scribe A is markedly inferior to D."[21] Dirk Jongkind says, "The work of scribe A and scribe B is not of a very high quality." And he affirms the words of Westcott and Hort about the Sinaiticus New Testament as accurately describing the work of scribe A, namely that it shows "all the ordinary lapses due to rapid and careless transcription" and a "bold and rough manner of transcription."[22] In some contrast to the scribal abilities of A and B, according to Jongkind "the bookhand of all three scribes is well formed, regular, and fairly standardized among the three."[23]

The corrections described in 1 and 2 above derive from the corrector called C by Tischendorf and subsequent investigators. This derivation is shown in both cases by the way the place of the correction in the text is indicated. The use of two arrows pointing in the same direction, one at the point of insertion, the other next to the text to be inserted, is characteristic of C corrections written in upper or lower margins. Likewise, the use of two wavy lines, one at the point of insertion, the other next to the text to be inserted, is characteristic of C corrections written in the side margins.[24] The C corrections are usually thought to have been made a considerable time after the writing of the original manuscript. According to Milne and Skeat, some assign them to the fifth, others to the seventh century.[25] At least some of the other corrections described above were probably made before Sinaiticus left the scriptorium.

The Meaning of 2 Peter in Codex Sinaiticus

I will discuss two ways in which the distinctive features of 2 Peter in Sinaiticus have the effect of giving the letter a meaning significantly different from that of the probable original text.

9–18, 26–27.

21. The first quotation is from *Scribes and Correctors*, 53, the second is from 54.

22. The first quotation is from *Scribal Habits*, 253; Jongkind quotes Westcott and Hort on 255. He quotes from Westcott and Hort, *New Testament*, 246–47.

23. Jongkind, *Scribal Habits*, 59.

24. Milne and Skeat, *Scribes and Correctors*, 46.

25. Milne and Skeat, *Scribes and Correctors*, 65.

1. Jesus as Distinct From God

The most important feature of the content of 2 Peter in Codex Sinaiticus is that it does not present Jesus as divine to the same degree as is done by the probable original text of 2 Peter. In 1:1 the text of Sinaiticus says that the addressees have received faith εις δικαιοσυνην του κυ ημων και σωτηρος Ιυ Χυ (for the justice of our lord and savior Jesus Christ) rather than εν δικαιοσυνην του θεου ημων και σωτηρος Ιησου Χριστου (by the justice of our God and savior Jesus Christ), as in the likely original text. Sinaiticus does not identify Jesus as God, while the probable original text does identify Jesus as God.[26] In addition, the statement that the addressees received faith "for the justice" of Jesus is less suggestive of an understanding of Jesus as divine than is saying that they received faith "by" his justice. The latter implies that Jesus is the one who bestows faith; the former suggests that faith allows one to have the justice that characterizes Jesus.

Another peculiarity of Sinaiticus that suggests it does not identify Jesus with God is the phrase τον θν και (God and) after προς in 1:3. Verse 3 begins with a reference to "his divine power"; other things being equal, the antecedent of "his" is likely to be Jesus, the person named immediately beforehand. Verse 3 goes on to say that "his divine power" has given author and addressees all things. In the likely original text of 2 Peter these are all things for life and piety, but in Sinaiticus they are all things for God and life and piety. The presence of "God" in this list suggests that even if Jesus has divine power, he is not God. His divine power has given all things for God, who is someone other than Jesus.

In light of Sinaiticus's text in 1:1, 3, it is also possible that in Sinaiticus "God" rather than "Jesus" is understood as the antecedent of "his" in the phrase "his divine power." This would further reduce any suggestion that Jesus is divine according to Sinaiticus's 2 Peter.

Another peculiarity of Sinaiticus that is congenial to its presentation of Jesus as someone distinct from God is its version of 1:14. In this verse Sinaiticus says simply that Jesus Christ revealed the imminence of Peter's death to Peter, while the likely original text says that ο κυριος ημων (our Lord) Jesus Christ revealed it. Insofar as the title "lord" implies the divinity of Jesus,[27] not using the title here avoids the presentation of Jesus as divine.[28]

---

26. Ehrman comments on the alteration of θεος into κυριος in Sinaiticus (and some other manuscripts) and implies that this is an anti-Patripassianist change (*Orthodox Corruption*, 266–67).

27. On this, see chapter 2, "The Christology of the Second Letter of Peter," 25–27.

28. Sinaiticus has the title "lord" in 1:1 where it is not found in the likely original text, but there, as we have seen, it replaces "God."

A final peculiarity of 2 Peter in Sinaiticus that is congenial to its presentation of Jesus as someone distinct from God is its version of the words of the heavenly voice to Jesus in 1:17. According to Sinaiticus the voice said ουτος εστιν ο υς μου ο αγαπητος εις ον εγω ευδοκησα (this is my beloved son in whom I am well pleased), while according to the likely original text the voice said ο υιος μου ο αγαπητος μου ουτος εστιν εις ον εγω ευδοκησα (my son, my beloved, is this one, in whom I am well pleased). The latter version suggests that the voice is indicating the identity of the son of God, while Sinaiticus's version suggests that the voice is disclosing the identity of Jesus. By making "my son" the predicate rather than the subject of the sentence, Sinaiticus makes the status of Jesus as son of God slightly less emphatic than in the probable original text.

In agreement with Sinaiticus's distinction between Jesus and God, three other peculiarities of 2 Peter in Sinaiticus emphasize the transcendence of God. (1) In 1:21 Sinaiticus describes prophecy by saying ελαλησαν αγιοι θυ ανθρωποι (holy human beings of God spoke), while the probable original text says ελαλησαν απο θεου ανθρωποι (human beings spoke from God). The text in Sinaiticus stresses the holiness of prophets and that they belong to God, but it does not say that their speech originated in God, as the likely original text does. (2) In 2:11 Sinaiticus has παρα κω (before the Lord), while the probable original text has παρα κυριου (from the Lord). The latter says that angels do not bring a slanderous judgment from the Lord, but Sinaiticus denies that angels bring a slanderous judgment before the Lord. This avoids any suggestion that God might be the source of a slanderous judgment. (3) In 2:13 Sinaiticus has κομιουμενοι (receiving), while the likely original text has αδικουμενοι (being wronged). Sinaiticus avoids all suggestion that the fate of the false teachers is unjust in any way.

2. A Clear and Explicit Text

A number of other features of 2 Peter in Codex Sinaiticus make the meaning of the likely original text clearer and/or more explicit. Thus in 1:4 Sinaiticus speaks of having escaped την εν τω κοσμω επιθυμιαν φθορας (the desire for corruption in the world) rather than της εν τω κοσμω εν επιθυμια φθορας (the corruption in the world by desire) as in the likely original text. The latter is a more complex and ambiguous expression than the former. The former makes it clear that desire for corruption is what needs to be escaped. This is in harmony with 2:10, which speaks of desire for defilement.

In 1:5 Sinaiticus has και αυτο δε τουτο (and indeed this very thing) while the probable original text has και αυτο τουτο δε (and for this very reason = therefore). In Sinaiticus αυτο ... τουτο is probably to be understood as the object of παρεισενεγκαντες (having brought in beside) and in apposition to σπουδην (eagerness); in the probable original text αυτο τουτο is an adverbial accusative introducing vv. 5–7 as the apodosis of the sentence in vv. 3–7.[29] In Sinaiticus vv. 5–7 can also be understood as the apodosis of the sentence, but one that has no introductory phrase. The expression in Sinaiticus is probably easier to understand than that in the likely original text. The latter seems to be unique in Greek literature, but the former is found in a few other places.

In 1:10 Sinaiticus has ινα δια των καλων εργων (in order that through good works) after σπουδασατε (be eager), something not found in the probable original text. This makes explicit that the addressees are to make their call and election secure through good works. Since ινα should be followed by the subjunctive, but Sinaiticus has the same verb as the likely original text, i.e., ποιεισθαι, a present middle infinitive, the sentence in Sinaiticus is ungrammatical. Perhaps the scribe and readers of Sinaiticus understand ποιεισθαι as ποιησθε, the second person plural present middle subjunctive. Obviously, this would involve substitution of ει for η, something not otherwise found in Sinaiticus's 2 Peter, and substitution of αι for ε, also found in 1:19.

In 1:17 the words of the heavenly voice in Sinaiticus (discussed above) are closer to the words of the heavenly voice in Matthew 17:5 (ουτος εστιν ο υιος μου ο αγαπητος εν ω ευδοκησα) than is the version of these words found in the likely original text of 2 Peter. This makes it easier to see the similarity of these words to the words in Matthew 17:5 than is the case in the probable original text.

Several features of 2:4–9 in Sinaiticus make the punishment suffered by sinners more explicit. In v. 4 Sinaiticus has σιροις ζοφου (pits of gloom), while the probable original text has σειραις ζοφου (chains of gloom). While the latter presents darkness as something with which the sinful angels can be chained, the former names the place to which they were delivered, i.e., dark pits. As Richard Bauckham argues, the text of Sinaiticus may presume knowledge of "the tradition of the fall of the Watchers as it was told in 1 Enoch."[30] According to this tradition, the fallen angels were confined in valleys (1 En. 10.12) or the abyss (1 En. 18.11; 21.7; 88.1, 3).

In the same verse Sinaiticus has κολαζομενους τηριν (to keep confined) where the probable original text has τηρουμενους (kept). The phrase used by Sinaiticus is also found in v. 9; the scribe may have been influenced by v. 9

---

29. On this, see chapter 5, "The Syntax of 2 Peter 1:1–7."
30. Bauckham, *Jude, 2 Peter*, 249.

in writing the phrase in v. 4. Use of the infinitive instead of the participle makes it clearer that the purpose of delivering the angels to pits of gloom was to keep them. The addition of κολαζομενους might simply develop the idea that the sinful angels are being kept, as indicated by the translation "keep confined." On the other hand, the participle might mean that the angels are being punished as they are being kept, either until judgment or as a judgment.

And in 2:9 Sinaiticus has πεφυλακισμενους (imprisoned) after δε (and), which is not found in the probable original text. If κολαζομενους later in the verse means "confined," Sinaiticus's πεφυλακισμενους emphasizes this idea, which is also implicit in τηριν (to keep), by adding a synonym. On the other hand, Sinaiticus may understand κολαζομενους as meaning "punished"; in this case, πεφυλακισμενους makes it explicit that the unjust are imprisoned while they are punished.

The punishment suffered by sinners is also more explicit in Sinaiticus's version of 2:12. In this verse Sinaiticus has καταφθαρησονται (will be utterly corrupted), while the probable original text has και φθαρησονται (will also be corrupted). Sinaiticus emphasizes that the corruption of the false teachers will be complete.

In 2:21 Sinaiticus has εις τα οπισω ανακαμψαι απο (to return to the things left behind from) after επιγνουσι (having fully known it), while the probable original text has υποστρεψαι εκ (to turn away from). The two are very close in meaning, but Sinaiticus makes it explicit that departing from the holy commandment means returning to a former condition.

In 3:9 Sinaiticus says that the Lord is patient δι' (on account of) rather than εις (toward) the addressees, as in the probable original text. According to Sinaiticus, the Lord's patience is not simply directed toward them but also is occasioned by them. It is their need for time to repent that elicits the Lord's patience. This is implicit in the likely original text, but Sinaiticus makes it explicit.

Finally, in 3:11 Sinaiticus has ουν (therefore) after τουτων (these) instead of ουτως (thus). This makes more explicit the meaning of the genitive absolute with which the verse begins.

III. Codex Vaticanus

Like Codex Sinaiticus, Codex Vaticanus is a parchment codex. Its pages are 10.6 inches by 10.6 inches (smaller than those of Sinaiticus) and have three columns per page.[31] In the New Testament each column has 42 lines. Also

31. The poetical books of the Old Testament are arranged in two columns per page.

like Codex Sinaiticus, Codex Vaticanus is a biblical codex. Although the first 46 chapters of Genesis are now missing, as are Psalms 105–135, the codex contained the entire Old Testament except for the Books of Maccabees. The last part of the New Testament is now missing, so the codex does not contain Hebrews 9:15–end; 1 and 2 Timothy; Titus; Philemon; and Revelation. However, it may originally have included these writings. Readers of this copy of 2 Peter would have known from the codex that they were reading part of the Bible.

The scribe who wrote 2 Peter in Codex Vaticanus was the best of the scribes who wrote the early copies of 2 Peter we are examining. The text of 2 Peter in Codex Vaticanus has remarkably few scribal errors. Most common are itacisms in which ει has been written instead of ι; this occurs 11 times (in 1:1, 4, 17, 20 [twice]; 2:6; 3:1, 3, 8 [twice], 17).

There is one case of misspelling where part of a word is omitted, namely εσχα instead of εσχατα in 2:20. In 2:14 ακαταπαστους has been mistakenly written instead of ακαταπαυστους. In 2:18 ματαιοτητης has been mistakenly written instead of ματαιοτητος. In 3:5 συνεστωσης has been mistakenly written instead of συνεστωσα.

A few errors have been corrected in the manuscript:

1. In 1:16 an ε has been written above the line before the ι in μεγαλιοτητος, making it μεγαλειοτητος. Likewise, in 2:1 an ε has been written above the line before αυτοις, making it εαυτοις.

2. In 2:7 a τ has been written above the θ in λωθ, making it λωτ. In the same verse a ρ has been written above the line over ερυσατο, making it ερρυσατο.

3. In 2:8 and 16 a γ has been written above the first ν in ενκατοικων and ελενξιν respectively, making them εγκατοικων and ελεγξιν.

4. When the letters of the text were traced over at a later point in its history, the ε in all of the itacisms mentioned above was not darkened. To this extent they were all corrected.

The scribe of 2 Peter in Vaticanus is the one called B, who wrote the entire New Testament. He also wrote part of the Old Testament; the rest was written by the scribe called A. Tischendorf suggested that scribe B of Vaticanus was the same as scribe D of Sinaiticus. By contrast, Milne and Skeat argue that the writing style of Vaticanus's scribe A is more similar to that of Sinaiticus's scribe D. Although the similarity is not great enough to be sure the same scribe wrote both, it is great enough to be sure they come from the same scribal tradition.[32] T. C. Skeat argues that is reasonable to assume that both texts come from the same scriptorium or at least the same place, i.e., Caesarea, about the same time.[33]

The Meaning of 2 Peter in Codex Vaticanus

There are so few distinctive features of 2 Peter in Vaticanus that reading it differs very little from reading the probable original text. Vaticanus has a couple of the distinctive readings that are also found in Codex Sinaiticus, but in Vaticanus they do not fit into a general theme the way they do in Sinaiticus. Thus, in 2:4 Vaticanus (like Sinaiticus) has σειροις ζοφου (pits of gloom), while the probable original text has σειραις ζοφου (chains of gloom). The latter presents darkness as something with which the sinful angels can be chained; the former names the place to which they were delivered, i.e., dark pits. In this way, Vaticanus is more specific than the probable original text about the punishment suffered by the angels. And in 2:11 Vaticanus (like Sinaiticus) has παρα κω (before the Lord), while the probable original text has παρα κυριου (from the Lord). The latter says that angels do not bring a slanderous judgment from the Lord, but Vaticanus denies that angels bring a slanderous judgment before the Lord. This avoids any suggestion that God might be the source of a slanderous judgment and so emphasizes the transcendence of God.

Vaticanus also has a couple of notable readings that are not found in Sinaiticus. However, once again they do not indicate a general theme of this copy of 2 Peter. In Vaticanus (as in P72) the first words of the letter identify its author as Σιμων Πετρος (Simon Peter) rather than Συμεων Πετρος (Simeon Peter), as in the most likely original text. This has the effect of making the author more recognizable as the Σιμων Πετρος mentioned in other New Testament writings, since this is the form of his name everywhere else but Acts 15:14. And in 2:13 Vaticanus has αγαπαις (love feasts), while the likely original text has απαταις (deceits). Perhaps under the influence of the parallel passage in Jude 12, Vaticanus locates the misbehavior of the false teachers specifically at formal celebrations of the Christian church; the likely original text is less specific about the meals at which the misbehavior

---

32. Milne and Skeat, *Scribes and Correctors*, 89–90.

33. Skeat, "Codex Sinaiticus, the Codex Vaticanus and Constantine" in Elliott, *Collected Biblical Writings*, 193–237, esp. 209–15. Others argue that Codex Vaticanus derives from Alexandria or even from Rome; arguments for both are found in Andrist, *Le manuscrit B de la Bible*. J. K. Elliott discusses all three possibilities and argues that Skeat is correct in "T. C. Skeat on the Dating and Origin of Codex Vaticanus" in Elliott, *Collected Biblical Writings*, 281–94.

occurs. Jude 12 is the earliest passage to use αγαπη (love) with this meaning, but this later became common usage. Another early instance is probably to be seen in Ignatius, *Smyrn.* 8.2.[34]

* * *

The most important differences among the three earliest copies of 2 Peter concern the way they present Jesus. Readers of 2 Peter in Codex Vaticanus found Jesus presented the same way as in the probable original text, i. e., as God yet distinct from God. Readers of 2 Peter in P72 found less emphasis on the distinction between Jesus and God and thus more emphasis on the divinity of Jesus than in the probable original text of 2 Peter (and in the Codex Vaticanus copy). Readers of 2 Peter in Codex Sinaiticus found a less explicit presentation of Jesus as God and thus more emphasis on the distinction between Jesus and God than in the probable original text of 2 Peter (and in the Codex Vaticanus copy). In conjunction with this, readers of 2 Peter in Sinaiticus also found a greater emphasis on the transcendence of God than is found in the likely original text.

Readers of 2 Peter in P72 also found it different in other ways than the probable original text. It presents the view that humans need salvation from desire rather than from corruption; is somewhat more consistently presented as a testamentary letter; views prophecy as something alongside scripture rather than part of it; and has a somewhat less complex eschatology than does the probable original text. Readers of Codex Sinaiticus found a text in which some of the probable original text's difficulties had been moderated and whose meaning was more explicit than that of the likely original text. Readers of 2 Peter in Vaticanus read a text very close to that of the probable original text.

Readers of 2 Peter in P72 did not read it as part of the Bible and did not read a text written by an expert professional scribe. Readers of 2 Peter in Codices Sinaiticus and Vaticanus did read it as part of the Bible and read a professionally copied text. But the work of the scribe of Vaticanus was much better than that of Sinaiticus.

---

34. On this, see Bauckham, *Jude, 2 Peter*, 84–85.

Appendix A

Itacisms and other errors based on replacing a letter or letters with similar sounding letters in P72

Itacisms of Various Kinds

1. ει for ι—forty-five times [1:1, 2 (twice), 3, 4 (four times), 5 (twice), 6, 8, 9, 10, 12, 13, 14, 16, 20 (three times); 2:1, 6, 7, 10 (three times), 13 (twice), 17, 18, 19, 20, 21, 22 (three times); 3:1, 3 (twice), 4, 7, 11, 14, 15]
2. ι for ει—twenty-nine times [1:3 (twice), 6 (twice), 7, 11, 12 (twice), 13, 14, 16, 20, 21; 2:1, 2 (twice), 3, 4, 5, 6, 7, 15, 21; 3:1, 10, 11 (twice), 12, 15]
3. ε for αι—twenty-six times [1:1, 4, 10 (twice), 11, 13, 19 (twice); 2:1 (twice), 5 (twice), 7, 8 (twice), 17 (three times), 18, 19 (twice), 21; 3:3 (twice), 13, 16]
4. αι for ε—two times [3:14, 17]
5. η for ει—three times [1:2, 6; 3:18]
6. α for ε—two times [2:15; 3:14]
7. υ for οι—eight times [2:8, 14, 22; 3:1, 10 (twice), 12, 16]

Other errors based on replacing a letter or letters with a similar sounding letter or letters include:

1. ο for ω (1:3) and ω for ο (1:19; 3:8—or is this a change from accusative to dative case?)
2. ο for ου (1:5)
3. νκ instead of γκ (1:6 [twice]; 2:8)
4. τ instead of π (1:9, 21)
5. inserting ν before τ (1:15)
6. δ instead of θ and ζ instead of δ (2:10)
7. η instead of α (2:10; 3:5)
8. ου instead of ω (2:13)
9. ν instead of μ before π (2:20; 3:3)

Appendix B

Itacisms and other errors based on replacing a letter or letters with similar sounding letters in Codex Sinaiticus

Itacisms of Various Kinds

1. ι for ει—forty-three times [1:2 (twice), 3 (twice), 5, 6 (three times), 7, 11, 12 (three times), 13 (twice), 17, 18, 19, 20; 2:1 (three times), 2 (twice), 4 (twice), 5, 6 (twice), 7, 9 (twice), 10, 11 (twice), 18, 21 (twice); 3:1, 4, 9, 12, 18]
2. ει for ι—three times [1:14; 2:11, 16]
3. ε for αι—five times [1:10; 2:17; 3:3 (twice), 13]
4. αι for ε—one time [1:19]
5. υ for οι—one time [3:10]

Other errors based on replacing a letter or letters with a similar sounding letter or letters include:

1. ν instead of μ before π (2:3)
2. νκ instead of γκ (2:8)

12

The Second Letter of Peter, Josephus, and Gnosticism

Jörg Frey has made a provocative and plausible case for 2 Peter's dependence on the Apocalypse of Peter.[1] In what follows, I will argue 2 Peter's possible relationship to two other items. Both have been proposed in the past but are presently rejected by scholars. The first proposal is that 2 Peter shows evidence its author had read Josephus; the second is that the false teachers opposed by 2 Peter were Gnostics.[2]

Second Peter and Josephus

Use of Josephus by 2 Peter was first argued by Edwin A. Abbott in 1882.[3] F. W. Farrar agreed that Abbott had proved a literary relationship between the two, but thought use of 2 Peter by Josephus was just as likely as the reverse.[4]

---

1. In Frey, "Second Peter in New Perspective."
2. At present, the meaning and adequacy of Gnosticism as a category is questioned by many, including Williams, *Rethinking "Gnosticism"* and King, *What Is Gnosticism?* Nevertheless, "Gnosticism" continues to be used, as it is in this essay, as a convenient name for the various groups criticized by Irenaeus and other such writers and the various views expressed in the Nag Hammadi texts and similar writings. A recent example of this usage can be seen in Pearson, *Ancient Gnosticism*.
3. Abbott, "Second Epistle of Peter I."
4. Farrar, "Dr. Abbott on the Second Epistle of St. Peter," 403–10.

Abbott's arguments were rejected by Benjamin B. Warfield and others[5] and have mostly been abandoned today.[6]

Abbott's purpose in arguing that 2 Peter had used Josephus was to show that 2 Peter was written too late to have been written by Peter.[7] His argument was based mainly on the use by 2 Peter of groups of uncommon words found in particular passages of Josephus's writings. Abbott argued that 2 Peter especially used two passages from Josephus's *Antiquities*, namely 1.14–26 and 4.177–93.[8] In further support of the idea that 2 Peter used these passages of Josephus, Abbott also mentioned two places where single words and isolated phrases are found in both 2 Peter and Josephus: 2 Peter 2:10 is similar to *J.W.* 3.475 and 2 Peter 1:19 is similar to *Ant.* 11.280. Finally, Abbott mentioned two places where the language of 2 Peter was not at all similar to that of Josephus, but where the two agree in supplementing the biblical narrative in the same way: 2 Peter 2:5 agrees with *Ant.* 1.74, and 2 Peter 2:16 agrees with *Ant.* 4.109.

In rejecting Abbott's argument, Warfield begins by denying that the two places where single words and isolated phrases are found in both 2 Peter and Josephus, and the two places where the two authors similarly supplement the biblical narrative, demonstrate, or even support, a literary connection between them.[9] Warfield responds to Abbott's main argument by observing that the method Abbott has used to argue 2 Peter used Josephus is "an exceedingly unsafe one"[10] and that Abbott has not made very good use of it. Warfield criticizes Abbott's use of his method on four grounds:

1. Abbott fails to distinguish among different kinds of evidence with different degrees of persuasive force. Warfield lists four different kinds of evidence in increasing order of persuasiveness:

    a. general resemblance of vocabulary

    b. common possession of a peculiar vocabulary

    c. a number of rare words grouped together in a brief context in one, found also in the other, either

---

5. Warfield, "Dr. Edwin A. Abbott," 421–44; Salmon, *Historical Introduction*, 547–56; Mayor, *St. Jude and St. Peter*, cxxvii–cxxx; James, *Peter and Jude*, xxv; Fillion, "Pierre (Deuxième Épitre de Saint)," cols. 409–10.

6. Bauckham, *Jude, 2 Peter*, 140.

7. Abbott, "Second Epistle of Peter I," 49–52.

8. Abbott, "Second Epistle of Peter I," discusses the first of these passages on 56–59 and the second on 59–61.

9. Warfield, "Dr. Edwin A. Abbott," 422–24.

10. Warfield, "Dr. Edwin A. Abbott," 428.

1. scattered through the writing, or
2. similarly grouped

   d. clauses or sentences occurring in both, either verbatim or nearly so, or with strongly marked similarities.

2. Abbott does not carefully remove from his list of similarities items that do not suggest borrowing. By this, Warfield mainly means words that are too common to suggest borrowing, but he also means words that might be accounted for by borrowing from another source.
3. Abbott does not distinguish between "what is sound and what is merely plausible."[11]
4. Abbott does not argue sufficiently for his explanation of the similarities between the two writings over against other possible explanations.

Despite all this, Warfield acknowledges that there are indeed similarities between 2 Peter and Josephus, though he denies that they indicate dependence of 2 Peter on Josephus.[12]

George Salmon's rejection of Abbott's argument is similar but much more sweeping. He first notes that Abbott's alleged similarities between 2 Peter and Josephus "relate entirely to words and not at all to the thoughts."[13] Salmon then argues that the similarities (1) do not appear in passages of brief compass; (2) are not in the same sequence and connection; and (3) do not involve unusual or startling words. He elaborates the last point at some length, especially observing that Abbott improperly regards any words that do not occur in the Septuagint as unusual. Finally, Salmon argues that the combinations of words to which Abbott appeals are of a commonplace character. Salmon concludes that Abbott "has completely failed to establish his theory."[14]

Salmon and those who follow him (James, Fillion, Bauckham) completely reject Abbott's argument, but this rejection seems excessive. Farrar responded to Salmon's arguments in some detail.[15] Farrar argues that the similarities between 2 Peter and Josephus (1) do appear in relatively brief passages, (2) in somewhat the same sequence, and (3) involve somewhat

---

11. Warfield, "Dr. Edwin A. Abbott," 433.
12. Warfield, "Dr. Edwin A. Abbott," 438–39, 443.
13. Salmon, *Historical Introduction*, 549.
14. Salmon, *Historical Introduction*, 556. James makes the same argument more briefly (*Peter and Jude*, xxv) as does Fillion, "Pierre (Deuxième Épitre de Saint)," cols. 409–10.
15. Farrar, "Second Epistle of St. Peter," 58–69.

unusual words and phrases. In addition, it is not accurate to say that the resemblances between 2 Peter and Josephus relate only to words and not at all to thoughts.[16] As we have noted above, even as Warfield criticized Abbott's argument, he admitted the existence of significant similarities between 2 Peter and Josephus. Likewise, Joseph B. Mayor does not think the connection between 2 Peter and Josephus is as close as Abbott suggests, but he acknowledges that there is a marked resemblance between the vocabulary and many of the ideas of the two writers.[17]

Abbott's critics have at least identified some weaknesses of his argument that must be acknowledged. As Salmon says, we certainly cannot regard vocabulary as unusual simply because it is not used by the Septuagint. We can agree with Warfield that the two places where 2 Peter and Josephus supplement the biblical narrative in similar ways do not suggest a literary relationship between the two. We can also agree that the strongest evidence for such a literary relationship consists of instances where (1) a number of rare words grouped together in a brief context in one, are found also in the other similarly grouped, and (2) clauses or sentences occur in both, either verbatim or nearly so, or with strongly marked similarities. The two passages on which Abbott mainly focused provide evidence of somewhat this kind.

One of these passages, *Ant.* 4.177–93, is one of Moses's farewell speeches. Abbott himself noted parallels to the vocabulary of this passage scattered throughout 2 Peter. His critics have rightly objected that many of these words are not very uncommon. However, a number of these parallels are found in 2 Peter 1:12–15, a passage that refers explicitly to 2 Peter as providing a farewell message from Peter.[18] These parallels, even if they do not involve very uncommon words, are more suggestive of a literary relationship.

	Ant. 4.177–93	2 Pet 1:12–15
a)	In the future Moses will not (οὐ μέλλω) be the Israelites' helper (177)	Peter will (μελλήσω) always remind those he addresses (v. 12)

---

16. Farrar, "Second Epistle of St. Peter," 62–65.

17. Mayor, *St. Jude and St. Peter*, cxxix.

18. Windisch (*Katholische Briefe*, 87–88) also notes some of these parallels, though he does not conclude there is a literary relationship between the two.

b)	Moses considered it right (δίκαιον ἡγησάμην) to continue working for the Israelites (178)	Peter considers it right (δίκαιον δὲ ἡγοῦμαι) to remind the addressees (v. 13)
c)	Moses provides a lasting memory (μνήμην) of himself (178)	Peter wants the addressees to have memory (μνήμην) of these things (v. 15)
d)	Israelites' possession of good things will rest assured (βεβαία) (180, cf. 192)	Addressees are established (ἐσηριγμένους) in truth (v. 12)
e)	Present (παρόντων) laws of the Israelites (181)	Present (παρούσῃ) truth of addressees (v. 12)
f)	As long as (ἐφ' ὅσον) the Israelites want God's protection (185)	As long as (ἐφ' ὅσον) Peter is in this tent (v. 13)
g)	Moses is at his exit from life (ἐπ' ἐξόδῳ τοῦ ζῆν) (189)	Peter refers to what will happen after his departure (μετὰ τὴν ἐμὴν ἔξοδον) (v. 15)
h)	Moses does not want to call painful memories to mind (εἰς ἀνάμνησιν φέρων) (189)	Peter wants to remind the addressees (ὑπομιμνῄσκειν—v. 12) (διεγείρειν ὑμᾶς ἐν ὑπομνήσει—v. 13)

Abbott mentions all of these items except "d," which is less persuasive than others because it involves synonyms rather use of the same words. This also applies to "h." The remaining items are more strongly suggestive of a literary relationship between the two passages. None of these words is really uncommon, and all suit the general situation of farewell. However, we can see from another farewell speech of Moses in Josephus, namely *Ant.* 4.309–19, that the terms are not inevitable in such a context. The latter passage includes only μνήμην (318).[19]

Probably the most striking item on the list is use of the term "departure" (ἔξοδος) for death (item "g"). Warfield argues that 2 Peter derived this term from Luke 9:31.[20] To me, this seems no more likely than that it was derived from Josephus.[21] Salmon argues that the presence of the term in Luke shows that it was in 2 Peter's linguistic sphere. This certainly makes it

19. *Ant.* 4.309–19 also uses πάρειμι several times, but not in the sense found in item "e."

20. Warfield, "Dr. Edwin A. Abbott," 432.

21. Bauckham (*Jude, 2 Peter*, 202) rejects dependence of 2 Pet 1:15 on Luke 9:31.

impossible to argue that 2 Peter must have derived the word from Josephus, but not that it might have been suggested by Josephus.

The other passage on which Abbott focused, *Ant.* 1.14–26, is part of the prologue to the *Antiquities*. As with *Ant.* 4.177–93, Abbott himself noted parallels to the vocabulary of *Ant.* 1.14–26 scattered throughout 2 Peter. A number of these parallels are found in 2 Peter 1:16–18. These parallels are most suggestive of a literary relationship.

	Ant. 1.14–26	2 Pet 1:16–18
a)	God the father and master (πατήρ τε καὶ δεσπότης ὁ θεός) (20)	God the father (θεοῦ πατρός) (v. 17)
b)	Unlike Moses, other legislators followed myths (μύθοις ἐξακολουθήσαντες) (22)	Peter and others did not follow myths (μύθοις ἐξακολουθήσαντες) (v. 16)
c)	In following myths these legislators gave the wicked a powerful excuse (22)	Peter clearly fears that people will use the mythical character of his teaching as an excuse
d)	The majesty of God (μεγαλειότητα) (24)	The majesty (μεγαλειότητος) of Jesus (v. 16)

Abbott mentions items "b" and "d," and they are the ones most suggestive of a literary relationship between 2 Peter and Josephus. This is especially true of "b." Neither of these words is rare, and their use together is not surprising, but I have not been able find any other passage in which they are in fact used together as they are here. Warfield argues that 2 Peter derived μεγαλειότητος from Luke 9:43.[22] Salmon again argues that the word was in 2 Peter's linguistic sphere and so need not have derived from Josephus.

Abbott did not mention another passage from Josephus, namely *Ant.* 9.51–59, that also has some similarity to 2 Peter 1:16–18. In this passage Josephus recounts an incident from the life of Elisha found in 2 Kgs 6:8–23.

	Ant. 9.51–59	2 Pet 1:16–18
a)	Elisha asked God to manifest God's power and coming (τὴν αὐτοῦ δύναμιν καὶ παρουσίαν) to Elisha's servant (55)	Peter and others made known the power and coming (δύναμιν καὶ παρουσίαν) of Jesus Christ (v. 16)

---

22. Warfield, "Dr. Edwin A. Abbott," 432.

| b) | In response to Elisha's prayer, God permitted Elisha's servant to see (θεάσασθαι) horses and chariots around Elisha (55) | Peter and others were eyewitnesses (ἐπόπται) of Jesus's majesty (v. 16) |

Item "a" is the weightier. It also involves the use of words that are not very uncommon, whose use together is not surprising. But I have not been able to find any other passage in which they are used together as they are here. Both cases also involve seeing ("b") something. Of course, exactly what is seen and what it signifies differs in the two cases.

Thus there is reason to think that there is a literary relationship between 2 Peter 1:12-15 and Josephus, *Ant.* 4.177-93, and between 2 Peter 1:16-18 and two different passages in Josephus, namely, *Ant.* 1:14-26 and 9.51-59. Warfield observes that there are at least four different ways to account for such similarities:

1. Second Peter borrowed from Josephus
2. Josephus borrowed directly or indirectly from 2 Peter
3. the resemblances are due to the influence of a writing known to, and affecting the language of, both
4. the resemblances are due to the common circumstances, surroundings, training and inheritances of the writers.

Warfield rejects the first explanation because he thinks it is almost certain that 2 Peter was composed earlier than 90, too early for the author to have used Josephus's *Antiquities*.[23] He does not think it possible to choose among the remaining three explanations. Mayor embraces the fourth explanation, attributing the similarities to the authors' being "Jews, trained on the old sacred books and familiar with later Jewish writings, such as Philo."[24] To me, it seems that the first explanation is the most likely. It seems unlikely that Josephus would have borrowed from 2 Peter, both because it seems unlikely that Josephus would have known 2 Peter even if it was already in existence at the time Josephus wrote, and because 2 Peter was probably written after the time of Josephus.[25] There is no direct evidence that a source common to 2 Peter and Josephus existed. And I am not sure how similar the circumstances, training and inheritances of the two writers were. This leaves 2 Peter's borrowing from Josephus the most likely of the four.

23. Warfield, "Dr. Edwin A. Abbott," 439-41.
24. Mayor, *St. Jude and St. Peter*, cxxix.
25. On the date of 2 Peter, see Callan, *Acknowledging the Divine Benefactor*, 35-37.

If it can be considered likely that 2 Peter used Josephus, some of the other points of similarity between them mentioned by Abbott can be considered supportive of this. Two of these are rather striking. In *Ant.* 11.280 a letter from Artaxerxes, king of Persia, refers to letters sent by Haman as something the recipients will do well to disregard (οἷς ποιήσετε καλῶς μὴ προσέχοντες). Second Peter 1:19 says that the prophetic word is something the addressees will do well to heed (ᾧ καλῶς ποιεῖτε προσέχοντες). The words that make up these clauses are not uncommon, and there is nothing striking about this way of combining them. But if on other grounds we have reason to think 2 Peter used Josephus, this similarity could be another instance of phraseology suggested to the author of 2 Peter by Josephus. Similarly, *J.W.* 3.475 says that the Jews, even if very bold and despisers of death (τολμηταὶ καὶ θανάτου καταφρονοῦντες), are a rabble rather than an army. Second Peter 2:10 speaks of people who despise dominion and then says that they are bold (κυριότητος καταφρονοῦντας. τολμηταί). These words might also have been suggested to the author of 2 Peter by his reading of Josephus.

And if it can be considered likely that 2 Peter 1:16-18 used Josephus, *Ant.* 1:14-26, the Josephus passage may also underlie 2 Peter 1:3-4 as Abbott suggested.

	Ant. 1.14-26	2 Pet 1:3-4
a)	Moses's conception of God's nature (φύσιν) (15)—Moses thought it necessary first to study the nature of God (θεοῦ ... φύσιν) (19)	Divine nature (θείας ... φύσεως) (v. 4)
b)	Moses always assigned to God actions worthy of his power (δυνάμει) (15)	Divine power (θείας δυνάμεως) (v. 3)[26]
c)	Moses wrote in regard to virtue (ἀρετῆς)—calamities befall those who step outside the path of virtue (20)—God possesses the perfection of virtue (23)	His own glory and virtue (ἀρετῇ) (v. 3)
d)	God grants those who follow him a happy life (βίον) (20)	Everything for life (ζωὴν) (v. 3)
e)	Obedience to piety (εὐσέβειαν) (21)	Everything for life and piety (εὐσέβειαν) (v. 3)

26. Josephus uses the phrase θείᾳ ... δυνάμει in *Ant.* 9.58.

| f) | Humans should strive to participate in (μεταλαμβάνειν) God's virtue (23) | You may become sharers (κοινωνοί) of divine nature (v. 4)[27] |

The parallels between *Ant.* 1:14–26 and 2 Peter 1:3–4 are less striking than the parallels between it and 2 Peter 1:16–18, though still considerable. The nouns φύσις, δύναμις, ἀρετή, and εὐσέβεια are found in both (a, b, c and e). Although they are not used in similar phrases, they are used in comparable descriptions of God and the way people should relate to God. Somewhat similarly, "d" and "f" use synonyms to present comparable ideas. These parallels would probably not themselves suggest dependence of 2 Peter on Josephus, but are supportive of such dependence established on another basis.

And finally, if it can be considered likely that 2 Peter used Josephus, *Ant.* 1:14–26, the Josephus passage may also underlie 2 Peter 2:9–10a as Abbott suggested. In the *Antiquities* passage Josephus twice summarizes the lesson to be learned from the history of the Jews. In section 14 he says the lesson is that those who follow the will of God receive happiness as a reward; those who do not, experience irretrievable disasters. In section 20 Josephus says the lesson is that God gives those who follow him a happy life, but brings great disasters on those who depart from virtue. In section 23 Josephus says God punished (ἐκόλασε) those who did not believe these doctrines. In 2 Peter 2:9–10a the author draws the conclusion from the Biblical stories he has summarized in 2:4–8 that the Lord knows how to rescue the pious from trial and to keep the unjust confined (κολαζομένους) for the day of judgment. In vocabulary this is not very similar to Josephus's summaries, and it has an apocalyptic character completely absent from Josephus. But like the Josephus passage, it summarizes the import of the Biblical narrative as an assurance of good things for those in harmony with God, and bad things for those who are not. Once again, this similarity would not in itself suggest dependence of 2 Peter on Josephus, but is supportive of such dependence otherwise established.

Second Peter and Gnosticism

At least since the publication of Hermann Werdermann's *Die Irrlehrer des Judas- und 2. Petrusbriefes* in 1913, many have argued that the false teachers opposed by 2 Peter were Gnostics. More specifically, they argued that the

---

27. Josephus uses κεκοινώνηκεν in section 18 to speak of the degree to which *Antiquities* partakes of natural philosophy. In *Ant.* 4.177 Moses addresses the Israelites as partners (κοινωνοί) in a long tribulation.

false teachers were Gnostics of the type that were opposed by Paul, especially in 1 Corinthians. Thus they were not understood as representatives of the Gnostic schools that appeared in the second century, but rather as incipient Gnostics or proto-Gnostics.[28] In 1977, however, Tord Fornberg argued that the false teachers were not Gnostics, but rather gentile Christians influenced by the deterministic view of the universe and moral standards current in their cultural context.[29] And even more importantly, in 1980 Jerome H. Neyrey argued that the false teachers were not Gnostics[30] and that there are significant similarities between the views of the false teachers and Epicurean polemics against Providence.[31] Since that time most commentators, including Jörg Frey,[32] have rejected the view that the false teachers are Gnostics and instead regard them as influenced by Epicureanism or popular philosophy more generally.[33]

For example, Richard J. Bauckham argues that the false teachers were influenced by Hellenistic religious debate and were not Gnostics. He gives two reasons for saying they were not Gnostics. The first is that there is no evidence the false teachers held "the cosmological dualism which is the essential mark of true Gnosticism"; the second is that there is no evidence the false teachers' "ethical libertinism was based on such dualism, or that their eschatological skepticism resulted from a Gnostic concentration on realized, at the expense of future, eschatology."[34] Gene L. Green also argues that the false teachers were not Gnostics and suggests that they were eclectics whose views combined at least four elements: 1) skepticism about the possibility of predictive prophecy, 2) the question of the immutability of the

---

28. Werdermann, *Irrlehrer*. Others who have taken this position include Bigg, *St. Peter and St. Jude*, 239–41; Windisch, *Katholische Briefe*, 98–99; Käsemann, "Apologia," 170–72; Schelkle, *Petrusbriefe*, 230–34; Kelly, *Peter and Jude*, 231; Grundmann, *Judas und Petrus*, 62–64. Charles Talbert ("II Peter and the Delay of the Parousia,") argued that the false teachers were second-century Gnostics but not representatives of the named schools of second-century Gnosticism.

29. Fornberg, *Early Church*, 65, 104–5, 119–20, 132. Fornberg explained those criticized by Paul in 1 Corinthians in the same way (see 104–5, 126).

30. Neyrey, "Apologetic Use," 506.

31. Neyrey, "Form and Background."

32. Frey, "Second Peter in New Perspective," 11.

33. On this development in the understanding of the false teachers, see Bauckham, "2 Peter: An Account of Research," 3724–28; Caulley, "'They Promise Them Freedom,'" 130–32.

34. Bauckham, *Jude, 2 Peter*, 156. Others who take similar positions include Perkins, *First and Second Peter*, 161–62; Davids, *2 Peter and Jude*, 132–36; Caulley, "'They Promise them Freedom'"; Donelson, *I and II Peter and Jude*, 209–10.

world, 3) the promise of freedom, and 4) embrace of immoral conduct.[35] Not all recent commentators have adopted such accounts of the false teachers. Terence V. Smith views them as Gnostics.[36] Henning Paulsen argues that little can be known about the false teachers.[37] Michael Green continues to maintain the view that the false teachers were incipient Gnostics, possibly influenced by the letters of Paul.[38] Daniel J. Harrington also suggests that the false teachers may be Paulinists.[39] Nevertheless, the view that the false teachers are Gnostics has largely been abandoned.

In what follows I will argue that the false teachers are best understood as Gnostics. It is, of course, true that there is no evidence the false teachers were cosmological dualists, or that their eschatological skepticism and ethical libertinism derived from Gnosticism. It is also true that Gnosticism is not the only way to account for the false teachers' eschatological and ethical positions. However, since it is known that there were Christian Gnostics and since Gnosticism is a viable explanation of the false teachers' views, the hypothesis that they were Gnostics remains a strong one. We do not have similar independent confirmation that there existed Christian groups with the characteristics attributed to the false teachers by Fornberg, Neyrey, Bauckham and Green.

How might Gnostic views account for the false teachers' eschatological skepticism and ethical libertinism? It seems fairly clear that some of those opposed by Paul in 1 Corinthians thought that salvation was a present reality with little or nothing to be awaited in the future (cf. 1 Cor 4:8; 15:12). And some of those he opposed were libertines (cf. 1 Cor 5:1; 6:15). Insofar as those opposed by Paul were incipient Gnostics, this libertinism and lack of future eschatological expectation can be seen as characteristic of Gnosticism.

The understanding of Gnosticism as characterized by emphasis on realized eschatology is explored at some length by Malcom Peel in his article "Gnostic Eschatology and the New Testament."[40] Peel points out that

---

35. Green, *Jude and 2 Peter*, 153–59. G. Green's second element is based on Adams, "'Where is the Promise of his Coming?'"

36. Smith, *Petrine Controversies in Early Christianity*, 92–93. Smith lists a number of earlier scholars who think the false teachers are Gnostics.

37. Paulsen, *Der Zweite Petrusbrief*, 95–97.

38. Green, *Peter and Jude*, 37–40; so also Knoch, *Erste und Zweite Petrusbrief*, 208–12; Harvey and Towner, *2 Peter and Jude*, 17, though they do not refer to the possible influence of Paul's letters.

39. Harrington, "Jude and 2 Peter," 235.

40. Peel, "Gnostic Eschatology and the New Testament," esp. 143–55. A more recent treatment of Gnosticism as characterized by realized eschatology can be seen in

the Nag Hammadi texts show future eschatology was not entirely lacking in Gnosticism, even if it is less prominent than realized eschatology.[41] Peel points especially to the expectation that in the future the scattered sparks of divine light will all be reunited with God, and the material world will come to an end.

One example of Gnostic future eschatology is provided by the Nag Hammadi Revelation of Peter, a text that seems to have some relationship to 2 Peter.[42] Smith suggests that the Revelation of Peter represents the kind of Gnosticism against which 2 Peter argues;[43] Birger A. Pearson argues that the Revelation of Peter depends on 2 Peter.[44] The Revelation of Peter recounts a conversation between Peter and Jesus shortly before Jesus's arrest and crucifixion. Peter describes several visions to Jesus, and Jesus interprets them. The central section of the document is a lengthy discourse of Jesus (NHC VII 73.10–81.3) that interprets the first vision Peter describes to Jesus. This discourse predicts opposition between the little ones who are the true followers of Jesus and other, false Christians. Jesus promises punishment of the latter and reward for the former. The false Christians will experience eternal destruction (NHC VII 75.21–22), will dissolve into non-existence (NHC VII 76.18–23), be cast into outer darkness (NHC VII 78.23–24), be punished (NHC VII 79.17). On the other hand, the little ones will receive a reward (NHC VII 80.15–16). Perhaps the single most striking element is the reference to the future παρουσία of Jesus in NHC VII 78.6. This, however, is only mentioned in passing; nothing is said about its significance or what will happen when Jesus returns.

In view of this, we can say more precisely that what is lacking in Gnosticism is not future expectation, but rather expectation of a future for the material world. While Gnostics may have expected the end of the material universe, they did not expect a new heaven and earth after that end. And they did not expect the physical return of the redeemer. Nor did they give credence to prophecy since it was an element of the material universe. Thus Gnosticism could well account for the eschatological views 2 Peter is concerned to oppose.

Pétrement, *Separate God*, 160–62.

41. Peel, "Gnostic Eschatology and the New Testament," 155–62.

42. This text is also known as the Apocalypse of Peter, but it should not be confused with the other text known as the Apocalypse of Peter, which Jörg Frey focuses on.

43. Smith, *Petrine Controversies in Early Christianity*, 126–41, esp. 137–41.

44. Pearson, "Apocalypse of Peter and Canonical 2 Peter."

In principle, Gnosticism allowed for ethical libertinism and Gnostics were criticized for it by the Church Fathers.[45] None of the Nag Hammadi texts seem to take a libertine position. This raises the question to what extent the Gnostics actually were libertines. But whether they were libertines, or were simply vilified for libertinism, Gnosticism could account for 2 Peter's ethical criticisms of the false teachers and their followers.

If we have established the likelihood that the false teachers were Gnostics, can we say what kind of Gnostics they were? J. W. C. Wand and Smith suggest that 2 Peter might be directed specifically against followers of Basilides.[46] I agree that there is some reason to think the false teachers may be followers of Basilides.

In the first place, Basilides, like other Gnostics, did not expect salvation of the material world. And like other Gnostics, he was said to be ethically libertine. The first of these is not explicit in accounts of Basilides's teaching, but is implied by the presentation of material creation as deriving from powers inferior to the true God (Irenaeus, *Haer.* 1.24.4) and the view that salvation belongs to the soul alone while the body is by nature subject to corruption (Irenaeus, *Haer.* 1.24.5).[47] In *Haer.* 1.24.3 Irenaeus describes Basilides's view that from the unoriginate Father originated successively five beings: Nous, Logos, Phronesis, Sophia and Dynamis. From Sophia and Dynamis originated powers, principalities and angels who made the first heaven. From them emanated other angels who made a second heaven. This happened again and again until a total of 365 heavens were made. The last of these is the one humans see. Smith thinks Basilides "maintained that the heavens would continue to be formed forever and would therefore never be destroyed" citing Irenaeus, *Haer.* 1.24.3.[48] This is possible, but not explicit

45. Rudolph, *Gnosis*, 252–57.

46. Wand, *St. Peter and St. Jude*, 142; Smith, *Petrine Controversies in Early Christianity*, 92–93. Smith thinks 2 Peter is directed both against the kind of Gnosticism represented by the Revelation of Peter and against the followers of Basilides. This seems to imply that the Revelation of Peter represents the teaching of Basilides, but Smith does not take up this implication. The idea that the Revelation of Peter might be Basilidean is entertained by Desjardins in "Introduction to VII,3," 208.

47. Like others, I derive my information about Basilides from the account of Irenaeus and the fragments of Basilides's teaching found mainly in Clement of Alexandria, *Stromateis*, and make little use of the very different account of Basilides given by Hippolytus. Bentley Layton suggests that Hippolytus's account may reflect later development of Basilides's teaching (Layton, *Gnostic Scriptures*, 418–19n2).

48. Smith, *Petrine Controversies in Early Christianity*, 93. Smith sees this as the principal reason for thinking 2 Peter might be directed against Basilideans. Because of uncertainty that this actually was Basilides's position, I give equal weight to the other items Smith mentions, all of which are discussed below. Irenaeus does say in *Haer.* 2.35.1 that Basilides's views imply that the heavens would continue to be formed forever, but it is

in Irenaeus, and I think it equally likely that Basilides would have expected such destruction. Second Peter's argument that this world will end and be replaced by a new heaven and earth would have been appropriate as a response either to the view that the heavens would continue to be formed forever, or to the view that they would be destroyed and not replaced. Basilides apparently expected what he called the restoration,[49] but its meaning for him is uncertain. Perhaps it referred to the reunion of the scattered sparks of divine light with God.[50]

Irenaeus explicitly asserts Basilides's libertinism (*Haer.* 1.24.5). However, judging from the surviving fragments of his teaching, if Basilides may be regarded as a libertine at all, it is only in the sense that he considered behavior a matter of indifference. Basilides apparently took the Stoic view that one should align oneself with the order in the universe. One should love all that is, desiring nothing and having nothing (Clement of Alexandria, *Strom.* 4.12 §86.1).[51] Basilides further argues that all suffering is a consequence of the sufferer's sins and thus part of the order in the universe. He applies this to martyrs, to children and to Jesus (Clement of Alexandria, *Strom.* 4.12 §81.2–83.2). Second Peter's argument that a virtuous life is necessary to continue in one's status as a person saved by Jesus would be appropriate as a response to libertinism or to the view that behavior does not matter.

Like some other Gnostics, Basilides denied the crucifixion of Jesus. According to Irenaeus, Basilides maintained that Jesus exchanged places and appearances with Simon of Cyrene at the time of the crucifixion, so that Simon was the one who was actually crucified, not Jesus. As Simon (who appeared to be Jesus) was crucified, Jesus (who appeared to be Simon) stood by and laughed (Irenaeus, *Haer.* 1.24.4). Partly because of the comment on the suffering of Jesus mentioned above, Pearson doubts Irenaeus's account. He suggests that Basilides thought the divine Nous-Christ descended into the human Jesus, probably at his baptism, and returned to the Father at Jesus's crucifixion.[52] Thus only the human Jesus suffered, not the divine

not clear that Basilides himself would agree.

49. See ἀποκαταστατικῆς in Clement of Alexandria, *Strom.* 2.8 §36.1; ἀποκατασταθήσεται in Hippolytus, *Haer.* 7.26.1–2; cf. ἀποκατάστασις in Revelation of Peter (NHC VII 74:9).

50. Note, however, that no explicit statement of an anthropology according to which at least some humans are trapped sparks of divine light is attributed to Basilides. On the meaning of ἀποκατάστασις for Basilides, see Pearson, "Basilides the Gnostic," 24; Méhat, "ΑΠΟΚΑΤΑΣΤΑΣΙΣ chez Basilide."

51. Pearson, "Basilides the Gnostic," 25.

52. Pearson, "Basilides the Gnostic," 23. Layton, however, seems to accept Irenaeus's account at face value ("Significance of Basilides," 144–45).

Nous-Christ. A similar view is presented in Revelation of Peter (NHC VII 81.3–83.15). Here Jesus interprets one of Peter's visions as a vision of the living Jesus smiling and laughing above the cross on which his fleshly part has been crucified. The reference in 2 Peter 2:1 to the false teachers as denying the master who bought them might refer to this view. Basilides does not see the death of Jesus as a saving action, but rather as a consequence of sin. Second Peter seems to understand Jesus's death as the price he paid to buy his followers.

Other links between Basilides and the false teachers of 2 Peter include:

1. Some sources suggest a connection between Basilides and Peter. According to Clement of Alexandria, *Strom.* 7.17 §106.4, Basilides derived his teaching from Peter via Glaucias.[53] And the teaching of Basilides reported by Clement in *Strom.* 4.12 §81.2–83.2 may be a comment on 1 Pet 4:12–19. Basilides may represent a Petrine tradition that 2 Peter considers false and tries to counter with the true teaching of Peter.

2. Basilides maintained that prophets came into being through the craftsmen of the world (Irenaeus, *Haer.* 1.24.5); cf. Revelation of Peter (NHC VII 71.6–9). The affirmation of prophecy in 2 Pet 1:19–2:10a, and especially in 1:20–21, might be intended to counter this.

3. Epiphanius, *Pan.* 24.5.2 says that Basilides referred to non-Gnostics as pigs and dogs (ὕες καὶ κύνες). Second Peter 2:22, which compares the followers of the false teachers and the false teachers themselves to a dog (κύων) and a sow (ὗς), might turn these epithets back against those who used them.

4. Origen, *Commentary on the Epistle to the Romans* (PG 1015A–B), says that Basilides has related Rom 7:10 to irrelevant, blasphemous myths (*ineptas et impias fabulas*). These myths concern reincarnation as a human being after having been a domestic animal or bird, and perhaps include an account of the ultimate origin of the soul. This might be an example of the things in the letters of Paul that are hard to understand that the ignorant and unstable twist to their own destruction according to 2 Pet 3:15–16.

---

53. Note, however, that Hippolytus, *Haer.* 7.20.1 says that Basilides derived his teaching from Jesus via Matthias.

Conclusion

I have argued there is reason to think the author of 2 Peter had read the writings of Josephus and was influenced by them at several points. I have also argued there is reason to think the false teachers opposed by 2 Peter were Gnostics, most likely followers of Basilides. Dependence of 2 Peter on Josephus and the Gnostic identity of the false teachers are old scholarly proposals that do not presently receive much support. I have tried to show that these proposals still have merit. The specific suggestion that the false teachers were followers of Basilides is a more recent proposal that I have also argued has merit.

Dependence of 2 Peter on Josephus adds one more to the already long list of literary sources of 2 Peter. As is widely recognized, 2 Peter 2:1–3:3 makes extensive use of Jude. Second Peter 3:15–16 refers to the letters of Paul, and 2 Peter 3:1 probably refers to 1 Peter. In addition, 2 Peter mentions passages from a number of Old Testament writings—Genesis, Numbers, Isaiah, Proverbs and Psalms—and passages from the Gospels of Matthew and John.[54] To this list Jörg Frey has argued that we should add the Apocalypse of Peter; now I have argued that we should add Josephus.

Dependence of 2 Peter on Josephus and the idea that the false teachers it opposes were followers of Basilides have implications for the date of 2 Peter. If 2 Peter depends on Josephus, it must have been written after the date of Josephus's writings. These are usually considered to have been completed c. 100. If 2 Peter opposes followers of Basilides, it must have been written after Basilides began teaching. In *Strom.* 7.17 §106.4, Clement of Alexandria says that Basilides arose during the reign of Hadrian (i.e., 118–38). Clement is arguing that heretical teachers like Basilides came after the time of the apostles so he has an interest in specifying a late date. However, opposing followers of Basilides probably requires that 2 Peter was written somewhat later than does dependence on Josephus. These implications for the date of 2 Peter are compatible with, and thus broadly supportive of, Frey's argument that 2 Peter depends on the Apocalypse of Peter, written c. 130–35. However, dependence of 2 Peter on the Apocalypse of Peter clearly requires that it be written at a later date than does dependence on Josephus, and may require a later date than does opposing followers of Basilides.

Dependence of 2 Peter on Josephus and the idea that the false teachers it opposes were followers of Basilides also have implications for the place where 2 Peter was written. Dependence of 2 Peter on Josephus most strongly suggests composition of 2 Peter in Rome where Josephus lived and wrote;

---

54. On this, see Callan, *Acknowledging the Divine Benefactor*, 15–18, and also chapter 9, "The Gospels of Matthew and John in the Second Letter of Peter."

opposition to followers of Basilides most strongly suggests that 2 Peter was written in Alexandria where Basilides was active. The latter is supportive of Frey's view that 2 Peter was written in Alexandria.

Although dependence of 2 Peter on Josephus might have been easiest if 2 Peter were written in Rome, there is some indication that Josephus's writings were rather widely dispersed and so could be used by those living outside of Rome. The earliest reference to Josephus seems to be found in a fragment of a lost writing of Irenaeus who wrote from Gaul in Greek about 180.[55] In this fragment Irenaeus mentions Josephus and paraphrases part of his account of the life of Moses found in *Ant.* 2.10. At about the same time (c. 169–83) Theophilus mentions Josephus in *Apology to Autolycus* 3.23 written in Greek in Antioch. Theophilus speaks of Josephus as having written about the Jewish war and says that Josephus gives information about the date of the law of Moses. Somewhat later Tertullian mentions Josephus in *Apology* 19 written from Carthage in Latin about 197. Tertullian speaks of Josephus as the vindicator of the ancient history of his people. About the same time Clement mentions Josephus in *Strom.* 1.21 §147.2–4 written from Alexandria in Greek c. 198–203. He speaks of Josephus as composing a history of the Jews and presents a chronology drawn from Josephus's works.

Not much later, other Greek writers mention Josephus: Hippolytus (170–235) in a fragment of a commentary on Jeremiah and Ezekiel written in Rome;[56] and Origen in several passages including *Contra Celsum* 1.16 written in Caesarea c. 248.[57] Minucius Felix, a Latin writer living in Rome who died about 250, mentions Josephus in *Octavius* 33.

This suggests that Josephus was widely known and that use of his writings might have been possible in many different places, including Alexandria. Of course, this does not make Alexandria any more likely than Rome, Gaul, Antioch, Carthage or Caesarea as a place where the author of 2 Peter might have used Josephus. And on the other hand, the teaching of Basilides was known outside of Alexandria. Irenaeus in Gaul is obviously aware of it in 180. It is commonly supposed that Irenaeus depends on a lost writing of Justin (cf. *First Apology* 26). If so, this suggests knowledge of Basilides in Rome c. 150.

---

55. Fragment XXXII (*ANF* 1:573).

56. *ANF* 5:177.

57. Other passages: *Contra Celsum* 1.47; 4.11; *Commentary on the Gospel of Matthew* 10.17.

Appendix A

Reading the Copies of 2 Peter in Codices Alexandrinus and Ephraemi Syri Rescriptus

Codex Alexandrinus (A)

a) The Form of the Text

Codex Alexandrinus[1] is a parchment codex. Its pages are 12.6 inches by 10.4 inches (slightly larger than those of Vaticanus) and have two columns per page. Each column has 49–51 lines. Codex Alexandrinus is another biblical codex. The codex contains the entire Old Testament as well as 3–4 Maccabees, Psalm 151, and some other non-biblical writings. It also contains the entire New Testament along with most of 1–2 Clement. Readers of this copy of 2 Peter would have known from the codex that they were reading part of the Bible.

The scribe who wrote 2 Peter in Codex Alexandrinus was less skillful than the corresponding scribe of Codex Vaticanus, but is second best of the scribes who wrote the early copies of 2 Peter we are examining. I count 29 itacisms and other errors based on replacing a letter or letters with similar sounding letters in 2 Peter.[2]

There are three words in 2:5 that are only partly written, probably because of damage to the manuscript. Thus only the N of Νωε, only εφυ of εφυλαξεν, and only ασε of ασεβων are visible.

---

1. The Codex Alexandrinus New Testament is available online at The Center for the Study of New Testament Manuscripts: http://www.csntm.org/Manuscripts/ManuscriptViewPage.aspx?id=203.

2. See Appendix B.

In 2:14 μοιχαλιας may be a misspelling of μοιχαλιδος, perhaps based on misunderstanding the word as it was read. Although μοιχαλιας is found at this same point in two other manuscripts, namely Sinaiticus and 33, it does not seem to be part of the vocabulary of the Greek language. Likewise, in the same verse ακαταπαστους may be a misspelling of ακαταπαυστους; although it is also found in Vaticanus, the former does not seem to be part of the vocabulary of the Greek language.

There are three grammatical errors in the manuscript. In 2:7 Alexandrinus has αναστροφη (nominative) instead of αναστροφης (genitive). In 2:10 it has καταφρονουντες (nominative) instead of καταφρονουντας (accusative). And in 3:16 it has αυτοις (masculine or neuter) instead of αυταις (feminine).

The only obvious corrections in the manuscript are erasures with nothing written over them, leaving a space. Such erasures can be seen in 1:3, 16; 2:12.

The scribe of 2 Peter in Alexandrinus is the one identified by Kenyon as hand IV. According to Kenyon four other scribes also contributed to Alexandrinus. Hands I and II wrote the Old Testament; hands III and V wrote the New Testament along with IV.[3] Milne and Skeat argue that Kenyon's three New Testament hands are strikingly similar to one another and to I in formation of the individual letters. This along with other less subjective points of agreement "leads almost unavoidably to the conclusion that all four, in spite of surface discrepancies, are the work of one scribe."[4] Thus Alexandrinus was written by two scribes, one of whom (named I by Kenyon) wrote 2 Peter.

b) The Content of the Text

(1) Most of the distinctive features of 2 Peter in Codex Alexandrinus have the effect of smoothing difficulties in the likely original text or making it more explicit. In many cases, these features are also found in Codex Sinaiticus; however, the first few are not. In 1:4 the text of Alexandrinus says that Jesus has given υμιν (you) the promises, while the probable original text says that he has given them to ημιν (us). The likely original text switches somewhat abruptly from speaking of "us" in vv. 3-4a to speaking about "you" in v. 4b; Alexandrinus speaks of "you" throughout v. 4. The promises have been given to "you" and through them "you" will become sharers of divine nature.

---

3. See Milne and Skeat, *Scribes and Correctors*, 91-93.
4. Milne and Skeat, *Scribes and Correctors*, 93.

In 1:5 Alexandrinus has και αυτοι δε (and you yourselves also) while the probable original text has και αυτο τουτο δε (therefore). In the likely original text these words introduce vv. 5–7 as the apodosis of a complex conditional sentence of which vv. 3–4 form the protasis. In Alexandrinus these words begin an independent sentence. Alexandrinus also signals this by writing the first letter of v. 5 that comes at the left margin (namely the δ in σπουδην) larger and in the margin itself. This is the way that Alexandrinus regularly indicates the beginning of a new section of the text. The lack of such a large letter in the left margin at the beginning of v. 3 shows that Alexandrinus does not see v. 3 as the beginning of a new section. It probably understands vv. 3–4 as a continuation of the letter greeting in v. 2, which does begin with a large letter in the left margin.

In 1:10 Alexandrinus adds ινα δια των καλων υμων εργων (in order that through your good works) to the probable original text after σπουδασατε (be eager); Sinaiticus adds the same clause but without υμων. Unlike Sinaiticus, Alexandrinus also has the verb ποιεισθε (= ποιησθε, i.e., the second person plural present middle subjunctive of "make" required by the ινα clause) where the likely original text has ποιεισθαι (i.e., the present middle infinitive). Alexandrinus also has παρακλησιν (comfort) where the probable original text has κλησιν (call) and Alexandrinus lacks ποτε (ever) at the end of the verse. Alexandrinus's version of this verse makes it explicit that the addressees are to make their comfort and election secure through their good works. The exchange of παρακλησιν (comfort) for κλησιν eliminates the redundancy of κλησιν και εκλογην (call and election); the omission of ποτε (ever) removes any suggestion that those who do these things are absolutely secure from future failings.

As was the case in Codex Sinaiticus, the words of the heavenly voice in 1:17 are closer to the words of the heavenly voice in Matthew 17:5 than is the version of these words found in the likely original text of 2 Peter. This makes the derivation of these words from Matthew 17:5 more explicit than in the probable original text.

Alexandrinus's version of 2:4 has σειροις ζοφοις (pits, darknesses) while the probable original text has σειραις ζοφου (chains of gloom).[5] While the latter presents darkness as something with which the sinful angels can be chained, the former names the place to which they were delivered, i.e., dark pits. In the same verse Alexandrinus (like Sinaiticus) has κολαζομενους τηρειν (to keep confined) where the probable original text has τηρουμενους (kept). Use of the infinitive instead of the participle makes it clearer that the purpose of delivering the angels to dark pits was to keep them. The addition

---

5. At this point, Sinaiticus has σιροις ζοφου (pits of gloom).

of κολαζομενους might indicate that the angels are being punished as they are being kept, either until judgment or as a judgment.

In 2:13 Alexandrinus (like Vaticanus) has αγαπαις (love feasts) while the likely original text has απαταις (deceits). Alexandrinus's (and Vaticanus's) version of this verse makes the location of the false teachers' misbehavior more specific.

Alexandrinus's version of 2:17 says that the punishment of the false teachers is eternal. In this verse Alexandrinus has a phrase εις αιωνα (forever) that is not found in the probable original text. This brings 2 Peter into complete conformity with Jude 13 which 2 Peter quotes at this point.[6]

In 2:21 Alexandrinus (like Sinaiticus) has εις τα οπισω ανακαμψαι απο (to return to the things left behind from) after επιγνουσιν (having fully known it) while the probable original text has υποστρεψαι εκ (to turn away from). The two are very close in meaning, but Alexandrinus makes it explicit that departing from the holy commandment means returning to a former condition.

In 3:10 Alexandrinus says that the earth and the works on it κατακαιησεται (will be burned up) while the probable original text says that they ευρεθεσηται (will be discovered). Alexandrinus's version is the more straightforward, simply making explicit what is implicit in the earlier part of v. 10. The meaning of the likely original text is more uncertain.

(2) Other distinctive features of 2 Peter in Alexandrinus, some of them found also in Sinaiticus, have the effect of emphasizing the transcendence of God. In Sinaiticus this emphasis has Christological significance; this does not seem true of Alexandrinus. Alexandrinus's version of 1:21, identical to that of Sinaiticus except that Alexandrinus has του before θυ which is not found in Sinaiticus, does not say that the speech of the prophets derived from God as the likely original text does. In 2:11 Alexandrinus does not have the phrase παρα κυριου (from the Lord) that is found in the probable original text. The latter says that angels do not bring a slanderous judgment from the Lord. The text of Alexandrinus avoids any suggestion that God might be the source of a slanderous judgment. Sinaiticus avoids this suggestion by having παρα κω (before the Lord) instead of παρα κυριου (from the Lord). In 2:13 Alexandrinus (like Sinaiticus) has κομιουμενοι (receiving) while the likely original text has αδικουμενοι (being wronged). Alexandrinus avoids all suggestion that the fate of the false teachers is unjust in any way.

---

6. On this, see chapter 1, "Use of the Letter of Jude by the Second Letter of Peter."

Appendix A

Codex Ephraemi Syri Rescriptus (C)

a) The Form of the Text

Codex Ephraemi[7] is a parchment codex. Its pages are 13 inches by 10.6 inches (very slightly larger than those of Alexandrinus) and have one column per page. Each page has 40–46 lines. Codex Ephraemi is another biblical codex. Only 64 leaves of the Old Testament survive, containing parts of Job, Proverbs, Qoheleth, Song of Songs, Wisdom and Sirach. The 145 leaves of the New Testament contain at least part of every New Testament writing except 2 Thessalonians and 2 John. Readers of this copy of 2 Peter would have known from the codex that they were reading part of the Bible.

The scribe who wrote 2 Peter in Codex Ephraemi seems to have been comparable in skill to the scribe of 2 Peter in Alexandrinus. I count 16 itacisms and other errors based on replacing a letter or letters with similar sounding letters in 2 Peter.[8]

A number of errors have been corrected in the manuscript. According to Robert W. Lyon, the original scribe of the manuscript made two corrections in the text of 2 Peter.[9]

1. In 2:14 the scribe originally repeated ουτος εστιν after ο υιος μου, then noticed this mistake, erased ουτος εστιν and replaced it with ο αγαπητος. He then left the rest of the line blank.

2. In 3:7 the scribe duplicated με in τηρουμενοι, but noticed the mistake, erased it and wrote over it.

Lyon lists other corrections made by the first corrector of the manuscript.[10]

1. In 1:5 an original τουτο δε was replaced with δε τουτο.
2. In 1:9 the α in an original μαυωπαζων was erased, leaving μυωπαζων.
3. In 1:13 an original σκηνω was replaced by τω σκηνω.
4. In 1:17 τοιασδε αυτω was replaced by αυτω τοιασδε.

7. I have had no direct access to Codex Ephraemi but only via Tischendorf, *Codex Ephraemi*.

8. See Appendix C.

9. Lyon, *Re-examination*, 293. The second of these was also noted by Tischendorf, *Codex Ephraemi*, 343.

10. Lyon, *Re-examination*, 318. All of these were also noted by Tischendorf (*Codex Ephraemi*, 342–43), but he did not explicitly identify numbers 2, 9, 11, 12, and 14 as the work of the first corrector. In addition, Tischendorf thought that number 4 was the work of the second corrector.

5. In 1:21 προφητεια was squeezed into a space originally containing a shorter word that can no longer be seen. Lyon thinks it might have been προφητια.
6. κολαζομενους τηρειν was added at the end of 2:4.
7. In 2:6 καταστροφη was added before κατεκρινεν.
8. In 2:12 και φθαρησονται has been converted into καταφθαρησονται.
9. In 2:22 κυλισμον was changed into κυλισμα.
10. In 3:3 προγινωσκοντες was changed into γινωσκοντες.
11. In 3:7 an εν before πυρι has been erased.
12. In 3:11 υμας was written twice and the second one was erased.
13. In 3:13 ωμεν εν οις δικαιο was rewritten in smaller letters to allow insertion of εν before οις. Tischendorf suggests that it may have been omitted originally because it was immediately preceded by the same letters (p. 343).
14. In 3:16 στρεβλωσουσιν was converted into στρεβλωσιν by erasing the letters σου.

Lyon lists still other corrections made by the second corrector.[11]

1. In 1:11 an original αιωνιαν has been changed to αιωνιον.
2. In In 1:17 εις ον εγω has been added after αγαπητος.
3. In 1:18 αγιω in τω αγιω ορει has been deleted, and τω αγιω has been added after ορει.
4. In 2:1 a σ has been written above παρειαξουσιν between ι and α, converting the word into παρεισαξουσιν.
5. In 2:3 the ε in εις has been overwritten to make it an ο, making the word οις.
6. In 2:11 a σ has been written above the ε in οντε, converting the word into οντες.
7. In 2:16 the final letter of an original ανουν has been erased and had a line drawn through it.

---

11. Lyon, *Re-examination*, 342. Tischendorf also noted all of these corrections (*Codex Ephraemi*, 342–43); however, he did not explicitly attribute numbers 4, 6, and 7 to the second corrector. In addition, he thought number 5 might be the work of the original scribe and attributed number 8 to the first corrector.

8. In 3:3 ν is written above the ω in εσχατω, converting the word into εσχατων.

9. In 3:13 a line has been drawn through the το before επαγγελμα.

Lyon, following Tischendorf, dates Codex Ephraemi in the first half of the fifth century. Different scribes wrote the Old and New Testament sections of the codex. It is uncertain whether more than one scribe wrote the New Testament.[12] The first corrector of the manuscript, whose corrections are listed above, did his work sometime in the sixth century. Erasing was his most frequent way of correcting the text. He either leaves a blank space where he has erased something, or writes the corrected text in the space, using letters noticeably smaller than those of the original scribe. In addition to correcting by erasing and rewriting, the first corrector also at times added small letters above the line. The second corrector of the manuscript, whose corrections are listed above, did his work in the ninth century. The second corrector either crossed out or encircled with dots what he wished to omit from the text.[13]

b) The Content of the Text

(1) As was the case with Codices Sinaiticus and Alexandrinus, a number of the distinctive features of Codex Ephraemi have the effect of smoothing difficulties in the likely original text or making it more explicit. In some cases the three deal with the same places in the text, but do so in different ways. In 1:4 Codex Ephraemi has της εν κοσμω επιθυμιας και φθορας (the desire in the world and corruption) rather than της εν τω κοσμω εν επιθυμια φθορας (the corruption in the world by desire) which is found in the likely original text. The latter, making use of two prepositional phrases enclosed between the article and the noun, is a more complex and ambiguous expression than the two nouns linked by και that are found in the former.

In 1:5 Codex Ephraemi (like Sinaiticus) has και αυτο δε τουτο (and indeed this very thing) while the probable original text has και αυτο τουτο δε (and for this very reason = therefore). This has the same meaning in Codex Ephraemi as it has in Codex Sinaiticus. As we noted in discussing the latter, the expression in Codices Sinaiticus and Ephraemi is probably easier to understand than the likely original text. The latter seems to be unique in Greek literature, but the former is found in a few other places.

---

12. Lyon, *Re-examination*, xvii–xix.
13. Lyon, *Re-examination*, xx–xxi, xxiv.

As was the case in Codices Sinaiticus and Alexandrinus, the words of the heavenly voice in 1:17 are closer to the words of the heavenly voice in Matthew 17:5 than is the version of these words found in the likely original text of 2 Peter. This makes the derivation of these words from Matthew 17:5 more explicit than in the probable original text.

As is the case in Sinaiticus and Vaticanus, Codex Ephraemi's version of 2:4 says that the sinful angels were delivered to σειροις ζοφου (pits of gloom) while the probable original text has σειραις ζοφου (chains of gloom). This specifies their situation in a way that may be similar to the description of the Watchers' situation in 1 Enoch. And in the same verse, Codex Ephraemi has κολαζομενους τηριν (to keep confined) after τηρουμενους (kept) while the probable original text does not. This may indicate that the sinful angels undergo punishment as they await the final judgment. The punishment suffered by sinners is also more explicit in Codex Ephraemi's version of 2:12, which has καταφθαρησονται (will be utterly corrupted) while the probable original text has και φθαρησονται (will also be corrupted). Codex Ephraemi emphasizes that the corruption of the false teachers will be complete.

In 2:17 Codex Ephraemi (like Alexandrinus) has a phrase εις αιωνα (forever) that is not found in the probable original text. Codex Ephraemi's version says that the punishment of the false teachers is eternal.

In 3:10 Codex Ephraemi has εν νυκτι (in the night) after κλεπτης (thief) while the likely original text does not. This brings 2 Peter into closer conformity with 1 Thess 5:2 which the author of 2 Peter quotes at this point. The text of Ephraemi adds the detail that the thief comes in the night, making the quotation more explicit and increasing the vividness of the simile. In the same verse Codex Ephraemi has αφανισθησονται (will disappear) while the probable original text has ευρεθησεται (will be discovered). Codex Ephraemi's version is the more straightforward, simply making explicit what is implicit in the earlier part of v. 10. The meaning of the likely original text is more uncertain.

In 3:12 Codex Ephraemi has της του κυ ημερας (the day of the Lord) instead of the likely original text's της του θεου ημερας (the day of God). In Codex Ephraemi 3:10 and 12 use the same expression not different ones. Also in 3:12 Codex Ephraemi has τακησεται (will be melted) instead of the likely original text's τηκεται (are melted). The former matches the future tense of λυθησονται (will be dissolved) earlier in the verse.

(2) As was also the case with Codices Sinaiticus and Alexandrinus, other distinctive features of Codex Ephraemi have the effect of emphasizing the transcendence of God. Once again the three deal with the same places in the text, but not always in the same way. In 1:21 Codex Ephraemi says ελαλησαν απο θυ αγιοι ανθρωποι (holy human beings spoke from God) while

the probable original text says ελαλησαν απο θεου ανθρωποι (human beings spoke from God). Codex Ephraemi's specification of prophets as holy human beings seems to imply that holiness is necessary for human beings to act on God's behalf as prophets. In 2:11 Codex Ephraemi (like Sinaiticus and Vaticanus) has παρα κω (before the Lord) while the probable original text has παρα κυριου (from the Lord). Codex Ephraemi's version avoids any suggestion that God might be the source of a slanderous judgment. Finally, in 2:13 Codex Ephraemi (like Sinaiticus and Alexandrinus) has κομιουμενοι (receiving) while the likely original text has αδικουμενοι (being wronged). Codex Ephraemi's version avoids any suggestion that God's treatment of the false teachers is unjust in any way.

Conclusion

Readers of Codices Alexandrinus and Ephraemi found a text in which some of the probable original text's difficulties had been moderated and whose meaning was more explicit than that of the likely original text.

Like readers of 2 Peter in Sinaiticus, readers of 2 Peter in Alexandrinus and Ephraemi saw a greater emphasis on the transcendence of God than in the probable original text. In Alexandrinus and Ephraemi, however, this does not seem to have the Christological significance it has in Sinaiticus.

Appendix B

Itacisms and other errors based on replacing a letter or letters with similar sounding letters in Codex Alexandrinus

Itacisms of various kinds:

1. ει for ι—twelve times [1:1, 14 (twice), 20; 2:10, 15, 17; 3:3, 4, 8, 9, 17]
2. ι for ει—nine times [1:13, 20; 2:1, 2, 4, 6 (twice); 3:1, 12]
3. ε for αι—two times [2:17; 3:13]
4. υ for οι—one time [3:10]
5. ει for η—one time [1:10]
6. η for ε—one time [1:17]
7. η for ι—one time [3:18]

Another error based on replacing a letter or letters with a similar sounding letter or letters is use of ν instead of μ before π (2:20; 3:3).

Appendix C

Itacisms and other errors based on replacing a letter or letters with similar sounding letters in Codex Ephraemi

Itacisms of various kinds:
1. ει for ι—five times [1:14; 2:1; 3:4, 8 (twice)]
2. ι for ει—three times [1:16; 2:15, 18]
3. ε for αι—four times [1:15; 2:17; 3:3, 13]
4. ε for α—one time [3:7]

Another error based on replacing a letter with a similar sounding letter is use of νκ instead of γκ (1:6 [twice]; 2:8).

Bibliography

The text and translation of Greek and Latin writers cited in these essays are taken from the Loeb Classical Library when possible.

Abbott, Edwin A. "On the Second Epistle of Peter I. Had the Author Read Josephus?" *The Expositor* 2 (1882) 49–63.

———. "On the Second Epistle of Peter II. Had the Author Read St. Jude?" *The Expositor* 2 (1882) 139–53.

———. "On the Second Epistle of Peter III. Was the Author St. Peter?" *The Expositor* 2 (1882) 204–19.

Abrams, M. H. *The Mirror and the Lamp: Romantic Theory and the Critical Tradition.* London: Oxford University Press, 1953.

Adams, Edward. "'Where Is the Promise of His Coming?' The Complaint of the Scoffers in 2 Peter 3:4." *New Testament Studies* 51 (2005) 106–22.

Aland, Barbara, et al., eds. *The Greek New Testament.* 4th rev. ed. Stuttgart: Deutsche Bibelgesellschaft, 1993.

Andrist, Patrick, ed. *Le manuscrit B de la Bible (Vaticanus Graecus 1209).* Lausanne: Éditions du Zèbre, 2009.

Bartchy, S. Scott. *Mallon Chresai: First-Century Slavery and 1 Corinthians 7:21.* Society of Biblical Literature Dissertation Series 11. Missoula, MT: Scholars, 1973.

Bauckham, Richard J. "2 Peter." In *Jude, 2 Peter*, 41–107. Word Biblical Themes. Dallas: Word, 1990.

———. "2 Peter: An Account of Research." In *Geschichte und Kultur Roms im Spiegel der Neuren Forschung Principat*, 3713–52. Vol. 25.5 of *Prinzipat: Herausgeber Hildegard Temporini.* Part II of *Aufstieg und Niedergang der Römischen Welt.* Berlin: Walter de Gruyter, 1988.

———. *God Crucified: Monotheism and Christology in the New Testament.* Grand Rapids: Eerdmans, 1998.

———. *Jude, 2 Peter.* Word Biblical Commentary 50. Waco, TX: Word, 1983.

Baumgärtel, Friedrich, and Johannes Behm. "καρδία κτλ." In *TDNT* 3:605–14.

Beare, Francis Wright. "The Text of 1 Peter in Papyrus 72." *Journal of Biblical Literature* 80 (1961) 253–60.

Bede. "*In epistulas VII catholicas.*" In *Expositio actuum apostolorum; Retractatio in actus apostolorum; Nomina regionum atque locorum de actibus apostolorum; In epistulas VII catholicas*, edited by David Hurst, OSB, 178–342. Corpus Christianorum Series Latina 121. Turnhout: Brepols, 1983.

Best, Ernest. *One Body in Christ*. London: SPCK, 1955.
Bibliorum Sacrorum Graecorum Codex Vaticanus B. Rome: Istituto Poligrafico e Zecca dello Stato, 1999.
Bigg, Charles. *A Critical and Exegetical Commentary on the Epistles of St. Peter and St. Jude*. International Critical Commentary. New York: Scribner, 1901.
Boehmer, Julius. "Tag und Morgenstern? Zu II Petr 1:19." *ZNW* 22 (1923) 228–33.
Brown, Raymond E. *The Gospel According to John I–XII*. Anchor Bible 29. Garden City, NY: Doubleday, 1966.
―――. *An Introduction to New Testament Christology*. New York: Paulist, 1994.
―――. *Jesus God and Man*. London: Chapman, 1968.
Bultmann, Rudolf, and Artur Weiser. "πιστεύω κτλ." In *TDNT* 6:174–228.
Burns, John Barclay. "Devotee or Deviate: The 'Dog' (*keleb*) in Ancient Israel as a Symbol of Male Passivity and Perversion." *Journal of Religion and Society* 2 (2000) 1–10. Online. http://moses.creighton.edu/JRS/toc/2000.html.
Cadbury, Henry J. *The Making of Luke-Acts*. London: SPCK, 1961.
Callan, Terrance. *Acknowledging the Divine Benefactor: The Second Letter of Peter*. Eugene, OR: Pickwick, 2014.
―――. "Reading the Earliest Copy of Galatians." *Conversations with the Biblical World* 35 (2015) 304–26.
―――. "The Style of Galatians." *Biblica* 88 (2007) 496–516.
Caulley, Thomas Scott. "'They Promise Them Freedom': Once Again the ψευδοδιδάσκαλοι in 2 Peter." *ZNW* 99 (2007) 129–38.
Charles, J. Daryl. *Virtue Amidst Vice: The Catalog of Virtues in 2 Peter 1*. Journal for the Study of the New Testament Supplement Series 150. Sheffield: Sheffield Academic, 1997.
Chase, F. H. "Peter, Second Epistle of." Vol. 3 of *Hastings Dictionary of the Bible*, 796–818. Edinburgh: T & T Clark, 1900.
Codex Sinaiticus: A Facsimile. Peabody, MA: Hendrickson, 2011. Online. http://www.codex-sinaiticus.net/en.
Conzelmann, Hans. *An Outline of the Theology of the New Testament*. Translated by John Bowden. New York: Harper & Row, 1969.
Cullmann, Oscar. *The Christology of the New Testament*. Translated by S. C. Guthrie and C. A. M. Hall. Philadelphia: Westminster, 1959.
Danker, Frederick W. "2 Peter 1: A Solemn Decree." *Catholic Biblical Quarterly* 40 (1978) 64–82.
―――. *Benefactor: Epigraphic Study of a Graeco-Roman and New Testament Semantic Field*. St. Louis: Clayton, 1982.
Davids, Peter H. *The Letters of 2 Peter and Jude*. Pillar New Testament Commentary. Grand Rapids: Eerdmans; Cambridge: Apollos, 2006.
Delling, Gerhard. "ἡμέρα." In *TDNT* 2:943–53.
Denniston, J. D. *The Greek Particles*. London; Indianapolis: Duckworth & Hackett, 1996.
Desjardins, Michel. "Introduction to VII,3: Apocalypse of Peter." In *Nag Hammadi Codex VII*, edited by Birger A. Pearson, 201–16. The Coptic Gnostic Library: A Complete Edition of the Nag Hammadi Codices 4. Leiden: Brill, 1996.
Dierauer, Urs. *Tier und Mensch im Denken der Antike: Studien zur Tierpsychologie, Anthropologie und Ethik*. Amsterdam: B. R. Grüner, 1977.
Dölger, Franz J. *Antike und Christentum*. Münster: Aschendorff, 1936.

Donelson, Lewis R. *I and II Peter and Jude: A Commentary*. New Testament Library. Louisville: Westminster John Knox, 2010.

Dunn, James D. G. *Christology in the Making: A New Testament Inquiry in the Origins of the Doctrine of the Incarnation*. Philadelphia: Westminster, 1980.

———. *The Theology of Paul the Apostle*. Grand Rapids: Eerdmans, 1998.

Ehrman, Bart D. *The New Testament: A Historical Introduction to the Early Christian Writings*. New York: Oxford University Press, 1997.

———. *The Orthodox Corruption of Scripture: The Effect of Early Christological Controversies on the Text of the New Testament*. New York: Oxford University Press, 1993.

Elliott, J. K., ed. *The Collected Biblical Writings of T. C. Skeat*. Leiden: Brill, 2004.

Elliott, John H. *1 Peter*. Anchor Bible 37B. New York: Doubleday, 2000.

Engberg-Pedersen, Troels. "Not an Iota, Not a Dot? On Correcting the Text of the New Testament (2 Peter 1:5)." Paper presented at the SBL Annual Meeting, New Orleans, LA, November 21–28, 1996.

Epp, Eldon Jay. *Perspectives on New Testament Textual Criticism: Collected Essays 1962–2004*. NovTSup 116. Leiden: Brill, 2005.

———. *The Theological Tendency of Codex Bezae Cantabrigiensis in Acts*. Society for New Testament Studies Monograph Series 3. Cambridge: Cambridge University Press, 1966.

Farkasfalvy, Denis. "The Ecclesial Setting of Pseudepigraphy in Second Peter and Its Role in the Formation of the Canon." *Second Century* 5 (1985) 3–29.

Farrar, F. W. "Dr. Abbott on the Second Epistle of St. Peter." *The Expositor* 2 (1882) 401–23.

———. "The Second Epistle of St. Peter and Josephus." *The Expositor* 3 (1888) 58–69.

Fauconnier, Gilles, and Mark Turner. *The Way We Think: Conceptual Blending and the Mind's Hidden Complexities*. New York: Basic, 2002.

Fillion, L. "Pierre (Deuxième Épitre de Saint)." In *Dictionnaire de la Bible* 5: cols. 398–413. Paris: Letouzey et Ané, 1912.

Fitzmyer, Joseph A. *Paul and His Theology: A Brief Sketch*. Englewood Cliffs, NJ: Prentice Hall, 1989.

Foerster, Werner. "σέβομαι κτλ." In *TDNT* 7:168–96.

Fornberg, Tord. *An Early Church in a Pluralistic Society: A Study of 2 Peter*. Coniectanea Biblica New Testament 9. Lund: Gleerup, 1977.

Fowler, Robert M. *Let the Reader Understand: Reader-Response Criticism and the Gospel of Mark*. Minneapolis: Fortress, 1991.

Frey, Jörg. "Second Peter in New Perspective." In *2 Peter and the Apocalypse of Peter: Towards a New Perspective*, edited by Jörg Frey et al., 7–74. Biblical Interpretation Series 174. Leiden: Brill, 2019.

Gerdmar, Anders. *Rethinking the Judaism-Hellenism Dichotomy: A Historiographical Case Study of Second Peter and Jude*. Coniectanea Biblica New Testament 36. Stockholm: Almqvist & Wiksell, 2001.

Giese, Curtis P. *2 Peter and Jude*. Concordia Commentary: A Theological Exposition of Sacred Scripture. St. Louis: Concordia, 2012.

Gilmour, Michael J. *The Significance of Parallels Between 2 Peter and Other Early Christian Literature*. Academia Biblica 10. Atlanta: Society of Biblical Literature, 2002.

Grant, Robert M. *Early Christians and Animals*. London: Routledge, 1999.

Green, Gene L. *Jude and 2 Peter*. Baker Exegetical Commentary on the New Testament. Grand Rapids: Baker Academic, 2008.

Green, Michael. *The Second Epistle General of Peter and the General Epistle of Jude*. Tyndale New Testament Commentaries 18. Grand Rapids: Eerdmans, 1987.

Grillmeier, Aloys, SJ. *From the Apostolic Age to Chalcedon (451)*. Vol. 1 of *Christ in Christian Tradition*. Translated by John Bowden. Atlanta: John Knox, 1975.

Grundmann, Walter. *Der Brief des Judas und der Zweite Brief des Petrus*. Theologischer Handkommentar zum Neuen Testament 15. Berlin: Evangelische Verlaganstalt, 1974.

———. "ἐγκράτεια κτλ." In *TDNT* 2:339–42.

Gunn, David M., and Paula M. McNutt, eds. *'Imagining' Biblical Worlds: Studies in Spatial, Social, and Historical Constructs in Honor of James W. Flanagan*. Journal for the Study of the Old Testament Supplement Series 359. Sheffield: Sheffield Academic, 2002.

Hahn, Ferdinand. *The Titles of Jesus in Christology: Their History in Early Christianity*. Translated by H. Knight and G. Ogg. London: Lutterworth, 1969.

Harrington, Daniel J. "Jude and 2 Peter." In *1 Peter, Jude, and 2 Peter*, by Donald P. Senior and Daniel J. Harrington, 159–299. Sacra Pagina 15. Collegeville, MN: Liturgical, 2003.

Harris, Murray J. *Jesus as God: The New Testament Use of Theos in Reference to Jesus*. Grand Rapids: Baker, 1992.

Harvey, Robert, and Philip H. Towner. *2 Peter and Jude*. The IVP New Testament Commentary Series. Downers Grove, IL: InterVarsity, 2009.

Hauck, Friedrich, "μένω κτλ." In *TDNT* 4:574–88.

Hays, Richard B. *Echoes of Scripture in the Letters of Paul*. New Haven, CT: Yale University Press, 1989.

Hengel, Martin. *The Son of God*. Translated by John Bowden. Philadelphia: Fortress, 1976.

Hiebert, D. Edmond. "The Prophetic Foundation of Christian Life." *Biblia Sacra* 141 (1984) 158–68.

Holladay, Carl R. *Theios Aner in Hellenistic Judaism: A Critique of the Use of This Category in New Testament Christology*. Society of Biblical Literature Dissertation Series 40. Missoula, MT: Scholars, 1977.

Hollander, John. *The Figure of Echo: A Mode of Allusion in Milton and After*. Berkeley: University of California Press, 1981.

Hofmann, Johann Christian K. von. *Die heilige Schrift neuen Testaments 7.2 Der zweite Brief Petri und der Brief Judä*. Nördlingen: Beck'schen, 1875.

Huizenga, Leroy A. *The New Isaac: Tradition and Intertextuality in the Gospel of Matthew*. NovTSup 131. Leiden: Brill, 2009.

Hurtado, Larry. *One God, One Lord: Early Christian Devotion and Ancient Jewish Monotheism*. Philadelphia: Fortress, 1988.

James, Montague R. *The Second Epistle General of Peter and the General Epistle of Jude*. Cambridge Greek Testament for Schools and Colleges. Cambridge: Cambridge University Press, 1912.

Johnson, Luke T. "The New Testament's Anti-Jewish Slander and the Conventions of Ancient Polemic." *Journal of Biblical Literature* 108 (1989) 419–41.

Jongkind, Dirk. *Scribal Habits of Codex Sinaiticus*. Texts and Studies Third Series 5. Piscataway, NJ: Gorgias, 2007.

Käsemann, Ernst. "An Apologia for Primitive Christian Eschatology." In *Essays on New Testament Themes*, 169–95. Translated by W. J. Montague. Studies in Biblical Theology 41. Naperville, IL: Allenson, 1964.

Keller, Otto. *Die Antike Tierwelt. 1 Säugetiere*. Hildesheim: Georg Olms Verlagsbuchhandlung, 1963.

Kelly, J. N. D. *Early Christian Doctrines*. New York: Harper & Row, 1960.

———. *The Epistles of Peter and of Jude*. Harper's New Testament Commentaries. New York: Harper & Row, 1969.

King, Karen L. *What Is Gnosticism?* Cambridge, MA: Belknap, 2003.

King, Marchant A. "Notes on the Bodmer Manuscript of Jude and 1 and 2 Peter." *Bibliotheca Sacra* 121 (1964) 54–57.

Knoch, Otto. *Der Erste und Zweite Petrusbrief. Der Judasbrief*. Regensburger Neues Testament. Regensburg: Friedrich Pustet, 1990.

Koester, Helmut. *History and Literature of Early Christianity*. Vol. 2 of *Introduction to the New Testament*. Philadephia: DeGruyter, 1982.

Kraus, Thomas J. "'Anders und doch Teil des Ganzen!?' oder Über Asianismus, das 'Verwunderliche' an 2 Petr und 'Verwunderliches' über ihn." In *Der zweite Petrusbrief und das Neue Testament*, edited by Wolfgang Grünstäudl et al., 231–53. WUNT 397. Tübingen: Mohr Siebeck, 2018.

———. *Sprache, Stil und historischer Ort des zweiten Petrusbriefes*. WUNT 136. Tübingen: Mohr Siebeck, 2001.

Kubo, Sakae. *P72 and the Codex Vaticanus*. Studies and Documents 27. Salt Lake City: University of Utah Press, 1965.

Kümmel, Werner Georg. *Introduction to the New Testament*. Translated by Howard Clark Kee. Nashville: Abingdon, 1973.

Layton, Bentley. *The Gnostic Scriptures: A New Translation with Annotations and Introductions*. Anchor Bible Reference Library. New York: Doubleday, 1987.

———. "The Significance of Basilides in Ancient Christian Thought." *Representations* 28 (1989) 135–51.

Lee, Simon S. *Jesus' Transfiguration and the Believers' Transformation: A Study of the Transfiguration and Its Development in Early Christian Writings*. WUNT 2. Reihe 265. Tübingen: Mohr Siebeck, 2009.

Leeman, A. D. *Orationis Ratio: The Stylistic Theories and Practice of the Roman Orators, Historians, and Philosophers*. 2 vols. Amsterdam: Adolf M. Hakkert, 1963.

Lips, Hermann von. "Schweine füttert man, Hunde nicht—ein Versuch, das Rätsel von Matthäus 76 zu lösen." *ZNW* 79 (1988) 165–86.

Lutz, Cora E. *Musonius Rufus "The Roman Socrates."* Yale Classical Studies 10. New Haven, CT: Yale University Press, 1947.

Lyon, Robert W. *A Re-examination of Codex Ephraemi Rescriptus*. PhD diss., University of St. Andrews, 1958. Slightly revised, 1994.

MacDonald, Dennis R., ed. *Mimesis and Intertextuality in Antiquity and Christianity*. Studies in Antiquity and Christianity. Harrisburg, PA: Trinity, 2001.

Marshall, I. Howard. "The Development of the Concept of Redemption in the New Testament." In *Reconciliation and Hope: New Testament Essays on Atonement and Eschatology*, edited by Robert Banks, 153–69. Grand Rapids: Eerdmans, 1974.

Martin, Dale B. *Slavery as Salvation: The Metaphor of Slavery in Pauline Christianity*. New Haven, CT: Yale University Press, 1990.

Martini, Carlo M., ed. *Beati Petri Apostoli Epistulae: Ex Papyro Bodmeriana VIII Transcriptae*. Milan: Pizzi, 1968.
Marxsen, Willli. *Introduction to the New Testament*. Translated by G. Buswell. Philadelphia: Fortress, 1968.
Mayor, Joseph B. *The Epistle of St. Jude and the Second Epistle of St. Peter*. London: Macmillan, 1907.
McNamara, Martin, and E. G. Clarke, trans. and notes. *Targum Neofiti 1: Numbers and Targum Pseudo-Jonathan: Numbers*. Vol. 4 of *The Aramaic Bible*. Collegeville, MN: Liturgical, 1995.
Meeks, Wayne A. *The Prophet-King: Moses Traditions and the Johannine Christology*. NovTSup 14. Leiden: Brill, 1967.
Méhat, André. "ΑΠΟΚΑΤΑΣΤΑΣΙΣ chez Basilide." In *Mélanges d'histoire des religions offerts à Henri-Charles Puech*, 365–73. Paris: Presses Universitaires de France, 1974.
Miller, Robert J. "Is There Independent Attestation for the Transfiguration in 2 Peter?" *New Testament Studies* 42 (1996) 620–25.
Milne, H. J. M., and T. C. Skeat, with Douglas Cockerell. *Scribes and Correctors of the Codex Sinaiticus*. London: British Museum, 1938.
Moo, Douglas J. *2 Peter and Jude*. The NIV Application Commentary. Grand Rapids: Zondervan, 1996.
Morgenthaler, Robert. *Statistik des Neutestamentlichen Wortschatzes*. Zurich: Gotthelf, 1958.
Moulton, J. H., and W. F. Howard. *A Grammar of New Testament Greek*. Vol. 2. Edinburgh: T & T Clark, 1920.
Mounce, Robert H. *A Living Hope: A Commentary on 1 and 2 Peter*. Grand Rapids: Eerdmans, 1982.
Murphy-O'Connor, Jerome. *Paul the Letter-Writer: His World, His Options, His Skills*. Good News Studies 41. Collegeville, MN: Liturgical, 1995.
Neyrey, Jerome H. *2 Peter, Jude*. Anchor Bible 37C. New York: Doubleday, 1993.
———. "The Apologetic Use of the Transfiguration in 2 Peter 1:16–21." *Catholic Biblical Quarterly* 42 (1980) 504–19.
———. "The Form and Background of the Polemic in 2 Peter." *Journal of Biblical Literature* 99 (1980) 407–31.
Niklas, Tobias, and Tommy Wasserman. "Theologische Linien im *Codex Bodmer Miscellani*?" In *New Testament Manuscripts: Their Texts and Their World*, edited by Thomas J. Kraus and Tobias Niklas, 161–88. Texts and Editions for New Testament Study 2. Leiden: Brill, 2006.
Norden, Eduard. *Die antike Kunstprosa vom VI. Jahrhundert v. Chr. Bis in die Zeit der Renaissance*. Leipzig: Teubner, 1898.
Oepke, Albrecht. "παρουσία κτλ." In *TDNT* 5:858–71.
Paulsen, Henning. *Der Zweite Petrusbrief und der Judasbrief*. Meyer Kommentar. Göttingen: Vandenhoeck & Ruprecht, 1992.
Pearson, Birger A. *Ancient Gnosticism: Traditions and Literature*. Minneapolis: Fortress, 2007.
———. "The Apocalypse of Peter and Canonical 2 Peter." In *Gnosticism and the Early Christian World: In Honor of James M. Robinson*, edited by James E. Goehring et al., 67–74. Sonoma, CA: Polebridge, 1990.

———. "Basilides the Gnostic." In *A Companion to Second-Century Christian "Heretics"*, edited by Antti Marjanen and Petri Luomanen, 1–31. Vigiliae Christianae Supplements 76. Leiden: Brill, 2005.

Peel, Malcolm. "Gnostic Eschatology and the New Testament." *Novum Testamentum* 12 (1970) 141–65.

Perkins, Pheme. *First and Second Peter, James, and Jude*. Louisville: John Knox, 1995.

Pétrement, Simone. *A Separate God: The Christian Origins of Gnosticism*. Translated By Carol Harrison. San Francisco: Harper, 1990.

Porter, Stanley E., and Andrew W. Pitts. "τοῦτο πρῶτον γινώσκοντες ὅτι in 2 Peter 1:20 and Hellenistic Epistolary Convention." *Journal of Biblical Literature* 127 (2008) 165–71.

Rahner, Karl. "Theos in the New Testament." In *God, Christ, Mary, and Grace*, 79–148. Vol. 1 of *Theological Investigations*. Translated by Cornelius Ernst. London: Helicon, 1961.

Reicke, Bo. *The Epistles of James, Peter, and Jude*. Anchor Bible 37. Garden City, NY: Doubleday, 1964.

Rengstorf, Karl H. "διδάσκω κτλ." In *TDNT* 2:135–65.

Robbins, Vernon K. "The Dialectical Nature of Early Christian Discourse." *Scriptura* 59 (1996) 353–62.

———. *Exploring the Texture of Texts: A Guide to Socio-Rhetorical Interpretation*. Valley Forge, PA: Trinity, 1996.

———. *The Invention of Christian Discourse*. Vol. 1. Blandford Forum, Dorset, UK: Deo, 2009.

———. "Rhetography: A New Way of Seeing the Familiar Text." In *Words Well Spoken: George Kennedy's Rhetoric of the New Testament*, edited by Duane F. Watson and Clifton C. Black, 81–106. Waco, TX: Baylor University Press, 2008.

———. "Socio-Rhetorical Interpretation." In *The Blackwell Companion to the New Testament*, edited by David Aune, 192–219. Malden, MA: Wiley-Blackwell, 2010.

———. *The Tapestry of Early Christian Discourse: Rhetoric, Society, and Ideology*. London: Routledge, 1996.

Robinson, John A. T. *Redating the New Testament*. Philadelphia: Westminster, 1976.

Rose, H. J. *Outlines of Classical Literature*. Cleveland: World, 1959.

Rowe, Galen O. "Style." In *Handbook of Classical Rhetoric in the Hellenistic Period: 330 BC–400 AD*, edited by Stanley E. Porter, 121–57. Leiden: Brill, 1997.

Royse, James R. *Scribal Habits in Early Greek New Testament Papyri*. New Testament Tools, Studies, and Documents 36. Leiden: Brill, 2008.

Rudolph, Kurt. *Gnosis: The Nature and History of Gnosticism*. Translated by R. McL. Wilson. San Francisco: Harper, 1987.

Russell, D. A. *Criticism in Antiquity*. Berkeley: University of California Press, 1981.

Salmon, George. *A Historical Introduction to the Study of the Books of the New Testament*. London: Murray, 1889.

Sanders, E. P. *Paul and Palestinian Judaism: A Comparison of Patterns of Religion*. Philadelphia: Fortress, 1977.

Schelkle, Karl H. *Die Petrusbriefe. Der Judasbrief*. Herders theologischer Kommentar 13/2. Freiburg: Herder, 1961.

Schmidt, Karl M. *Mahnung und Erinnerung im Maskenspiel: Epistolographie, Rhetorik und Narrative der Pseudepigraphen Petrusbriefe*. Freiberg: Herder, 2003.

Schrenk, Gottlob. "δίκη κτλ." In *TDNT* 2:174–225.

Schutter, William L. *Hermeneutic and Composition in First Peter.* WUNT 2/30. Tübingen: Mohr (Siebeck), 1989.

Segal, Alan F. *Two Powers in Heaven: Early Rabbinic Reports about Christianity and Gnosticism.* Studies in Judaism in Late Antiquity 25. Leiden: Brill, 1977.

Senior, Donald. *1 and 2 Peter.* New Testament Message 20. Wilmington, DE: Glazier, 1980.

Sidebottom, E. M. *James, Jude, and 2 Peter.* New Century Bible. London: Nelson, 1967.

Smith, Terence V. *Petrine Controversies in Early Christianity: Attitudes towards Peter in Christian Writings of the First Two Centuries.* WUNT 2. Reihe 15. Tübingen: Mohr (Siebeck), 1985.

Soden, Hans Freiherr von. "ἀδελφός κτλ." In *TDNT* 1:144–46.

Sorabji, Richard. *Animal Minds and Human Morals: The Origins of the Western Debate.* Ithaca, NY: Cornell University Press, 1993.

Spicq, Ceslas. *Les Épitres de Saint Pierre.* Sources Biblique. Paris: Gabalda, 1966.

———. *Theological Lexicon of the New Testament.* Translated and edited by J. D. Ernest. Peabody, MA: Hendrickson, 1994.

Spitta, Friedrich. *Der zweite Brief des Petrus und der Brief des Judas.* Halle: Waisenhaus, 1885.

Starr, James M. *Sharers in Divine Nature: 2 Peter 1:4 in Its Hellenistic Context.* Coniectanea Biblica New Testament 33. Stockholm: Almqvist & Wiksell, 2000.

Stauffer, Ethelbert. "ἀγαπάω κτλ." In *TDNT* 1:21–55.

Swain, Simon. *Hellenism and Empire: Language, Classicism, and Power in the Greek World AD 50–250.* Oxford: Clarendon, 1996.

Τα Ιερα Βιβλια: *Codex Vaticanus Graecus 1209 (Codex B) phototypice expressus iussu Pauli PP VI Pontificis Maximi: Η Καινη Διαθηκη.* Civitate Vaticana: Opera Curatorum Bibliothecae Vaticanae, 1965. [facsimile of Codex Vaticanus New Testament]

Talbert, Charles H. "II Peter and the Delay of the Parousia." *Vigiliae Christianae* 20 (1966) 137–45.

Terian, Abraham. *Philonis Alexandrini De Animalibus: The Armenian Text with an Introduction, Translation and Commentary.* Chico, CA: Scholars, 1981.

Testuz, Michel, ed. *Papyrus Bodmer VII–IX.* Geneva: Bibliotheca Bodmeriana, 1959.

Thurén, Lauri. "The General New Testament Writings." In *Handbook of Classical Rhetoric in the Hellenistic Period: 330 BC–400 AD,* edited by Stanley E. Porter, 587–608. Leiden: Brill, 1997.

———. "Hey Jude! Asking for the Original Situation and Message of a Catholic Epistle." *New Testament Studies* 43 (1997) 451–65.

———. "Style Never Goes out of Fashion: 2 Peter Re-Evaluated." In *Rhetoric, Scripture and Theology. Essays from the 1994 Pretoria Conference,* edited by Stanley E. Porter and Thomas H. Olbricht, 329–47. Journal for the Study of the New Testament Supplement Series 131. Sheffield: Sheffield Academic, 1996.

Tischendorf, Constantinus. *Codex Ephraemi Syri Rescriptus.* Lipsiae: Tauchnitz, 1843.

Trobisch, David. *The First Edition of the New Testament.* Oxford: Oxford University Press, 2000.

———. *Paul's Letter Collection: Tracing the Origins.* Minneapolis: Fortress, 1994.

Turner, Nigel. *A Grammar of New Testament Greek.* Vol. 4. Edinburgh: T & T Clark, 1976.

Vögtle, Anton. *Der Judasbrief/Der 2. Petrusbrief.* Evangelisch-Katholischer Kommentar zum Neuen Testament 22. Düsseldorf: Benziger; Neukirchen-Vluyn: Neukirchener, 1994.

———. *Die Tugend-und Lasterkataloge im Neuen Testament: Exegetisch, Religions-und Formgeschichtlich Untersucht.* Münster: Aschendorfschen Verlagbuchhandlung, 1936.

Waldis, Joseph. *Sprache und Stil der grossen griechischen Inschrift vom Nemrud-Dagh in Kommagene (Nordsyrien): Ein Beitrag zur Koine-Forschung.* Heidelberg: Carl Winter's Universitätsbuchhandlung, 1920.

Wand, J. W. C. *The General Epistles of St. Peter and St. Jude.* London: Methuen, 1934.

Warfield, Benjamin B. "Dr. Edwin A. Abbott on the Genuineness of Second Peter." *Southern Presbyterian Review* 34 (1883) 390–445.

Wasserman, Tommy. "Papyrus 72 and the Bodmer Miscellaneous Codex." In *The Epistle of Jude: Its Text and Transmission*, 30–50. Coniectanea Biblica New Testament 43. Stockholm: Almqvist & Wiksell, 2006.

Watson, Duane F. *Invention, Arrangement, and Style: Rhetorical Criticism of Jude and 2 Peter.* Society of Biblical Literature Dissertation Series 104. Atlanta: Scholars, 1988.

———. "The Oral-Scribal and Cultural Intertexture of Apocalyptic Discourse in Jude and 2 Peter." In *The Intertexture of Apocalyptic Discourse in the New Testament*, edited by Duane F. Watson, 187–213. Society of Biblical Literature Symposium Series 14. Atlanta: Society of Biblical Literature, 2002.

Webb, Robert L. "Intertexture and Rhetorical Strategy in First Peter's Apocalyptic Discourse: A Study in Sociorhetorical Interpretation." In *Reading First Peter with New Eyes: Methodological Reassessments of the Letter of First Peter*, edited by Robert L. Webb and Betsy Bauman-Martin, 72–110. Library of New Testament Studies 364. London: T & T Clark, 2007.

Werdermann, Hermann. *Die Irrlehrer des Judas-und 2. Petrusbriefes.* Gütersloh: Bertelsmann, 1913.

Westcott, Brooke Foss, and Fenton John Anthony Hort. *The New Testament in the Original Greek: Introduction, Appendix.* 2nd ed. London: Macmillan, 1896.

Wilamowitz-Moellendorff, Ulrich von. "Asianismus und Atticismus." In *Rhetorika: Schriften zur aristotelischen und hellenistischen Rhetorik*, edited by Rudolf Stark, 350–401. Hildesheim: Georg Olms Verlagsbuchhandlung, 1968.

Williams, Michael Allen. *Rethinking "Gnosticism": An Argument for Dismantling a Dubious Category.* Princeton: Princeton University Press, 1996.

Windisch, Hans. *Die Katholische Briefe.* Handbuch zum Neuen Testament 15. Tübingen: Mohr (Siebeck), 1951.

Wisse, Jakob. "Greeks, Romans, and the Rise of Atticism." In *Greek Literary Theory After Aristotle: A Collection of Papers in Honor of D. M. Schenkeveld*, edited by J. G. J. Abbenes et al., 64–82. Amsterdam: VU University Press, 1995.

Wohlenberg, G. *Der erste und zweite Petrusbrief und der Judasbrief.* Leipzig: A. Deichert, 1915.

Wolfson, Harry A. *Philo: Foundations of Religious Philosophy in Judaism, Christianity, and Islam.* Cambridge, MA: Harvard University Press, 1968.

Young, Frances. "Two Roots or a Tangled Mass." In *The Myth of God Incarnate*, edited by John Hick, 87–121. London: SCM, 1977.

www.ingramcontent.com/pod-product-compliance
Lightning Source LLC
Chambersburg PA
CBHW051638230426
43669CB00013B/2346